SILVER ACE

The Intelligences team

Dr. Dov Yanai

Cover image, illustrations and graphic consulting: Natali Yanai- Dibner

Cover Design: Studio 'Almog'

Layout: Dalit Rahamim - Studio 'Almog'

Produced by Orly Levy

Orion Publishing House

www.orion-books.co.il

03-5030822

POB 5330 Holon 5815251

ISDN: 978-965-91288-5-3

Printed in April 2015

SILVER ACE

The Intelligences team

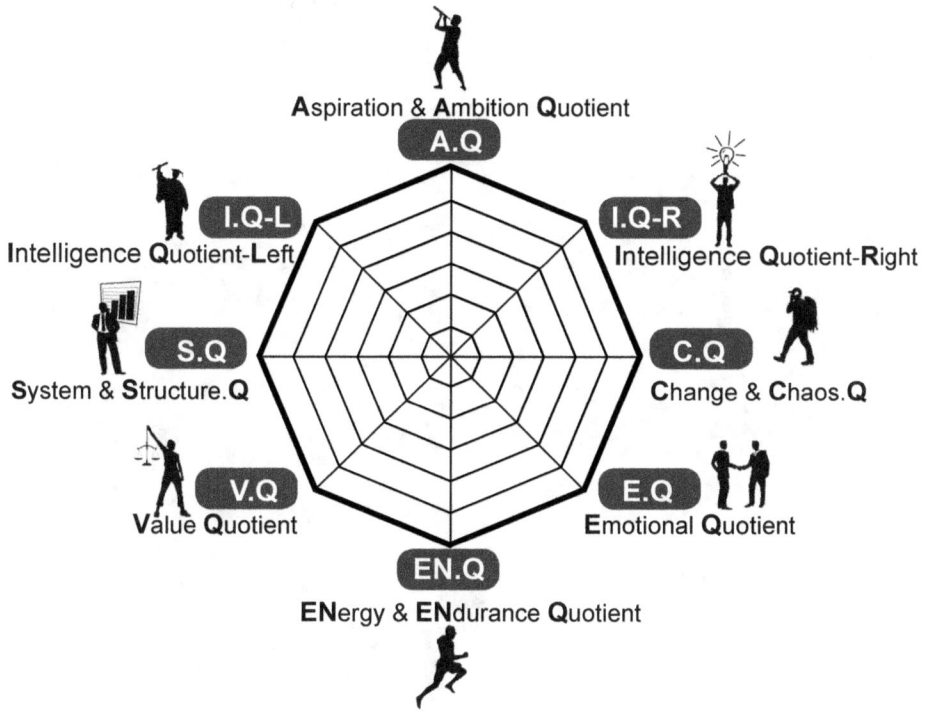

Dr. Dov Yanai

Orion Publishing House

Dedicated to my parents that
"Gave me the roots and allowed me the wings"

Contents

Preface

The author as a SILVER ACE

"And God created man in His own image"

(Genesis 1:27)

The notion of creating "in His own image" represents the process of divine creation, but to the same extent, it describes human creation which isn't necessarily objective.

Man's search after a doctrine or truth in any given field is expressed through his own characteristics, namely the connection between objective truth and the man who subjectively found it.

When I had time to write a few words about the author, i.e., myself, after years of elaborating on the SILVER ACE theory, it occurred to me that the principles of the model were actually what defined **me**, my actions and my activity throughout my life as the "master of connecting the impossible," as my daughter once remarkably described it.

Throughout my life, I have felt the need to find connections between sky and earth, roots and wings, rationality and mysticism, chaos and order, emotions and principles, feminine and masculine, Yin and Yang.

I understood, in retrospect, that this wasn't about impossible connections but rather the preferred connections unique to that individual. I understood also that man is the sum total of his actions and felt the need to live the whole spectrum of my human abilities that comprised me. I've always felt that manifesting one facet alone of the limited expression of the "I," is equivalent to walking on one's strong leg, namely, limping! My life has been a journey in the realization of the Ace who is Me: Between left (logical and scientific: the study of mathematics and physics) and right (irrational, intuitive, mystical, emotional); between spirituality (the study of psychology, philosophy, and theology) and materialism (the study of economics and business management); between establishing organizations, constructing buildings and computers, and dwelling in eastern monasteries occupying myself with the study of spiritual esoteric learning; between science and consciousness; between attending corporate board meetings, managing companies, organizations and business initiatives, and professional model development dealing with future-required qualifications.

Along my path, in study and work, I was always eager to crack "the secret" of Man, to understand him and develop analytical tools for his diagnosis and further development. I have evaluated people for various jobs from America to China, from Siberia in the then USSR to multinational corporations. I learned that despite cultural differences, it is always simply people we are talking about – we're all human beings. Cultural differences are only on the surface; clothes are different, but under the Scotsman's kilt or the Indian's sari is a human being.

The life I have lived in different cultures – in monasteries or in cults of the East, working with construction workers in Canada, or as a sailor on a ship – has taught me to listen to people and get to know them as individuals without referring to their culture.

I believe that Man's essence is the sum total of his deeds, and that is how I have lived my life. I looked for more ways to express myself as an occupational adventurer in the human dimensions of the SILVER ACE; this indeed defines me and my endeavors.

The 21st century human skill characteristics in the SILVER ACE model are unique in connecting different sciences, theories, cultures and worlds. Readers will be exposed to approaches from Western and Eastern culture, from physics and mathematics, Buddhism and Judaism, from spiritual teachings as well as from modern management theories.

Once, at a management conference, I spoke about "Managing Human Energies in the Organizational Field" based on the SILVER ACE. I spoke about organizational chakras and meridians, about Einstein's energy equation and about human energy. At the end, one of the senior executives of an accounting and business consulting firm came up to me and said, "You haven't said anything that I hadn't already heard from other sources, but you did manage to put all my bits of information into one holistic model and connect, organize and set all the pieces into one picture." I thanked him for his acknowledgement and for helping me define the uniqueness of my professional work as reflected in this model. Indeed, the model enables us to connect pieces of knowledge from different fields into a useful holistic system.

I believe human truth to be one, even though it can be multifaceted. If the theory is correct, it will find its expression in different cultures, dimensions and times.

The search for connections between directions and tendencies and their overall meaning, as well as the search for relationships within the variety and dimensions of life, was the guiding principle in the writing of this book, as it is of my entire life. To me, the essence of human uniqueness is not in Man's being a highly developed machine, one-dimensional and limited, but rather in the width and depth of the wondrous weave of expression at its full human potential.

Science Fiction?!

It is the end of the 21st century, the **singularity** point has been reached, it is the **cyborgs' time,** that of the "**compuman**."

After all the information and memory of every single human being had been transferred to a computer, computers rapidly developed the ability to produce generations of highly sophisticated "offspring," with the computing skills of an entire community, which combined human biological and neurological components using advanced and sophisticated processing systems. As they developed tremendous processing abilities, those cyborgs gradually replaced the human race and took control over the world maintaining their human appearance.

* * *

An important assembly was underway in the Computer Intelligence Hall, where the cyborgs used to meet for debates and decision making.

"I am truly honored to open the 21st century meeting of senior advisors," declared the assembly chair Billa, named after one of the mythological fathers of the computer race, Bill Gates. For the occasion, Billa chose to appear in the form of the perfect woman: Her figure, facial features, clothes and hairdo were carefully selected from a variety of options to represent her status and her immense computing powers. Like all cyborgs of the latest generation, Billa was endowed with a thinking capacity equal to a country's entire population at the turn of the last century. Thousands of years of knowledge derived from scientific research were stored in her memory. Billa knew everything a human being possibly could in every possible field: Literature, philosophy, music, electronics, visual arts, science, along with all their derivatives and combinations. The knowledge of these fields was available to all members of the council of advisors, which humans once called government or parliament. These senior advisors attending the conference chaired by Billa were the most highly developed and knowledgeable cyborgs with the keenest processing faculties. The criteria for admittance to that elite group were unequivocal – only the most knowledgeable and highly capable were eligible to attend – which is why elections or disputes over "The Throne" never occurred. As supported by results, this selection method was absolutely the right one.

"Today we discuss an issue that has been on my mind for quite some time now," Billa went on. "That is, the creatures commonly known as '**human beings**.'"

Erupting voices in the audience indicated that this in itself was no novelty.

"They are not our enemies," Billa continued. "As opposed to some of my colleagues here, I honor them as our ancestors. We all have positive memories of them, and I was even named after one of them. But in view of the tremendous and rapid development in our capabilities, I wish to raise before this honorable forum the question of whether they possess skills and abilities that we do not, in which case they would be indispensable to us.

"The Neanderthals became extinct because they had neither existential uniqueness nor skills superior to those of the Homo sapiens. From a historical point of view, they will always have their place, but in day-to-day reality, they have become irrelevant. We must examine whether this is also the case with humans today.

"We, the processors, write software better and faster than they ever did. For years now, we have had no need for humans for skills such as driving, housekeeping, service provision or production. There was a time when humans excelled at providing services, but nowadays we cannot compare them to the service provided by a virtual agent in direct communication with all existing information centers. In the past, humans believed they held an advantage over us because they were the ones who created us, but we have managed to regenerate ourselves without their involvement. Prior to today's assembly, we established a professional inspection committee to investigate the question of whether there was anything that humans do better than us that would justify our need for them."

"It's in our best interest to preserve them as a source of historical knowledge," a voice resonated from the plenum.

"It's in our interest to preserve them, but not as a source of knowledge," replied the chairwoman. "They are not needed for that purpose because we have already absorbed, stored and preserved all existing human knowledge. You all remember we conducted Operation Human Reservoir, in which we scanned every single human brain and created a copy of everything we found to ensure that all information, memories and images are never lost."

"We have performed numerous tests, a battery of which humans formerly used for job applicants," said the Scientist computer, head of the committee examining the issue.

"We then selected groups from among the humans and the computer populations to take these tests. We tested intelligence, languages, technical comprehension, reading speed and comprehension, mathematics, geometry, planning and time management, knowledge of ethics and philosophy, performance pace and level of accuracy, among many more. A meaningful gap was found in all criteria in favor of computers. Even the older generation processors defeated the humans. It should be noted that we did not test those skills and functions in which we indisputably surpass them, such as performing a task at a steady pace without signs of fatigue, performing complex tasks meticulously, memory capacity, information retrieval speed and finally, areas such as medicine, particularly surgery, in which we are clearly superior. On behalf of all the multidisciplinary members of the scientific committee and myself, I can end by saying that our objective scientific examination didn't indicate any skills in which humans outperformed computers!" the Scientist computer concluded his presentation.

"In this case," said the chairwoman, "given that a historic decision is about to be made, it is important that we have a consensus. I therefore suggest that this decision be backed up by our **Super Brain**. Let us web our brains," Billa invited the members. The chairwoman was referring to a process in which all participants in the assembly join together in a network forming a mega-processor that sorted out all data and information with the aim of reaching an optimal and unanimous decision. This practice was a replacement of the primitive process of votes and decisions by majority, which had often resulted in unwise half-measures.

The members immediately began wiring their arms together to form the Super Brain. While everyone awaited a decision, the Super Brain froze and contradictory data appeared on the Super Screen. Indignant cries were heard as neither consensus nor harmony was achieved.

"I demand that those who are strongly opposed speak up," said Billa.

Slowly and quietly, a giant computer rose. His name, **RAV,** which means MULTI in the ancient Hebrew language and was derived from his multidisciplinary, multidimensional, omnipotent, and most of all multigenerational, nature. He held the memories of generations of computers. Everybody quieted down to hear what he had to say. Within the computer community, Rav's thought process was perceived as unique. Ever since he initiated the operation to scan human knowledge and information, he was considered an expert on the human race.

"At the turn of the century," he began in an authoritative voice, "humans raised this very question. Indeed, computers had only just come into existence, but they were gradually biting into human occupation spheres. Back then, some humans already claimed that they no longer held an advantage over computers; on the other hand, others were required to outline all human aptitude and proved that humans possessed skills and abilities that we didn't. Hence, we need them," he concluded in a powerful voice.

The attendees were in shock. "Is that so?" "How?" "What for?" Questions came from the audience.

"Humans can be used as the interfaces to worlds beyond our reach or understanding," Rav asserted. "Granted, they are neither super-processors nor do they have our computing powers, memory or decisiveness, but the structure of the human brain and its functioning enable them to create a connection with other worlds surrounding us."

Tension in the air was tangible.

"What do you mean; what worlds are you referring to?" someone's voice boomed, breaking the silence.

"I will try to explain, but it's complex," replied Rav. "It's like a bird trying to tell a fish about the forest landscape in the mountains. The bird is the fish's interface to what is going on there because the fish will never be able to get there. Humans are like that same bird looking at us. With the help of their unique brains, they can fly to the heights of the mountains and establish connections to worlds with which we cannot interact: Worlds of muse and creativity, intuition and chaos, the ability to 'think with one's gut' and to feel with one's heart. All of this is of crucial importance."

"Why is it so important? Those are primitive systems, not rational ones!" objected one of the participants.

"That's true," Rav agreed, "but that is where inventions, flashes of genius, breakthroughs, art, and even shrewd business decisions come from. It's a world of poetry devoid of logic, which is essential to original and creative thinking. That's what enabled Albert Einstein to imagine himself in a train moving at the speed of light. In those worlds, Michelangelo imagined the sculpture inside the rock, and Mozart heard in his mind's ear the symphony he put down in writing later on. We may be able to produce more efficiently, but they surpass us with their ability to dream, to desire, to imagine, to understand incomprehensible and senseless things and give them a new meaning. We can copy their creations by means of an exact production line, but in order to do this we need humans and their phenomenal ability to reach these worlds. We have no access to the world of emotions, passions and creation and we were not conceived to understand and express the ability to love."

"That's enough!" the representative of the scientific committee suddenly roared. "That's enough! We have thoroughly examined this issue, and we all know that love is primitive!"

"I agree," Rav said, "but, nonetheless, I believe that passion and love are crucial skills enabling humans to develop relations and networks of special qualities that we have no knowledge of. Their ability isn't limited to the connection between reason and intuition, or between art and engineering; they rather have the ability to be an interface between sky and earth, between material worlds and spiritual ones. I don't really know what it is but I see them connect to what they call the spiritual world. They have faith."

"Faith? There is no such thing!" the attendees sneered. "Explain yourself. Define faith in terms that we can understand!"

"Faith is the **ability to change probability**. By believing in something, they increase its chances to occur. Faith is an ability that generates change in matter. According to research we have conducted, humans' belief generates changes that are manifested materially," Rav tried to explain. "Humans have the particular ability to constitute a sort of interface between these worlds, including the future one. Some of them have actual gut feelings as to what would happen in the future. Do you remember Steve Jobs, one of our revered ancestors? His instincts were the foundation for the advent of new things, and the need for these particular things is something that we haven't been able to predict, despite all our processing abilities. Only humans are able to connect with faith and love. Such abilities are what constitute humans' superiority over processors.

"I'm not so sure the human race is in the process of extinction. It may just be possible that their ability to be an interface between different worlds is of the utmost importance to evolution. Humans just might have an advantage over us."

With the outbreak of disputes and clamor in the auditorium, Billa was forced to end the meeting and the issue at hand remained unresolved. No decisions were taken.

Introduction to SILVER ACE

Examining how people express themselves through their work is what I have worked at for the past four decades, diagnosing individuals and checking their compatibility with various organizations, positions, roles and careers. As a psychologist and futurist, the mysteries of the human mind in an era of chaos and change fascinate me. I attempt to understand who is to become the "Ace of the show" in the world of activity and career, whom to invest in and how to bring all their treasures into ultimate expression in the 21st century career world, where competition and quality guarantee excellence.

Career is not merely an undertaking for the sake of making a living but is rather the totality of one's performance and the ultimate expression of self.

When we ask, "What do you do?" out of curiosity, what we really have in mind is, "Who are you? What is your essence?" A person is not merely his intentions or dreams, but rather the sum total of his activities and occupations, namely his dreams and intentions that have materialized in reality. Therefore, evaluation relates to the totality of a person's activities because this is his projection on the wall of his life. The further we progress from mere survival to higher phases of self-fulfillment, the more accurately our multifaceted activities express us.

What is the secret of success? Are the components of success in the past, present and future identical?

The technological revolution leads to cultural, organizational, occupational and economic changes, which alters the skills and aptitudes needed for success in the professional world. New professions appear daily while others are pushed aside and reduced, and the human work force is replaced by machines and computers. In order to succeed in the 21st century, a few skills are no longer enough; there is an ever-growing need for a new and highly complex array of skills and abilities that function harmoniously when connected to systems of high sophistication and complexity.

The profile of the successful person is becoming more intricate and the nuances of the human and business array ever more diversified. Although many theorists and researchers try to define the "Ace" in the professional world, I have yet to find a model that extensively and adequately refers to all components that make up the business and human array that actually define an "Ace." It is common knowledge that to succeed, people need specific knowledge in their field: An accountant has to understand finances; a computer programmer has to understand computing. But in addition to this, there is also a set of a universal, more general index or measure that determines if a man will turn Ace. The technological revolution brought about the need to develop a model that would address such a multidimensional complexity—a model that would successfully exhibit the overall definition with a minimum of characteristics and supply a holistic response to the myriad skills required for a person to succeed in the career world of the 21st century.

The SILVER ACE model represents the personal development process, empowerment and potential realization and answers the questions "Who has the best chance to become an Ace?" and "What does an organization, team or person lack that would have made it function like an Ace?" To this end, it uses measures employed by analysts in the human resource field. Whoever is gifted with these measures at a high and balanced level is worthy of investment.

The model displays a comprehensive definition with minimal characteristics:

1. The individual

2. The team

3. The occupations and jobs

4. The organizations

These characteristics enable the identification of the weak points and obstacles of imbalance between the items as well as constitute a basis for individual development, empowerment and potential fulfillment and the construction of teams for the formation of synergy that creates an Ace team.

The power of the model lies in its logical, analytical and holistic organization of all the human skills required for success in the 21st century, combining scientific knowledge in various fields – psychology, neurology and physics, and human knowledge derived from different cultures, philosophies and alternative medicine. Its main purpose is to put the pieces of the puzzle of human potential into one cohesive picture.

One of the main messages of the book is **"Be the Ace You Are."** Man, whoever he is, is looking to find and use his overall potential and aptitudes. People are like Aces of different size and glow, and the challenge is for them to realize the stars that they are. Those who are true to themselves and their origins will succeed.

Thinking in Future Tense

When I was young, I loved dreaming of remote places where no one had ever set foot, somewhere along the lines of the places in stories such as Robinson Crusoe and Tarzan. Upon growing up, I turned the future into such a place for me. A voyage into the future leans on many axioms – scientific, technological and sociological among others – but still remains largely speculative. Jennifer James, author of Thinking in the Future Tense (1997), equates future activity with a situation in which we are given puzzle pieces that form a complex image but are not given the picture to guide us. In this case, all we can do is look for the frame. We will probably be unable to put the pieces into a coherent picture and will only have fragments that could be connected to a few possible scripts.

If this analogy is accurate, why is it at all important that we think about what's to come? The answer lies in a phrase that may sound somewhat simplistic – the future today is no longer what it used to be. The development rate and change potency in the past do not even come close to those the person living in the 21st century has to deal with. It was plausible in the past to say, "There's nothing new under the sun," whereas nowadays, the change rate is at a rollercoaster's zooming and dizzying speed. The sheer reference/allusion to the dimension of time has undergone a drastic change. Einstein turned it into the Fourth Dimension, Freud took the past into the present, and the dimension of time has seeped into the psychological discourse. To understand a person at present, the past has to be allowed into the present. Psychotherapists amend the past in the present. Just as the past has an impact on the present, so does the future. Since about the middle of the 20th century, we have been operating under a futuristic stream of thought coming from the United States, a future-oriented nation, and in an economic world in which corporate values are not determined by their present status but according to forecasts of their future success.

Attitude toward the future is important not only at the national and corporate levels but at the individual level as well. The children we raise are the arrows we shoot into the future. If we ignore the future, we will be like those who shoot arrows with their eyes closed or according to a remembered past picture of the target. There is no way of knowing what the future has in store for us, but we must think about the world where we are raising our kids. We must decide what kind of a reality we will educate them for and endeavor to endow them with the skills they will need to succeed in that world. Many parents raise their children according to their own past and present whereas these children will live in a different world. The SILVER ACE model attempts to enable a view of the overall skills and tools our children will need in order to successfully face the future.

> The central question that will challenge the future occupational world, which the SILVER ACE model tries to come to grips with, is: **Is there human superiority?**

Since the dawn of human history, man has striven to find tools, devices and animals to replace him at his work. The knife was used instead of teeth, tools instead of hands, the mule pulled the plow, the ox turned the millstones, the horse and the automobile replaced legs, and so forth. Man happily adopted and used all the means he could find to make his life easier and relieve himself of his tasks and chores. Indeed, if the other (tool, device or animal) can do it in my place, why should I do it myself? That's the dream of heaven on earth – to not work and to have the genie in the bottle or a capable robot to execute your will.

Rapid technological development intensifies the problematic character of this question since more and more domains we used to think of as our very own are being gradually taken over. This is the crisis of occupations, some of which are taken over by computers, while new ones are generated and developed. Occupational history follows the Darwinist drama, where human activities don't survive because they've been entrusted to all sorts of machines, robots and computers. Everything that a computer does better than man will pertain to its domain, and the greater the power and abilities of processors, the more they will bite into fields of human activity. The technological revolution also entails a revolution in human activities, which are gradually taken over by tools, processors and technological devices. The Darwinist drama of occupational survival is confronted by ever-changing conditions, and only suitable activities and skills will survive.

The issue of human superiority over computers can be addressed as a struggle for survival during the process of "computers taking over our work." This struggle against change is doomed, just like the battle waged against the machines that "robbed us of our livelihood" at the beginning of the Industrial Revolution. Slogans such as "break the machines" did not stop the industrialization process, and the response came with a surge of human capabilities which had not surfaced before. Technological development can also be regarded as an extraordinary evolutionary process: The refinement of human uniqueness. If machines, robots and virtual agents perform considerable parts of human roles, what is it that will keep the spark and uniqueness of humans? What is human exclusivity? What is the pre-eminence of man above computers?

The SILVER ACE model, which is a conceptual model, seeks to identify the required skills for success in the occupational world of the 21st century. In its very essence it relates to the present and future realities – it strives to answer these questions.

- **Which skills are required for success at present and in the future?**

- **How can we identify a person as an "Ace"?**

- **Who is worth hiring and nurturing by the organization?**

- **How does one form winning teams?**

- **What is the secret of winning organizations?**

- **Which professions and occupations will be in demand in the future: Which skills do they require?**

Trends and Changes in the Occupational World

The occupational world has been undergoing accelerated changes in the last few centuries.

The first transition was from the agricultural era which dominated the world for thousands of years, towards the industrial era which reached its apex at the beginning of the 20th century. The era of services reached its peak around the end of the 20th century, and the era of knowledge and information systems has been developing in an accelerated pace since the end of the 20th century and has yet to reach its pinnacle.

	Knowledge Year 2000	Services Year 1950	Industrial Year 1850	Agricultural 70,000 B.C.
Leadership style	Autocratic	Authoritarian	Human relations	Cooperation
From control	►► ►► ►► ►► ►► ►► ►►			to freedom
Cultural values	Survival	Security	Belonging	Self-esteem
From materialism	►► ►► ►► ►► ►► ►► ►►			to idealism
Technological base	Agriculture	Production	Social organization	Information systems
From simple	►► ►► ►► ►► ►► ►► ►►			to complex

The occupational world follows Darwin's laws: The "fittest" professions will survive, while others will either transform in order to survive or disappear. This is the basis of the occupational drama we are witnessing. In the past, when most humans were occupied with agriculture, the basic question was, "In what way was man superior to the animal?" Over time, all activities animals were capable of performing shifted from humans to them. The Industrial Revolution raised the question of man's superiority over the machine, and all activities the machine could perform were eventually pulled out of human hands to such an extent that hundreds of functions and professions disappeared.

The 21st century is characterized by the incorporation of computers and robots into our lives in general, and into the occupational world in particular. In comparison to the past when occupations were passed on from father to son with hardly any change in context, the advent of computers has changed the entire occupational and professional map. Even if a job's title remains the same, its characteristics and essence have changed entirely; for example, the printing press worker with ink-stained hands is replaced by a modern compositor who uses a computer for the same purpose. The computer replaced human muscle, animals and machines, as well as the human brain, so that people now need to develop an entirely new set of skills.

At the very beginning of humankind, the main predictor of success was muscle or strength. For Jacob to gain the title of "Father of Israel," he had to prove himself by fighting with the angel. Only after having proven himself did he win the title. The intelligence component emerged as a possible indicator of success as the importance of physical prowess gradually declined. When David had to prove himself in combat against Goliath, physical strength alone was no longer sufficient but was still a part of success, thus David had to show his ability to analyze the situation and come up with an original advantage: The power of creative intelligence.

The notion of "Intelligence Quotient" was defined by Alfred Binet in 1905 to serve as a means to measure the degree of mental retardation of patients being admitted for treatment in institutions specializing in mental retardation. The intelligence quotient soon became a key concept in the prediction of success, and institutions, schools and parents are still using it today. The psychometric aptitude test's dominance in the admission process at higher education facilities only perpetuates this perception that I.Q. is key. But we have learned over the years that the world is full of people with a high I.Q. who cannot realize their potential. Ted Kaczynski, a child prodigy who enrolled at Harvard University at the age of 16 and earned a PhD in mathematics by the age of 20, utterly lacked any social skills. His eventual contribution to society was the activation of a bomb at a bustling public facility, killing and injuring many people (incidentally, researchers claimed the explosive device was clearly assembled by a genius...).

In his Emotional Intelligence (1997), Daniel Goleman talks about an additional prediction indicator needed and suggests the emotional intelligence quotient, the E.Q. He rightly argues that emotional intelligence is of far greater importance in daily, mundane matters than intelligence is. Robert Cooper and Ayman Sawaf, in Observation and Insight (1998), take the concept of emotional intelligence a step further and turn it into a comprehensive ensemble of all characteristics that do not fit into the notion of intellect. To them, this form of intelligence includes emotions and intuition, the value system and human energy. Paul Stoltz, in Adversity Quotient (1997), refers to an important new dimension essential to the prediction of success, which is the way one copes with situations of stress and failure.

The technological revolution brought about dramatic changes in the occupational world in the last century and especially so in the last few decades. The world is gradually becoming more complex, and indicators of future success can no longer be limited to a single theory but rather must comprise a system of predicting indicators that are inter-related forming a net. We need new types of organizations, new approaches to occupations, new schools and new ideas that will be compatible with such changes. Success criteria in the occupational world are closely linked with the characteristics of that world and to understand them, one must understand the processes the occupational world is undergoing and where it is heading.

Changes in the World of Occupations and Skills

Occupational world	Skills
• from physical ability ➡	• to creative thinking
• from permanence and order ➡	• to change and flexibility
• from I.Q. ➡	• to E.Q.
• from calculation ➡	• to intuition
• from memory ➡	• to knowledge and wisdom
• from operating by the book ➡	• to creativity out of the book
• from knowledge ➡	• to wisdom

The End of the Muscle Era

- **The end of the labor and muscle era**

- **From doing to creating**

- **From calculating to thinking**

- **Robots and knowbots**

- **Computerized agents**

- **From information – to knowledge – to wisdom**

- **From gender-related occupations to unisex occupations**

Until the beginning of the 20th century, "work" implied physical muscle exertion in farming or craft. It is not accidental that the English language uses the term "labor," a concept connected with the pain of childbirth and strenuous physical effort. Even physics defines "work" as the application of power over distance, therefore, people who lacked physical strength could not succeed in the occupational world and labor was considered the domain of the "common" public.

At the beginning of the 20th century, a paralyzed child had absolutely no chance of succeeding in the occupational world and only a slight survival chance, whereas in the 21st century, a disabled person can take on many different roles and even reach senior positions.

Rodin's famous sculpture The Thinker exemplifies how deeply the concept of "labor" as a function of effort is rooted in us. To demonstrate the great effort expended in thinking, a human sits naked with muscles bulging, even though the process of thought requires no muscles at all!

Knowledge and memory – Memory is an example of a skill which once was of paramount significance but has become much less important. In the past, the knowledge required for traditional farm work or craftwork was static and cyclical. Tasks were repeated year in and year out, and changes occurred only during transition from season to season: The required equipment was installed in the winter, seeds were sown in the autumn, and the crops were harvested in the spring, which is why the only form of knowledge required of the worker was memory. Knowledge was passed on from master to apprentice, from father to son verbally, hence those who had a good memory were considered intelligent. Nowadays, memory is no longer considered the main criterion for success: The computer has clearly defeated humans in this competition.

From specification to robotization – The Industrial Revolution regarded the worker as part of a machine: He wasn't required to think but to carry out instructions as a specific part of a process. Most workers were expected to do their manual jobs, while the thinking was left in part to engineers or managers, though in a compartmentalized and fragmented way. This approach led to a form of dehumanization of the worker and resulted in the downfall of that revolution. Charlie Chaplin depicted the absurdity of the man-machine in his movie Modern Times (1936). The Industrial Revolution worker was basically a sort of precursor to the robot of the future.

Robots are not necessarily humanoid devices, the way they are usually seen in movies; they are machines that perform tasks that humans used to do in an earlier time. The word "robot" derives from the Russian term rabota, which means "work" or "working machine." Many jobs have disappeared from production plants and are now performed by robots. In this sense, even the washing machine can be regarded as a kind of robot which made the laundresses' jobs vanish. The robotic revolution is only at the beginning, but with the gradual development of technology, more and more mechanical and technical human skills will be taken over by robots. Nowadays, the development of robotic drivers is already at an advanced stage and in the future, robotic drivers will replace the human driver. The robot replaces production laborers and their physical work skills, whereas the computer replaces human thinking. The combination of the robot with the computer will generate our society's future labor force.

From computing to creation – Since computers are also capable of thinking, Man should express his wisdom, which goes far beyond the capacity to process information. Since the beginning of the 21st century, much creativity has been reflected in a series of new types of jobs connected with the internet. In fact, new jobs and positions that we could not conceive of in the past are born every day, hence the ever-growing difficulty to prepare the next generation for the occupational world.

The gender drama of the occupational world

From an occupational point of view, there was a balance of interdependence between males and females for many years. The profession of "woman" was defined as someone who had a whole world of knowledge that was vital for existence. Men were dependent on women and needed them for their daily existence, for their cooking and baking, laundering, sewing, preserving food and raising livestock, no less than women needed men. For generations, recently widowed men found themselves in existential distress, as they didn't know how to go about performing basic survival tasks. Such delicate occupational balance of interdependence existed for thousands of years, to be disrupted only following the technological revolution of the 20th century.

This balance was first breached in the beginning of 20th century with the invention of electric appliances – refrigerators, baking ovens and washing machines – as well as the establishment of textile and processed food factories. All of these have released men from their dependence on women for their survival. The technological revolution and the transition to modern society rendered the job of "housewife" no longer a survival necessity. Contrary to common belief, the feminist revolution came with the undermining of the status of women as they lost their power base along with men's dependence on them. Women were forced to empower themselves elsewhere, in domains that had been so far under absolute male dominance.

Thanks to the very technology that originally breached women's equilibrium, a growing number of occupations, which had been considered masculine, opened to them as well. When performing tasks that did not demand physical strength, men held no advantage over women. The machines, even the heaviest ones, are controlled by computers, which women can also operate. The beginning of the 21st century enabled the occupational world to be free of gender-related stereotypes. As masculine activities are gradually given a more feminine character and vice versa, the need for attributes regarded as feminine, such as communication skills, intuition, empathy, and feminine management styles, has grown.

Changes in Organizations and Jobs

Compared with occupation and profession, a job is an organizational function that is derived from the work within the organization itself. Changes in economy, media and transport generated dramatic changes in the organizational structure, which entailed changes in job descriptions as well as the skills required for their performance.

Transition from a rigid organization to an elastic and plastic one – In the distant past, prior to the Industrial Revolution, organizations and jobs remained nearly unchanged over hundreds of years within the family framework. The Industrial Revolution disrupted the family occupational chain, and millions of farmers and craftsmen became industrial workers. The structures of organizations established following the Industrial Revolution were rigidly structured, and jobs were clearly defined in accordance with the functions required to operate machinery.

Global media and technology have created a new environment requiring more flexible organizations, capable of adapting themselves to rapid and complex competitive conditions. This often means actual elastic flexibility, requiring an organization to expand or shrink quickly. Such flexibility is expressed in downsizing and outsourcing processes, requiring that the organization maintain constant focus on its core activity, specializing and fulfilling its other needs through external sources.

Internet communication changes the organization from elastic to a plastic one, which is an organization capable of reform. Elasticity is a situation in which the original form and function of the organization are preserved and maintained but size changes. The plastic change implies the ability to undergo a complete and total transformation: No longer turn a big triangle into a small one but from triangle to circle. For instance, the ability of an organization to move into new domains of activity after changes in the market, and consequently, to restructure its entire nature.

Global organizations – We live in a Global Village, a term coined in 1959 by Marshall McLuhan, a Culture and Technology professor at the University of Toronto. Formal barriers of walls and borders have fallen, thus thinking in terms of globalization is gradually growing, and it is now possible to plan in one location, produce in another and market in a completely different one.

Large and compact organizations are, therefore, needed. There seems to be a contradiction in terms here, but the subtle play between large size and compactness is one of the key factors determining success of organizations. How can one hold the advantage of size through mergers and establishment of mammoth structures, and at the same time be compact and keep high responsiveness, flexibility and sensitivity towards the client? One solution is the creation of a federation of small, independent units, all of which share responsibility, identity and values. Many future organizations will be based on a nucleus group and peripheral ones. The core group will retain highly tight relationships and will be characterized by a high trust level and functional flexibility. On the other hand, there will be varying degrees of contact between groups, blurring the borders between constructors, suppliers and workers in the peripheral groups. Organizational fringe borders expand and blur up to the existence of virtual workers who work with the organization but operate from an unknown and irrelevant location.

The effect of future organizational structures on human functioning –

1. In a classic, hierarchical organization, a person's suitability for a position is examined according to the job description.

2. In an elastic and flexible organization, ability to change in various fields at work, from ability to show flexibility, adaptation through ability to learn, develop and grow is tested.

3. In the changing and future plastic organization, where total changes are possible, the human potential of its people is one of the assets around which the new organization will be built anew. The renewed organization will draw on the full human potential of its people and will foster the workers' own fulfillment and self-realization. This relates to the overall potential and passion of all the people comprising the organization regardless of their specific role or organizational goal and is becoming of central importance.

Promoting creativity, entrepreneurship and sensitivity

New organizations speak of turning workers into entrepreneurs and owners of their business units. As a result, a variety of new methods of rewarding worker-entrepreneurs has evolved. A high level of entrepreneurship will enable the organization to be flexible and adjust to the environment and changing needs.

Creativity is gradually becoming a key element in the lives of individuals as well as organizations. There will be no profit without creativity. Only an organization that succeeds in inserting creativity into its products, services and production processes will succeed in gaining a relative advantage. A life-loving organization must develop a market and client sensitivity at all levels of the organization and in all its employees. Market-customer sensitivity, which in the past was the sole domain of marketing and sales departments, has now reached all the employees of the organization. Customers, for their part, relate to all employees as representatives of the entire organization regardless of their position, which is why lack of customer sensitivity on any employee's part would reflect lack of sensitivity of the entire organization.

Organization management and leadership

Management style in agricultural society was autocratic and highly controlled. Transition to an industrialized society turned management into an authoritarian model, whereas in a service-oriented society, emphasis is placed on human relations. In the present knowledge society, management style will be cooperative. Transition, therefore, will be from absolute control to management allowing considerable freedom. The manager thus becomes a developer and educator, who interferes less and aims to enable every worker to fully realize their potential. The change in management and leadership style is also connected to the organization's cultural change itself: From an organizational culture of survival and security to one of belonging with the service-oriented companies, up to an organizational culture in which the acknowledged worker is central.

Changes in the career world

A career is a continuous series of jobs or occupations that constitutes a person's professional life. The word "career" comes from the French term carrière, relating to the roles and activities of a person on a time continuum much like a wagon race. Changes in the world of occupations, organizations and roles naturally bring about changes in the way careers are perceived.

A carriage race, like any other, deals with racing along predefined tracks. We used to treat one's career as if it were a train. A person would get on at a certain station and move on predetermined tracks towards known stations and destinations. Today, a career is more like a cross-country rally which requires maximal flexibility in dealing with varied goals and challenges. Every person actually has a few different career paths: Sequential, parallel, or at different levels.

Modern career perceptions refer to a career multilayered "cake" enabling a person to sustain a few careers simultaneously, prioritizing them as he would, enabling him to prefer one career over another at different times, without actually changing his career. In fact, it is a multicareer in relation to time and multicareers occurring simultaneously. There may be a number of central domains in a "career wheel," and sometimes only one of them is the person's source of income.

My mother studied chemistry at France's École Polytechnique, but not one day in her life did she practice her profession, having chosen to dedicate her time to raising her children and running her household. Many people of her generation said, "I wanted to, but couldn't, I didn't have the time." Our generation has a slightly different approach, as Frank Sinatra sang, "I did it my way." In this day and age, a person does not have to give up opportunities or choose between them. Nowadays, we have the will and the way to live all possibilities simultaneously all the time. Faith Popcorn, an American futurist and marketing consultant who owns her own prediction company and produces periodic reports on future trends, dubbed this process "99 Lives": Live all 99 levels of your life; strive to be everything you want simultaneously. Realize your aspirations. Don't give up and don't procrastinate.

An interesting notion characteristic of today's new career world and whose relevance is constantly growing is "I, Inc." or "Me, Ltd." The person is a business of its own; a multitasked, experienced and able one-person company that enters collaboration contracts with other groups. Working as an employee is, then, an individual case of a periodic contract with one sole client. The terms "employee" and "self-employed" are indistinct and blurred. Is a company manager who owns shares of the company he works at as an employee, self-employed or owner of the company? There is a wide variety of alliance opportunities starting at working from home and going up to work by output or as a partner receiving share allocation. People view themselves as independent business entities, as do companies that aspire to view their workers as independent people who assume responsibility over their careers. The old-school employee, who handed responsibility over his career to his employer, is on the brink of disappearing altogether, just as the term "tenure" has lost its supremacy. Job security exists only as long as the company is secure in the market. As long as the worker has value for the company and vice versa, the worker is responsible for the creation of his own market value.

In their book Future Wealth (2000), Stanley Davis and Christopher Meyer discuss future wealth in light of the fundamental change occurring in the human resource market, one that is reflected in the shift from "worker" to "player." They expect that we will invest in the "human resource stock exchange" rather than in company stocks in the future. Companies will invest in their workers in terms of financial investment expected to yield rather than in training and development. The market will identify people with special skills and will buy a percentage of their future profits, thus securing a future partnership. Many managers and company owners regret in retrospect not having identified their talented workers' potential to become Aces; they gave up on them without finding a way to invest in them and create a long-term partnership. These workers later spread their wings and became owners of start-ups and large companies. This new environment calls for analysts capable of assessing people's potential in the same way they analyze companies and their role in the capital market – analysts who will determine who is worthy of investment, which "Ace stocks" will increase in value and what the ingredients of Acehood are.

The SILVER ACE model aspires to serve as an analysis basis in the stock exchange of human qualifications.

Changes in the perception of time

Since career is a sequence of a person's occupations over a time continuum and in parallel scopes, changes in the grasp of time and space deeply affect it. The changes the dimension of time is undergoing can be defined as the "unbearable elasticity of time in the career domain." Such changes are expressed in two ways:

1. **Time is shrinking** – The rate of change is growing exponentially and shortens the relevance span of our professional knowledge. What we learned once has rather quickly become irrelevant, and man is required to adapt himself continuously to a new reality. Not only is the concept of "tenure" gradually disappearing, so is job stability and the idea of "occupation" itself as well as structured, well-defined career paths.

2. **Time is lengthened** – Life expectancy has risen from 35 to 80 years at least in the last few centuries and with a healthy lifestyle and advanced medicine, many actually live to be 100 and more. There are those who believe that scientific breakthroughs will enable a normal life even beyond the age of 140: Futurist Ray Kurzweil strives to make his life a living example of this possibility.

Those born in the 21st century already have a great chance of being alive in the next century, and a career range of almost a hundred years may become a fact: It will probably change people's outlook of employment over time.

One example of the impact of longer living is the irrelevance of the term "retirement." Anyone who can afford it, who is holding a key position as a CEO or whose services are still in demand, pursues his activity long after the official age of retirement. Warren Buffett and Leonard Cohen, among others, are examples of such active longevity.

Human development and learning in the ever-changing career world

The previously mentioned quick changes necessitate the constant need to learn, acquire knowledge and evolve as a person. The training and study industry has been one of the fastest developing industries in the past decades, much like the whole domain of human development, including coaching, therapy, workshops and courses, which are in higher demand. People will have numerous careers in their lives, depending on their added market value and the market demand, for which they will learn and train more than once.

The Key Question in the Occupational World for the 21st Century

Is man superior to computers?

The 21st century - The processors' revolution and singularity point

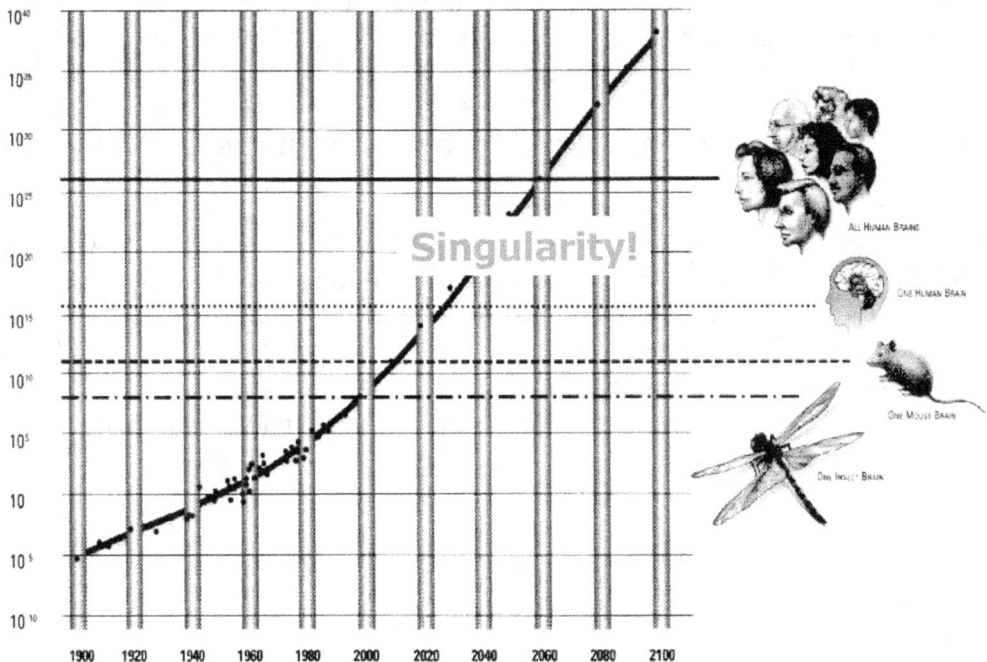

As early as 1965, Gordon Moore, co-founder of the Intel Corporation, devised "Moore's Law," affirming the cost-performance ratio of computer processors would double every two years. Today, fifty years later, it can be safely said that such a ratio doubles in even shorter time periods. One can see the difference between the enormous computers of the past, which cost millions and filled huge rooms, and the palm-sized computers with similar, not to say superior, processing capacities. Almost everyone can afford to purchase these computers, and forecasts bring up biological and quantum computers the size of single cells.

Processors accelerated the development rate and have given rise to the concept of "a future singularity point," where computers will have identical, if not superior, thinking ability to that of man. Although there is an ongoing debate between futurists and scientists revolving around the date and intensity of such a revolution, it is no doubt, a future tendency.

The concept of "**singularity**" was first coined by mathematician Irving John

Good (1916-2009) and became widely known. Thanks to science fiction author Vernor Vinge, who published an essay entitled "The Imminent Technological Singularity" in 1993. Ray Kurzweil, futurist and scientist, later published books in this field and is considered the strongest proponent of the theory. Kurzweil went even further, predicting it will happen in 2045.

Computers are more intelligent and more efficient than humans in completing many different tasks, some of which were considered far beyond computers' ability, like playing chess, and others seemingly exclusively compatible with the human mind. Future potential is connected to the gradual augmentation of computing capacity, miniaturization and the human/computer interface. A future system based on joining humans and computers is called a "cyborg" and will connect directly to the human's nervous system, muscles and brain, causing them to operate as one single system.

Computer scientists working on artificial intelligence and robotics discussed the notion of "intellect explosion," where intelligent machines will create other intelligent machines. The idea was first raised by mathematician Irving John Good in 1965 and was later followed by Vernor Vinge, who said humans will one day create a machine, the superior intelligence of which will be higher than their own, whereby an extremely rapid change will bring the human era to an end. This vision, presented in books and films of the time, seemed plausible and scary to many scientists. Others, like Ray Kurzweil, praise clever, even spiritual machines and find their use of great advantage for life expectancy and the creation of wealth. Many scientists have, therefore, asked whether artificial intelligence should be restricted. They believe the way technology is progressing will change the labor market, when increasingly machines will replace human workers in many different areas, forcing humans to live near machines that imitate human behavior.

Against the background of the processor revolution, we foresee that many occupations and professions will disappear from the human landscape and move into computing, virtual agents, robots and "knowbots" (knowledge robots). Everything that computers are able to do will be entrusted to them. Skills like memory and calculation are downgraded by computers, just as the appearance of cars on the scene did to human muscle force.

In light of the computing revolution over the years, the question **of how humans are superior to the computer**, is finding its way into the center of human essence in the 21st century. In the middle of the 20th century, mathematician Alan Turing offered a test, named after him, which checks whether a person could differentiate between human and computer activity. He argued this was the criterion for the existence of artificial intelligence. For years, it was generally maintained that there was no chance for it to ever happen, but in 2011 an impressive experiment was conducted using chat-software based on artificial intelligence people could communicate and correspond with. The users were deceived, some of the time, so that they were unable to tell the difference between conversation generated by software and actual human interaction.

As a holistic model, the SILVER ACE represents the human skills of the 21st century, examining those skills, the importance of which will grow and gather strength in light of both the development and proliferation of computing, and those skills whose relevance will decline, enabling people to map out their futures and assess their singularity in relation to computers as well.

The SILVER ACE Model

Human skills for the 21st century

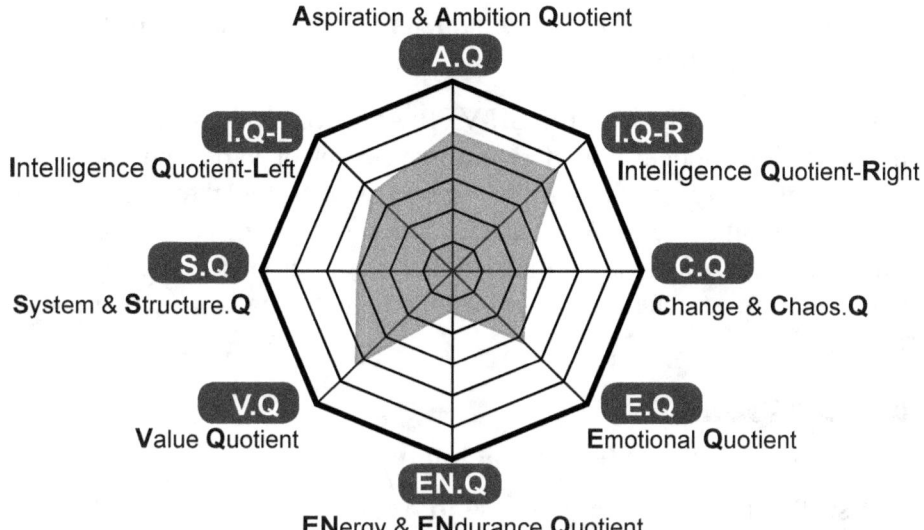

The SILVER ACE model was first presented two decades ago and was immediately adopted by professionals and practitioners in organizations in Israel and worldwide. The model, which speaks the language of both the right and left sides of the brain, has also been successful in helping engineers apply engineering-type order to the human domain. Over the years, the model changed and developed with the emergence of new needs, knowledge and questions, which required that its objectives evolve as well.

In its early stages, the SILVER ACE model was called "The Future Skills Model." It addressed the professional skills required in the future and tried to bind the accumulated skills, both old and new, into one single system that would be in demand in the future. The name of the model was later changed to "The are the Aces made of?." This ambivalent name deals with the basic foundations of celestial bodies, regardless of their size and radiance on the one hand, and with "stars" in the sense of "talent" on the other. The model dealt with the question of who among the "stars" was worth investing in as a worker, entrepreneur or business, a kind of analytical model for investment in "human shares" or those of companies.

This is a conceptual and theoretical model that defines and maps connections between the defined parts of a system, and concretizes the order, the organization and the forces operating within this system. The atom model and Freud's structural model of the psyche are examples of such a model. The objective of the model is to "put things in order," to place all terms into a clear road map that clarifies the picture. This is not another personality theory or morphological psychology, but the organization of the required quotients for success and their interrelation.

Some people mistakenly took the SILVER ACE for a diagnostic rather than a characterization model, as if it represented a set of valid and trustworthy tests. Although there are a number of assessment tools for some of the quotients comprising the SILVER ACE, which will be discussed further on, there are others for which assessment tools do not yet exist. (Therefore, there is a questionnaire attached as an appendix to help readers perform a self-assessment.)

Model Components:

1. **Two dimensions/axes – horizontal and vertical**

2. **Eight skills/quotients that give rise to Aces**

1. **Axes/Dimensions**
   These constitute the core of the model; each quotient is organized around and characterized by these axes:

   A. **Horizontal** – The characteristics axis; characterizing the right and left brain metaphorically, standing for cerebral thinking versus thinking with one's heart, expressing the horizontal dimension in the two-dimensional model. The Left-Right division gives the different quotients their unique characters.

   B. **Vertical** – The energy axis; from survival to self-realization.

   The concept that energy lies at the basis of the model draws from both modern physics and Eastern medicine. The vertical axis represents the energy facet of each quotient. Each location in the model is defined by its position on both axes and is expressed by energy and characteristic.

2. **Skills/Quotients**
   All eight skills/quotients are distributed around the two-dimensional circle of the model.

The colored zone at the center represents an example of a person's/a job's/an organization's characteristics as defined by the model. Each quotient represents an index for a particular domain.

An index is a complex of characteristics relating to and having an effect on a certain domain. The cost of living index, for instance, is affected by all the components relating to the expenses in our lives, just as the cost of building index represents a variety of resources connected with construction.

Just like other indices we are familiar with, the SILVER ACE model isn't about potential but about actual abilities and features.

Holistic model

The SILVER ACE is a holistic model structured in the form of a network in which each dimension is imbued with significance by its location in the system in relation to the others. That is, no quotient is more or less important than another; the quotients function as a system of indices constituting a dynamic texture that can turn a person or an organization into a star. The quotients are organized in a structure, and connecting the dots between them forms an octagon. The shape and surface area of the octagon generate a SILVER ACE pattern unique to each person, job or organization, providing information about characteristics, strengths and weaknesses as well as the aspects that need to be developed.

Just like any other model, the SILVER ACE does not demonstrate reality nor does it invent a new reality; instead it organizes the reality in such a manner that it becomes clearer and possible to observe with a different perspective. The key standards of an effective model are its functionality, clarity, simplicity and efficiency.

To meet these criteria, the theoretical model is connected with the following data:

The significance of space – The model's directions in space: Right-to-left and bottom-to-top are significant.

The significance of relationships – There are three types of relationships between the quotients:

1. **Neighbors**: As **Neighbors**, there is a reciprocal effect of each quotient on its neighbor. Neighbors influence each other.

2. **The balance within the levels**: There is a balance between each factor and its counterpart on the right or the left on either side of the vertical axis. A large gap between opposite factors can be critical and will require development in the future. There are three level balances in the model.

3. Counterbalance: This is the link between diametrically opposed factors. There are three opposed balances in the model (aside from the horizontal axis in which both types of links exist).

Abraham Maslow, in Motivation and Personality (1954), examines the question of whether conflicting aptitudes can coexist within the same person. Can a person be positioned only on one single point of the continuum between the need for system and structure and the need for change and breaking out of frameworks? Maslow argues that healthy people have this dichotomy resolved.

The SILVER ACE model promotes the concept that a person can simultaneously be on opposite points of the continuum and meet their contrasting needs.

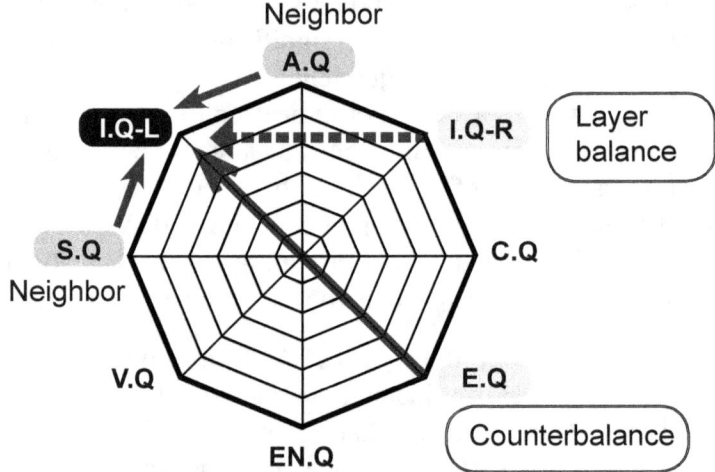

There are six opposing-balancing pairs:
1. Three level balances between right and left;
2. Three counterbalances, diametrically opposed.

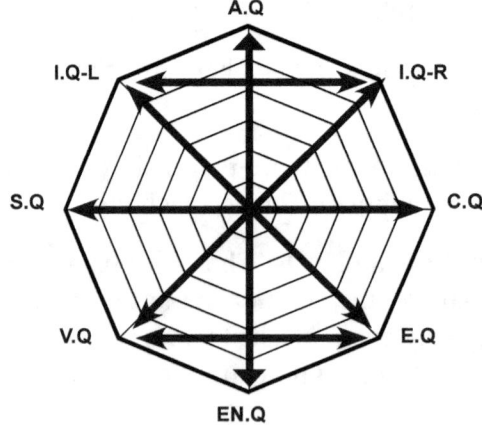

These pairs can be compared to the wings of an airplane. Each wing provides lift on its own, but taking off and flying is impossible without the two of them. If one wing gets larger that necessitates the similar growth of the other or the airplane will become unbalanced and will not fly. All Ace qualities, both individual and organizational, are based on balance not only between right and left but also between the various balancing elements in the model. Without equilibrium, the potency of a certain quotient can turn from a blessing into a curse.

The meaning of size – The larger a person's map surface area, the higher the star quality. A star is a person who has abilities in seemingly opposed areas. The SILVER ACE model is not based on "either/or" but on having both, hence the importance of size.

The meaning of shape

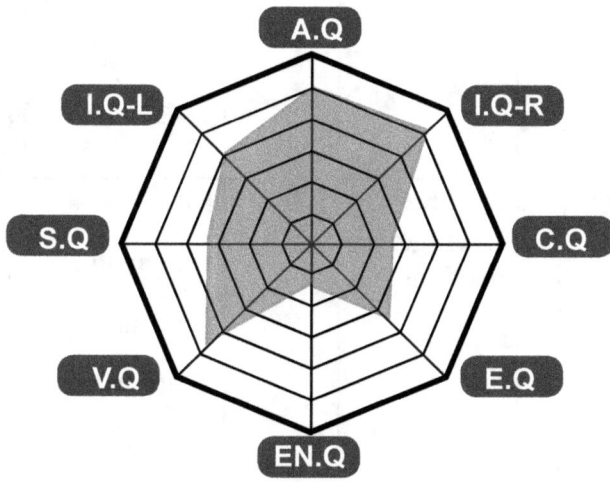

Unlike classic personality profiles based on a series of data, tables and scales, the SILVER ACE presents a person as an icon, a graphic shape. In this manner it is very easy to understand a person's attributes, strengths and weaknesses, the extent of balance between attributes, and the eventual need for development. The figure above illustrates a person or an organization with an especially high intelligence and system and structure coefficient, but that lacks creativity and has an underdeveloped interpersonal approach, which makes it hard to cope with situations of change and uncertainty. This describes an intelligent but rigid person or organization that has potential but remains stagnant.

SILVER ACE Quotient Table

Level	Symbol	Name	Letter	Key Words	Definition
Spiritual	**A.Q.**	**Aspiration** & **Ambition** quotient	**A**	Actualization Ambition Aspiration Aim Assurance Achievement	All measures connected with the degree of ambition, challenge and goals. Addresses the question of realizing one's mission and vision, self-confidence, adherence to goals, faith in one's chosen path.
Cognitive Right	**I.Q.-R**	**Right-intelligence** quotient	**I-R**	Intuition Imagination Innovation Illumination Incubation Irrational Icon Image Relativity Right	All measures representing intuitive and creative thinking, abstract, parallel and lateral vision. Invention, strokes of brilliance, irrationality, associative, relative and artistic thinking. Imagination, humor.

Level	Symbol	Name	Letter	Key Words	Definition
Cognitive Left	**I.Q.-L**	**Left-intelligence** quotient	**I-L**	Intelligence Logic Linear Learning Linguistic Left	Vertical thinking, logical, sequential and analytical thinking, classic I.Q., wisdom, capacity to study, analyze, draw conclusions, engineering, computing and mathematics.
Behavioral Right	**C.Q.**	**Change** **&** **Chaos** quotient	**C**	Chaos Change Chance Concurrent Conflict Complexity Curiosity Courage	Dealing with change, situations of uncertainty and chaos. Refers to aspects of functioning with flexibility and ability to improvise. Simultaneous performance, complexity, ability to deal with conflict, courage in the face of change, and curiosity.

Level	Symbol	Name	Letter	Key Words	Definition
Behavioral Left	**S.Q.**	**System** **&** **Structure** quotient	**S**	System Structure Stability Simple Standard Sorting Short	Ensemble of indices characterizing a person in relation to being systematic: Orderliness, structuring space and time, focus, clarity, simplicity, standard and stability.
Social/ **Emotional** Right	**E.Q.**	**Emotional** **intelligence** quotient	**E**	Emotion Empathy	Level of emotional maturity and readiness, awareness of emotion, empathy and sympathy, sensitivity to others and the ability to work in a team.

Level	Symbol	Name	Letter	Key Words	Definition
Social/ Emotional Left	**V.Q.**	**Value** quotient	**V**	Value Virtue	Level of one's value system and maturity, internal measure of integrity, commitment, fairness, dedication and impartiality. An inner law and rules.
Energy	**EN.Q.**	**Energy & Endurance** quotient	**E**	Energy Engine Endurance	Dynamism and vitality; towards action and the different Q's. Quotient of endurance and efficient energy preservation.

The impact of the letters and meaning of the name

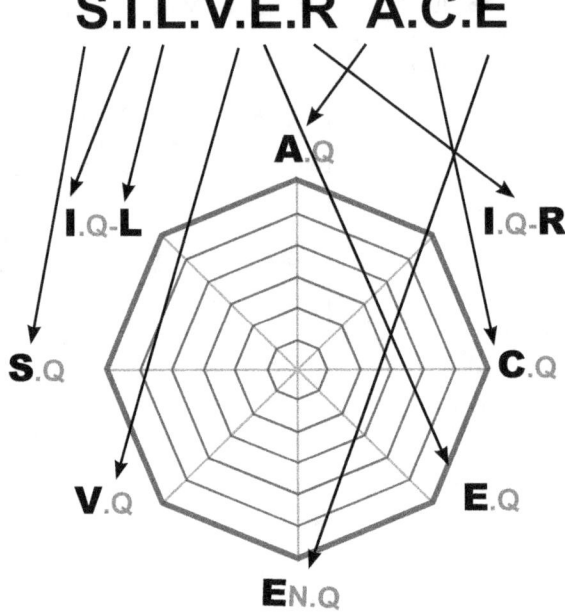

The name of the model represents the complexity and the uniqueness of human skills. The word "ace" is defined in Webster's English dictionary as a "skilled person, outstanding, champion, extraordinary, excellent," and therefore refers to success and triumph. It also represents the human aspiration to realize one's personal potential. One of our main human strengths is the need to express the maximal potential of our skills.

The range of different SILVER ACE skills also provides an answer to the key question of the 21st century occupational world: In what ways is man superior to computers? The concept of "S.I.L.V.E.R .A.C.E" also symbolizes the other human characteristics; human skills are reflected as well in association of ideas, aesthetics and harmony, which integrate the poetic factor into the scientific content characterizing the model.

Humans make associations through words and symbols, which is why letters of the alphabet are so often used when representing content. A scientist may well wonder what this has to do with a professional model. What is the connection between letters, words and the characteristics of each quotient and its name? This is not a poetic and lyrical approach designed to emphasize the range of human emotions over the logical, scientific side. The composition of the name also represents the importance of words, the magic of associations in human thinking. The combination of poetic and scientific skills is uniquely human, and this unparalleled pairing is the main message of this model and this book.

The name "SILVER ACE" expresses these characteristics too. Each quotient in the model is associated with representative key words, and most of them begin with the letter symbolizing it. For instance, the S.Q., the system and structure quotient, is characterized by a series of key words beginning with "S" (standards, structure and system, among others). All of these letters combined compose the name of the model, **SILVER ACE**, beyond the meaning of the word itself.

The Silver ace as a synergetic team of intelligences

Success is achieved when the eight intelligences of the Silver ace are reviled and expressed with most of their potential and act as a synergetic team.

. The term *synergy* comes from the Greek word *synergos*, , meaning "working together". **Synergy** is the creation of a whole that is greater than the simple sum of its parts

"Working together" as a team of different and contradicting intelligences, which allows room for harmonious communication between conflicting areas, by understanding the contribution and importance of each other.

SILVER ACE as a unifying language

unifying language for the characterization of:

- the individual

- the job

- the organization

- the team

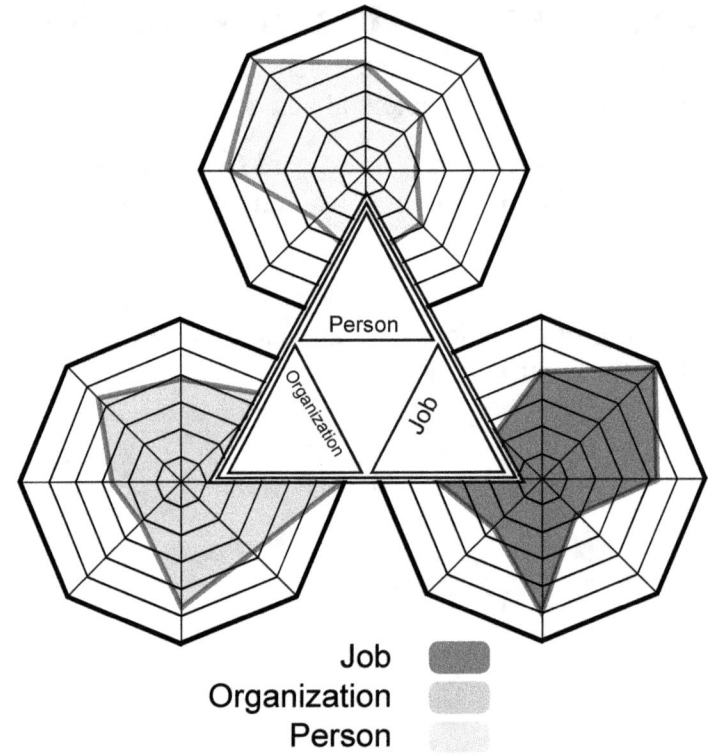

Job
Organization
Person

Different languages emerge from different theories and fields of knowledge, each containing a world of concepts and connections that describe each of the terms above: The language of classic engineering to describe organizations and organizational structures, the language of psychology to describe individuals and their skills, the language of sociology to characterize teams, and a functional language to describe occupations and jobs. The existence of this mixture of languages does not facilitate recognized, unified and efficient communication. How do you translate the requirements of a job and the organizational environment in order to characterize the person required for the job?

The SILVER ACE model offers a homogeneous language to describe and characterize the organization, the team, the individual, the occupation and the job. It is a language with defined letters, accepted words, connections and a defined syntax. The SILVER ACE language makes it possible to characterize a team and describe a job using the same terms we would use to define the person. The model makes possible a graphic representation identical for each concept and the examination of overlapping elements, such as the characteristics of a job, a person or an organization.

SILVER ACE as an educational concept

There is no shortage of knowledge and information in our world. In the past, learning was based on knowledge accumulation and its processing, whereas nowadays it is difficult, if not impossible, to keep up with the pace at which knowledge is developing. This is driving a dire need for change in academic teaching methods: Schools must move from transferring knowledge to providing tools for knowledge acquisition. Students will then be able to continue the process on their own even after they complete their formal studies, ensuring that they will be capable of dealing with vast amounts of frequently updated knowledge and information. Schools will need to teach how to study; they must make learning a pleasant experience with much more emphasis on **how** than on **what**.

Traditional learning is mainly based on developing the left brain, with particular emphasis on I.Q. Psychometric and psycho-technical tests have high predictive validity, but developing the left brain alone doesn't prepare the student for the skills and life of the future. Even though the computer still beats humans in the I.Q.-L battle, it is very important to develop programs for enhancing emotional intelligence. Developing creativity, initiative, management skills, and the ability to cope with change and with order – namely knowledge and wisdom – is much more important than learning by rote. Schools and societies that wish to prepare the next generation for the future should develop all eight factors while understanding the relative importance of each, proffering a complete set of skills for life. The main message is the deep need to develop the entire array while stressing the importance of developing and maintaining balances.

Comparison with other typological theories

Ned Herrmann's Whole Brain

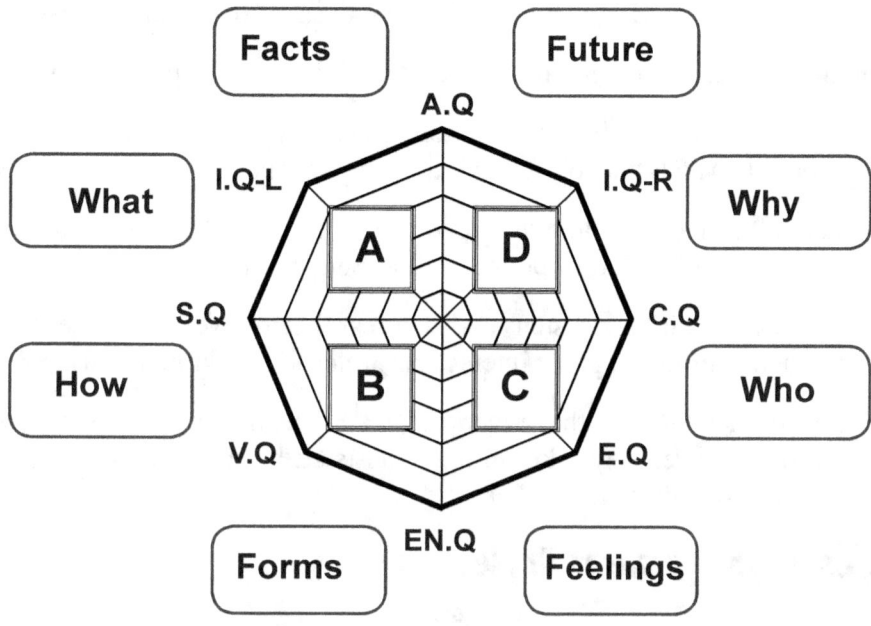

William Edward (Ned) Herrmann (1922-1999), a physicist and musician, was the head of the management education department at General Electric. He is known for his research on creative thinking and the elaboration of the "whole brain" method. Herrmann devoted twenty years of his life to implementing his theory of learning and teaching methods. The two axes of his model represent the four quadrants of the brain he describes: The lower brain, the upper brain, the right brain and the left brain.

The lower brain – This is the stem of the brain – the area responsible for all involuntary, instinctive activity that regulates vital functioning. The brain stem is also known as "the animal brain" for its manner of functioning and because it is present in all animals. It is sometimes referred to as the "reptilian brain" since it constitutes a part of our evolutionary past.

The upper brain – The upper brain is also known as the "new brain" since it developed in the later stages of our evolution. It constitutes the cerebral cortex in which complex thought processes occur pertaining to understanding and consciousness. This type of cerebral activity represents some of humankind's highest capacities.

The right and left brain – This division is better known than others. Even though Ned Herrmann discusses this division of the brain, it is important to state that we are not dealing with neurophysiology but with the metaphorical sense of the right-left and lower-upper division of the brain, which refers to different functions and modes of thinking (see above). Ned Herrmann developed his "Whole Brain" typology on the basis of this overall perspective.

Herrmann divides people into four types according to four modes of thinking:

A: Analytical thinkers gather information then analyze and examine processes and ideas based on facts and logic. Analytical thinkers pose the question "**What**?"

B: Sequential thinkers deal with forms, details, step-by-step solutions of problems, organization and implementation. Sequential thinkers ask "**How**?"

C: Interpersonal thinkers listen and express themselves; they search for interpersonal meaning and group interactions. Interpersonal thinkers ask "**Who**?"

D: Creative thinkers look at the bigger picture, concentrating on looking toward and seeing the future; they take initiative assisted by metaphors, images and creativity. Creative thinkers ask "**Why**?"

Adizes' Management Styles

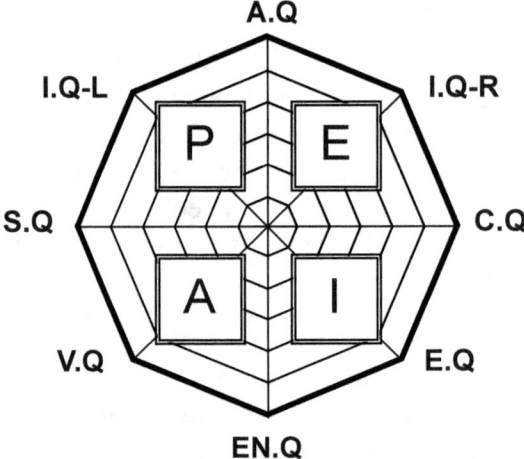

Professor Ichak Adizes' widely popular management model, first published in his book How to Solve the Mismanagement Crisis (1980), is basically a synergetic model. In his model, correct managerial decisions are made thanks to four characteristics representing different management types and styles constituting the cornerstones of every organization and function. These four types comprise descriptions of individuals, functions and organizations alike.

P (Productive) – generates results

Performance oriented and focused on action and results; tends towards "putting out fires"; quick, efficient and results-oriented style of decision making. Characteristic questions: "What? How much? How many?"

A (Administrative) – administers and generates processes

By-the-book, methodical manager; cautious, analytical, logical, and rigidly procedural; makes decisions in strict accordance with precedents or rules of logic; defines new procedures. Characteristic questions: "How? When?"

E (Entrepreneurial) – the initiator

Creative; breaks away from conventional wisdom and other customs; enthusiastic, makes others enthusiastic too; charismatic; makes decisions on the spur of the moment; erratic. Characteristic question: "Why?"

I (Integration) – the integrator

Creates harmony; relates to people and builds teams; interpersonally sensitive. Characteristic question: "Who?"

The SILVER ACE expands Adizes' approach to managerial types. For each depicted managerial style, the model makes it possible to examine which types of skills should be activated in order to succeed. The dominant factor for the productive type is logical-quantitative thinking (I.Q.-L); the dominant factors for the entrepreneur are intuition and creativity (I.Q.-R); the dominant factor for the integrator is emotional intelligence (E.Q.); and as for the administrator, the dominant factors are a combination of system and structure (S.Q.) and value (V.Q.).

Jung's Personality Model

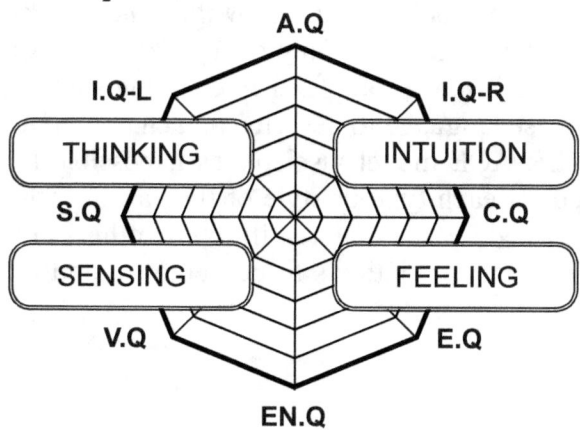

Carl Gustav Jung (1875-1961), the Swiss psychiatrist and psychoanalyst, one of Freud's leading disciples and one of the founders of modern psychology, describes two dichotomies of opposite functions representing the structure of the brain:

First: **Thinking** versus **Feeling**

Second: **Intuition** versus **Sensation**

Jung demonstrated his approach by the contemplation of a picture of the Madonna holding the baby Jesus and described how one could look at the picture in different ways: One can consciously **think** about the picture and wonder whether the depicted characters actually portray a real life; one can **feel** attraction or repulsion, love or compassion towards the characters; one can **sense** the picture as an object (perceive the oil paint on the canvas, the sitting figure, the color of the background, the texture of the colors, and so on); finally, the picture can also arouse very significant associations or **intuitions** (the sacred and profound relationship between the earth and mothers as the creators of new life).

Jung's approach sets the four functions around a circle whose structure largely overlaps that of the SILVER ACE as shown in the diagram above. These four archetypes – thinking, feeling, sensation and intuition – served as a basis to develop the MBTI (Myers-Briggs Type Indicator) assessment system, a questionnaire that describes a person in relation to the four archetypes deriving a complex array of typologies.

General summary

The models presented here represent a typology of four archetypes/functions, which in turn represent the four quadrants of the circle. Some of them place the individual at a single point in space, while others locate the individual in four dimensions by means of a "key of four." The SILVER ACE is built upon a "key of eight," a more complex key enabling spatial characterization and a rich and diverse language to describe and characterize types, roles and styles. The SILVER ACE model also makes it possible to examine which skills are required for each type or style of the various other models. Some types are characterized by one major skill, while others are endowed with a profile of several principal quotients to be demonstrated through types and archetypes.

The Horizontal Axis

The right and the left hemispheres

Two brains: Two different central processing units (CPU) operating on different principles

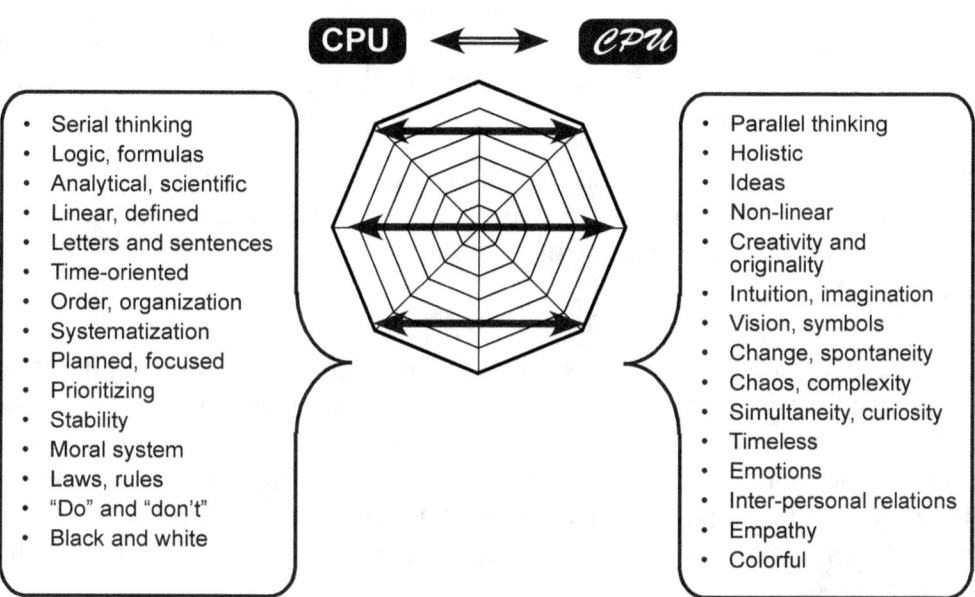

- Serial thinking
- Logic, formulas
- Analytical, scientific
- Linear, defined
- Letters and sentences
- Time-oriented
- Order, organization
- Systematization
- Planned, focused
- Prioritizing
- Stability
- Moral system
- Laws, rules
- "Do" and "don't"
- Black and white

- Parallel thinking
- Holistic
- Ideas
- Non-linear
- Creativity and originality
- Intuition, imagination
- Vision, symbols
- Change, spontaneity
- Chaos, complexity
- Simultaneity, curiosity
- Timeless
- Emotions
- Inter-personal relations
- Empathy
- Colorful

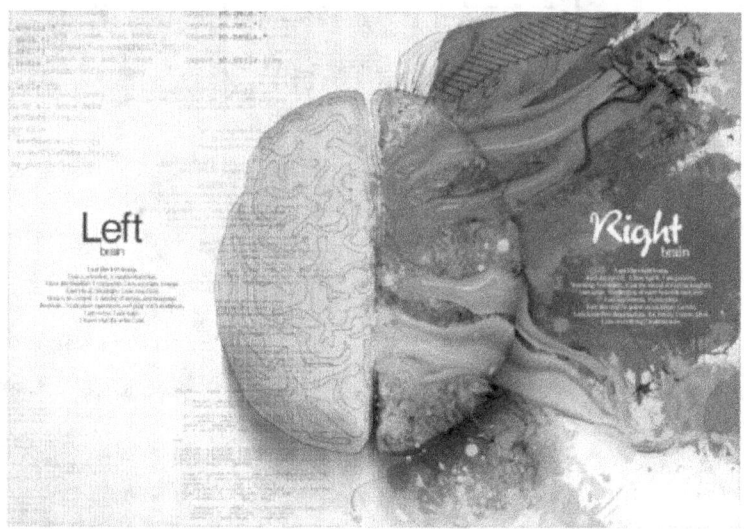

A Mercedes ad representing the right and left sides of the brain

The horizontal axis shifts from right to left and represents the duality between the two opposed and complementary poles. Many names have been given to the dual complexity in every person. We have chosen to use as our image the right and left sides of the brain. This dual approach is found in many teachings and theories, and in a certain way, the SILVER ACE feeds off all of them: neurological, biological, psychological, anthropological and philosophical approaches – feminine versus masculine, the yin versus the yang.

In the SILVER ACE model there are three pairs of quotients that have a right and a left expression on all three central strata, whereas the two other quotients situated on opposite ends of the vertical axis have no expression of right or left.

The use of the terms "right" and "left" here holds no value judgment (feminine - masculine) or political judgment (right wing - left wing), nor in the literal physiological-neurological sense of location.

Right and left in the human body

The metaphor of right and left is visually expressed in the following diagram of the structure of the human eye: Two of the main components of vision, the rods and the cones, are each connected to a different part of the brain. The cones, responsible for focus, are connected to the left side of the brain, being more involved in the perception of detail. The rods, connected to the right side of the brain, are in charge of the bigger picture, including background and surroundings.

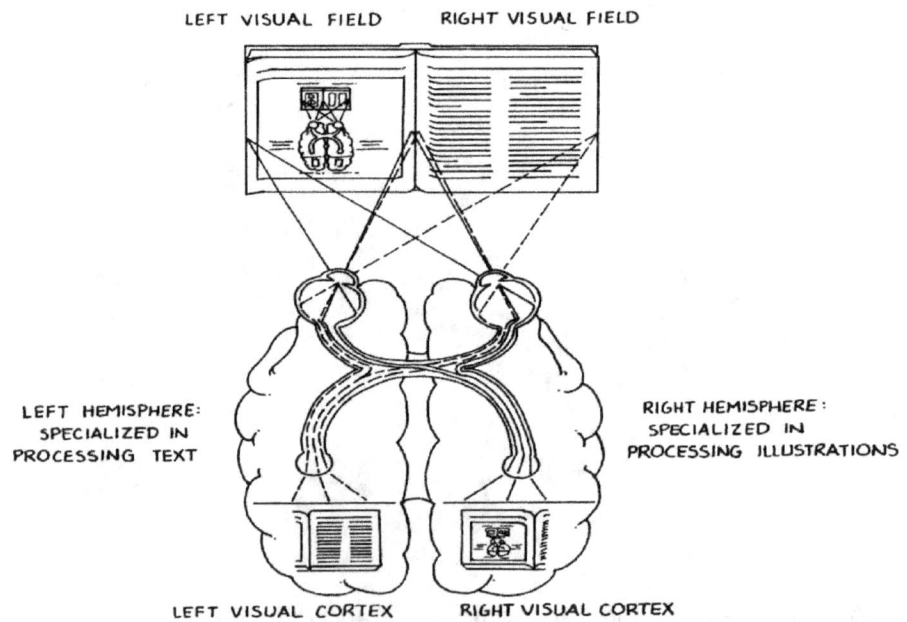

LEFT VISUAL FIELD   RIGHT VISUAL FIELD

LEFT HEMISPHERE:
SPECIALIZED IN
PROCESSING TEXT

RIGHT HEMISPHERE:
SPECIALIZED IN
PROCESSING ILLUSTRATIONS

LEFT VISUAL CORTEX   RIGHT VISUAL CORTEX

The limbs are also connected to the brain, but each one receives its commands from the opposite side. Here, we can also distinguish different and unique types of activity for each part of the brain. Recognizing that most human beings are right-handed, the right hand will serve more to gather and pick things up, while the left hand will hold them. In all paintings of the Madonna and her baby, she is cradling the child with her protecting left arm. In contrast, throwing a spear-like object, or cutting with a sharp tool is normally done with the right hand, which is controlled by the left brain lobe. Such characteristics are at the root of the two basic human behaviors – hunting and gathering.

In the 19th century, neurologists and brain specialists noticed that tumors or wounds in the right side of the brain cause different mental phenomena than those observed in the left side. Over time, it was discovered that the left side of the brain is in charge, among other things, of our capacity to use language, mathematical faculty and the sense of time, while the right side is mainly responsible for body image and its perception, orientation in space, motor skills and identifying people. By the 1960s, it was widely understood that the left hemisphere conducts rational and logical thinking, while the right hemisphere manages thinking which is more intuitive and creative.

The division of the brain in two hemispheres is unique to humans. In all other species of animals, even the most developed, there is no division between right and left; if you throw a banana at a monkey, it may catch it once with the left hand then with the right with no preference of one hand over the other. If you throw a ball at a human, he will catch it with his dominant hand – usually the right.

Researchers have discovered that the human brain actually operates as two separate brains. The hemispheres process different kinds of information and distinctly divide the work. The left side thinks in an analytic, reductionist manner, and operates in a linear, orderly way, while the right side of the brain thinks in a holistic manner, with associative and simultaneous thinking based on images and shapes. Nonetheless, it would be inaccurate to imagine that there is a small artist sitting in the right side and a small mathematician in the left and that depending on the situation only one of them is active. In fact, in most cases both parts of the brain are active, but there is an inclination towards one side over the other in relation to the content of the activity. Think of it like a computer with two processors (CPU [Central Processing Unit]) that work in different ways, based on different principles, but work in parallel by dividing tasks and workload.

The left brain – The sequential, serial processor operates in a linear and analytic way, in control of reasoning as well as linear and goal-oriented thinking. The left brain is involved with written language and mathematics, both being linear processes: It is impossible to begin a sentence in the middle and move backwards, and it is impossible to understand a mathematical formula if it is not written in order. The left brain deals with implementation, with the operation of tools, analyzing situations and discerning details within the whole picture. For generations, Western civilization gave preference to the left brain, thus it is tightly linked to such concepts as laws, definitions, principles and order.

The right brain – This is the parallel processor. The right brain operates in a holistic manner and deals with synthesis rather than analysis. It is decentralized and disorganized, and it handles emotions, associations and patterns (gestalt). It is intuitive, illogical and thinks in terms of shapes and icons, associations and sensations. It is able to recognize a familiar face even after many decades despite physical changes that have occurred over time. Through it one can sense the "other," interpret irrational sensory and nonverbal messages and get the complete picture beyond its details. The right brain constitutes a gateway to the worlds of dreams and mysticism.

Simon Baron-Cohen, professor of developmental psychology at Cambridge University and author of The Essential Difference: Men, Women and the Extreme Male Brain (2006), believes that the brains of men and women are biologically different. The female brain is designed first and foremost for empathy – the natural and spontaneous connection to the thoughts and feelings of another person; whereas the male brain tends towards understanding systems and building them. He concludes his book by saying that men love charts and women love people.

M.R.I. – magnetic resonance imaging, showing brain activity areas – tests show that men and women differ in their approaches to tackling problems. Men, in general, tend to start off by activating broad areas of brain activity to be reduced and focused later on in the process, while women prefer operating ever-widening areas of cerebral activity. Female strategy expands the circles, while male strategy reduces and focuses.

The origins of the right-left dichotomy

Dualism in Philosophy

Dualism is a concept that describes every belief or philosophical, scientific or theological system that perceives the entities in the world and the world itself as based on two categories or elements. This approach draws everything from two, sometimes conflicting, basic principles. Striking contrasts are, for example, body-soul, causality-purposefulness, matter-spirit, and object-subject. Various social and philosophical theories deal with duality in general and with the right-left and body-soul duality more specifically. Plato, for one, distinguished between the world as perceived through the senses and the world of ideas; Descartes claimed that the activities of one's soul and body are two distinct and separate qualities; Kant distinguished between the world of phenomena and the "thing" itself.

The Yin and Yang concept

Yin/Yang represents the cultural understanding of the ancient Chinese tradition, which is also expressed in modern management theories. The Yin/Yang concept originally referred to male and female forces, the Yin representing the female and the Yang representing the male. This division represents the main cosmic forces present in everything that maintain a dialogue of harmony and struggle. The Chinese, for example, believe in duality as a form of drama  between two forces operating at the core of all existence and creation. Although these two forces are seemingly opposed, they are in fact complementary; the tension between them creates perfection. This duality is present in every phenomenon and human value, and each aspect contains the core of the other. The togetherness and wholeness these create is obvious in the Yin/Yang symbol.

History as the story of the relationship between right and left cultures

In his book The Alphabet Versus the Goddess: The Conflict Between Word and Image (1999), neurologist and researcher Leonard Shlain presents the drama in the relationship between the two parts of the brain as representative of a battle between cultures, religions and the sexes. Shlain reviews the history of mankind as a chain of skirmishes between the left and the right brain. In his opinion, the past 500 years of Western civilization reflect the dominance of the left brain. According to Shlain, the Age of Enlightenment began with the invention of printing and the clock, thus ending the right-brain dominance that characterized the medieval era. The invention of printing made reading and writing, left-brain activities par excellence, accessible to all.

In the middle of the 20th century, a counterrevolution began: Right-brain culture returned to prominence with the use of graphic print, photography, television and movies – and later, the computer and the internet; these are all aspects of visual media, the dominion of the right brain. They now dominate interpersonal as well as multinational communication. Today, it is hard to imagine an idea without a clear illustration. In our minds, the atom bomb comes up first as the image of a mushroom cloud, and only later does additional information accompany it. The young grow up with television and the internet, training daily, intensively, in developing the right brain.

Concurrently, science is flourishing, especially computer science, based on left-side thinking; yet we are also witnessing widespread awareness of the need for personal empowerment, spirituality and the return to nature – characteristics based on right-side thinking. In this combination, nothing is done at the expense of the other but embodies the principle of "this and that, and the more the better." The 21st century is the epoch of the holistic mind: both sides of the brain operating simultaneously and interactively.

This interesting drama of the struggle between right and left is occurring in computing. On a certain level, the world of computing and programming is the prototype of the **left** brain as it is orderly, highly logical and technical, but making computers more user-friendly is accomplished with graphic icons and symbols based on intuition and association, which are the characteristics of the **right** brain. The computer, which at first served as database and computing tool, led to the internet – a system functioning seemingly without rules, based on both simultaneity and endless creativity. It is a universe through which we surf without a logical structure, through associations and links. This system was created and is enjoyed by the generation that grew up in front of a television set and a computer screen, the generation whose right brain is highly developed. Facebook often uses visual representations and creation of interpersonal ties, thus, the members of the Facebook generation keep their right brains fit on a daily basis.

In his book A Whole New Mind: Why Right-Brainers Will Rule the Future (2009), researcher Daniel Pink argues that the analytical left-brain era has exhausted itself and is coming to an end. Creativity will make the breakthrough to a new path as that would be expressed through the computer man who would liberate his right brain (see Steve Jobs). As Dr. Asher Idan, a researcher whose expertise is in technological culture, has seen "the future of careers and the labor market in arts and creation rather than engineering." Professor Nicholas Negroponte, head of the MIT Media Laboratory, who is quoted in Pink's book said, "In situations of engineering stagnation, breakthroughs are accomplished by people who aren't engineers."

Right and left in the SILVER ACE model

The model assumes that the healthy state of an individual or an organization is a state of energy intensification and healthy energy flow, in which both processors can be developed and run at full power in different or opposite directions simultaneously, so that a person can be both very creative and emotional as well as very logical and goal oriented. This is the real Ace.

The ability to combine such mental characteristics and use them in a balanced way offers maximal employment of the potential of human thought, which is precisely the challenge an Ace faces. Without right-brain intelligence, source of the creative aspect and breaking of conventions, there can be no true genius; still, brilliant ideas have no meaning if they cannot be proven by mathematical calculations and scientific predictions. Therefore, the characteristics of right and left are not opposites but counterbalances. The uniqueness of humans is in their ability to activate and orchestrate different processors. Healthy energy flow on the horizontal axis comes from the right side, the feminine, creative and intuitive side, moving towards the logical, organized and methodical left side. This is the movement from the side in which things originate towards the other side where they become established as a theory which can be realized.

Albert Einstein is the embodiment of the energy flow between right and left. Einstein is known as a physicist and mathematician, but he was also an avid violinist. The right side of his brain enabled him to imagine riding a train faster than the speed of light, while the left side was occupied in a search for a mathematical solution to the problem of traveling beyond the speed of light. No breakthrough is possible without the existence of two developed processors and the aptitude to move between them. The left brain does not break through paradigms or change what already is but rather seeks to preserve, which is why emotion, creation and change will remain one-time occurrences unless the left side turns them into patterns and frameworks.

Beyond right and left?

It is important to understand and place that which is "beyond" the confines of the model, beyond its right and left but still part of it. Beyond the right is the world of chaos, disorder, the world of muses and sirens, and a place where new and brilliant ideas and gut feelings sprout and grow. It is the primeval idea from which everything new that hadn't previously existed grows. From there it then moves over to the left side in order to create a concept, a manifestation or an action. Beyond the human left side is the "expert" system, a system that turns ideas into an algorithm which can be replicated, a system that doesn't depend on anyone whatsoever.

An idea or a flash of inspiration emerges from chaos then becomes reality in the human domain, in time turning it into an independent system with clear rules. Therefore, humankind serves as an interface between the world of computers, machines and formulas, and the world of muses, creativity and emotions. It is this ability to coordinate and mediate between these very different worlds that makes humans unique.

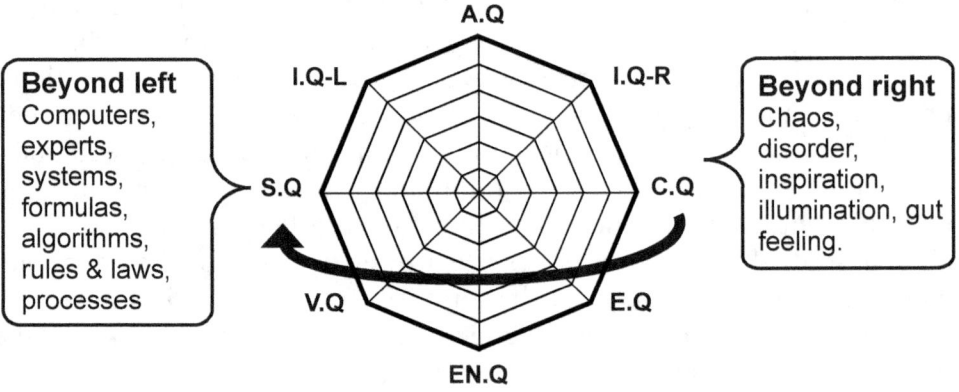

The vertical axis

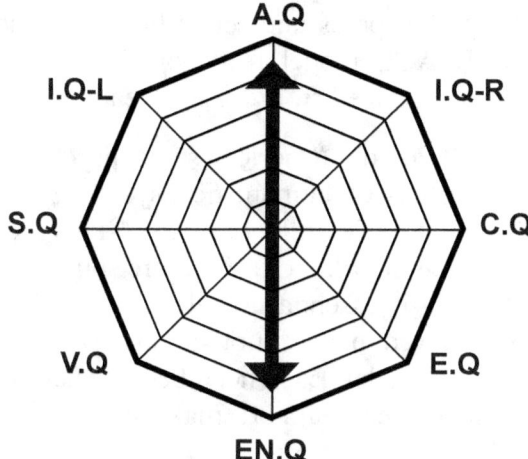

The vertical axis, which is the center of the SILVER ACE model, is a five-rung ladder.

Two vectors always affect any person climbing a ladder: Gravity, which is a vector going down, and the passion to climb, which is the vector going up. Both are vital and important as there can be no climbing without gravity and the desire to climb up.

Two forces operate on the vertical axis:
1. Downwards

2. Upwards

1		2	
Existence		Self-realization	
Adaptation		Vision	
Present		Future	
Physical		Spiritual	
Survival		Fulfilling one's potential	

The origins of the vertical axis

The vertical axis as a ladder moving from the material to the spiritual appears in different teachings, philosophies and scientific approaches. As previously mentioned, the SILVER ACE model feeds off Maslow's theory of needs combined with approaches derived from Eastern teachings of energy.

Abraham Maslow (1908-1970), the American social psychologist, is considered one of the principal theorists of humanistic psychology. He developed the eponymous theory, "Maslow's Hierarchy of Needs." This hierarchy, illustrated as a pyramid, postulates that in order to fulfill more spiritual and exalted needs connected with the "self" it is essential to fulfill the needs at the base of the pyramid first. Maslow believed that our motivations center on needs, which are organized in a hierarchical ladder. Each need becomes dominant in turn until it is satisfied, and then its power wears off, making room for the next need.

The Maslow Needs Scale with its five levels:

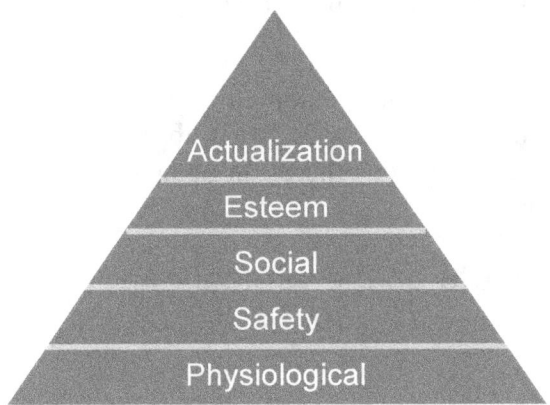

1. At the base of the pyramid are the basic physical needs such as sleep, food, water and air for breathing. At the second level of the pyramid is security for sleeping quarters, for secure employment and health.

2. The need to belong comes at the third level. It is a social need that includes the desire to belong to a group and to be part of it, to love and be loved. This step relates to consolidating self-identity.

3. The fourth level refers to the need for social recognition, the need to feel respected by others, attain status and with it admiration and social regard.

4. The fifth and last level reflects the need for self-realization based on the individual's ability to realize one's unique skills thus expressing the unique and personal potential.

In the 21st century, people are more occupied in fulfilling the higher needs in the pyramid, especially those of realizing their aspirations, what Maslow calls self-actualization. An in-depth study of Maslow's theory shows that it is not just a hierarchical ladder. Human purpose is much more complex and interactive than the metaphor of climbing a ladder. It is more like widening circles since man is also in search of love and even the meaning of his existence. We operate for the simultaneous realization of the full range of our needs.

How needs and passions differ

The Maslow Needs Scale identifies human needs which must be satisfied. Having satisfied one need, one is free to satisfy a higher one. Once fulfilled, one can forget about it and move on to the next. The need to eat or drink is satisfied by drinking or eating. Likewise, the need to belong and the need to feel socially safe are satisfied when certain conditions are met. Need is satisfied from the outside in; in other words, bringing in something from the outside that satisfies the need we feel within us.

In addition to Maslow's Needs Scale, the SILVER ACE model's vertical axis integrates the notion of human energy. The intensity of human energy manifests itself through human passion.

The distinction between needs and passions was addressed and discussed by the French Jewish philosopher Emmanuel Levinas in the 20th century: While a need is finite and works its way from outside inwards, passion is infinite and arises within a person and radiates out. For example, our desire to eat "gourmet" food persists even after having satisfied the basic need for food; the desire for love also persists even after having attained a sense of safety and belonging.

One of the rules defined by the legendary investor Warren Buffett says, "Without passion, you don't have energy. Without energy, you have nothing!"

In the SILVER ACE model, passion is the main energy motor putting skills and potential into motion.

Comparative table between need and passion:

Need	Passion
finite	infinite
from the outside inwards	from the inside outwards
limited energy	continuous energy

The Eastern Theories of Energy Centers

The seven chakra centers

7. Crown
6. Third eye
5. Throat
.4 Heart
3. Solar plexus
2. Sex
1. Root

Oriental teachings attribute humans with a hierarchical scale of energy centers.

The term "chakra" derives from Sanskrit and refers to energy centers located in the human body in charge of the functioning of different parts of the body and the soul. Energy is perceived as the life force, the Chi. According to Oriental medicine, an illness is a disruption of the equilibrium of the body's energy systems. The chakras are organized in ascending order from physiological to spiritual, starting with the root chakra and the sacral chakra, both connected with sex and existence, with the corresponding energy located in the pelvis The chain of chakras then makes its way up through the solar plexus and the heart chakras, the centers of emotion, further up through the throat chakra, which is the center of communication, followed by the chakra of intellect (the third eye) and the highest chakra (the crown chakra), the center of spiritual insight located at the very top of the head.

This scale includes many elements remarkably similar to Maslow's Scale of Needs and the SILVER ACE's vertical axis.

Flows and blocks of energy

The SILVER ACE considers its quotients similar to energy centers, like chakras or meridians. Each quotient is an energy center in charge of a certain skill or characteristic. In Eastern medicine, a person is deemed healthy when all energy centers are filled with energy flowing freely among them. A sick person has energy blocks, thus he lacks active energy in some energy centers. The essence of healing medicine opens the blockages and stirs up energy centers.

So does the SILVER ACE. It deals with healthy energy flow and the prevention of pathological energy blocks. Unlike the above mentioned models which embody a one-dimensional scale of one energy center per rung, our model consists of three right-left pairs which must keep a healthy energy flow from right to left and feminine to masculine, as an energy blockage will cause atrophy, stagnation and impasse.

Levels of the vertical axis in the SILVER ACE model

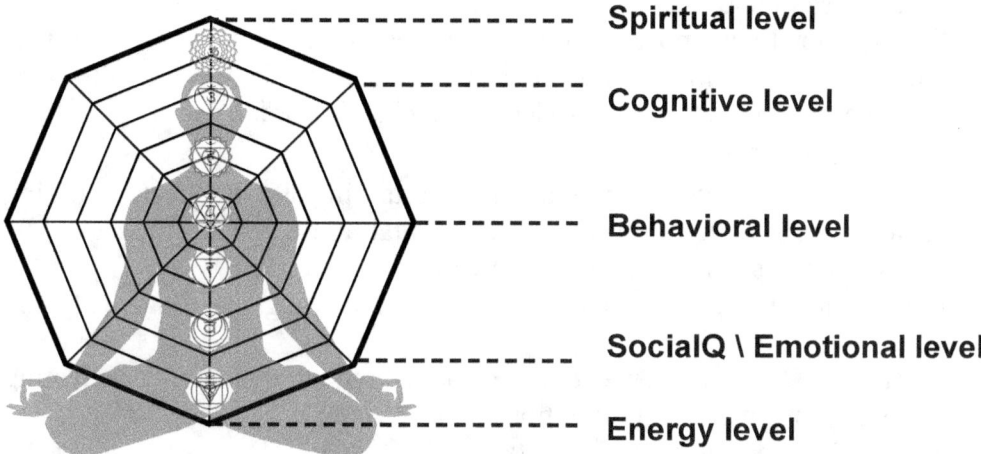

Spiritual level

Cognitive level

Behavioral level

SocialQ \ Emotional level

Energy level

The vertical axis of the SILVER ACE is a five-level/five-step ladder parallel with Maslow's Hierarchy of Needs or the chakra system of energy centers. The three middle levels are associated with different quotients (right and left), while the base level (raw energy) and the top level (spiritual energy) are each associated with one quotient only.

1. **The Energy level**
   This integrates the **EN.Q.** the Energy and Endurance quotient, which represents energy vital to living and survival.
   This quotient is responsible for generating, managing and consolidating energy, preventing its loss and ensuring its flow through all other parts of the model. This level consists of only one quotient with no right-left characteristics.

2. **The Social/Emotional level**
   This level characterizes a person's emotional and moral maturity and has two faces, thus including both right and left with energy flowing from emotional to moral. This level integrates the personality quotients that are essential to any effective society, organization, or business.
   E.Q.: The Emotional Intelligence quotient – emotions and empathy;
   V.Q.: The Value quotient – principles and rules.

3. **The Behavioral level**

The behavioral level represents one's spheres of activity and performance. It is situated between the emotional/social level and that of the intellectual/cognitive, both of which impact behavior. This is the central horizontal axis of the model, where the distinction between right and left is most pronounced. In this level, there is the greatest tension between the edges and it is the most sensitive to lack of balance; it embodies two quotients.

C.Q. – Chaos and Change quotient;

S.Q. – System and Structure quotient.

The behavioral axis moves between the edges, from chaos, change, conflicts and simultaneity, to methodical, efficient, sequential, uniformity and simplicity. The energy flows from right to left, from chaos to order.

4. **The Cognitive level**

This level integrates characteristics pertaining to intellect, thinking methods, information processing, and mental and cognitive processes. Its role is to process information in two ways:

1. Left - Identifying patterns and laws, understanding, learning, analyzing and drawing conclusions.
2. Right - Breaking conventions, stepping out of frameworks, creating novelty, originality and intuition.

It embodies the following quotients:

I.Q.-L – The left intelligence quotient, which deals with reduction, concentration, clarity and goal setting.

I.Q.-R – The right intelligence quotient, based on widening one's perspective and creating broadening associative connections.

In addition to rational and logical thinking, it refers to thinking through the heart, intuition, the third eye, art and creativity. One cannot be a star without a variety of thinking modes guiding one's actions. This domain is identified with the head. The cognitive level is situated between the behavioral and the spiritual levels; it influences the former and is influenced by the latter. Energy flows from right to left.

5. **The Spiritual level**

The top level is the domain of spiritual energy, which is equivalent to the top level of Maslow's Needs Ladder and marks aspirations and the power of self-realization. This is the crown chakra, the point of connection between man and the realms of personal psychology and thought. It holds the **A.Q.**, the quotient of ambition, vision, mission, aspirations, the need for achievement and self-realization. Here, there is also separation between left and right. The right-left separation, which reaches its peak in the behavioral level, becomes redundant in the spiritual level and resumes a state of uniformity, as it does in the raw energy level, the EN.Q.

The Eight Quotients of the Model

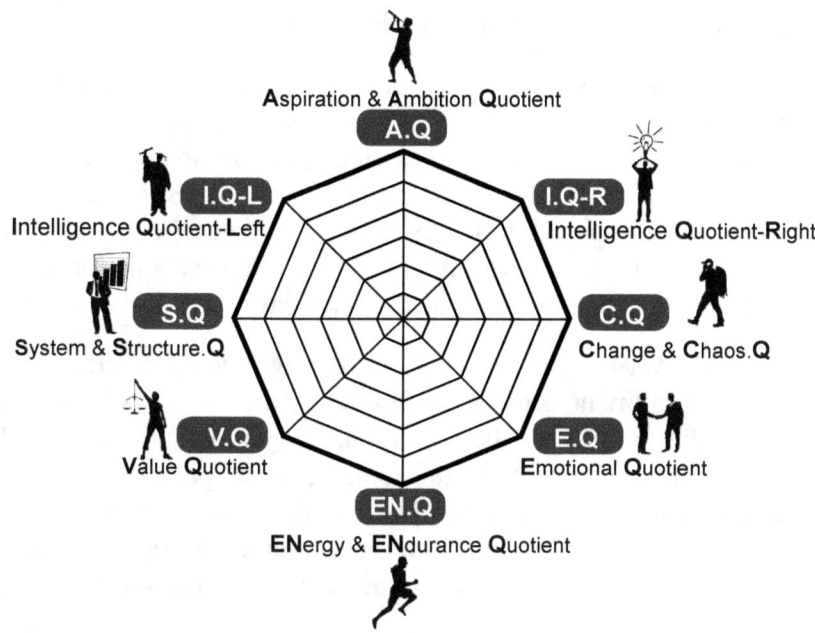

The model quotients by their different layers:

1.   **Energy** - with the energy and endurance quotient;
2.   **Social/emotional**- with the emotional intelligence quotient and the value quotient
3.   **Behavior** - with the system and structure quotient;
4.   **Cognitive** - with the classic, creative and intuitive I.Q.;
5.   **Spiritual** - with the aspiration and vision quotient.

The 8 Q's in the book:

Q.-1   **EN.Q** - ENergy & ENdurance Quotient

Q.-2   **I.Q.-L** - Left- Intelligence Quotient

Q.-3   **I.Q.-R** - Right- Intelligence Quotient

Q.-4   **C.Q** - Change & Chaos Quotient

Q.-5   **S.Q** - System & Structure Quotient

Q.-6   **E.Q** - Emotional Quotient

Q.-7   **V.Q** - Value Quotient

Q.-8   **A.Q** - Aspiration & Ambition Quotient

The Energy Level

The energy level is the base of the SILVER ACE model.

It is analogous to the basic existential stage of Maslow's Hierarchy of Needs and the basic chakra responsible for generating one's get-up-and-go; it therefore represents our survival strength, our existence in the present and our will to preserve existence. This level creates, manages and intensifies energy, causing it to flow through all parts of the model. It is directly connected with the physical side, the state of one's health, strength, physical force and potential; therefore there are those who see it as the physical aspect of human skills.

The raw energy level has not been as extensively studied as other levels, and there is still an argument over which domain it belongs in. Some think this level is part of the physical-medical domain, just as the spiritual level belongs with the philosophical- transcendental domain. In the past, these two domains were out of the scope of occupational psychology, which is why no satisfactory assessment tools were developed. But in recent years the importance of the raw energy level and the central role it has in the achievement of success have gained more recognition.

The energy transformation scale

Energy is the foundation of our existence; therefore, the energy axis is the central axis of existence and of the model.

Every organism and living creature is a sophisticated and unique system of energy transformation processes (permutation, change and metamorphosis): from the leaf to the caterpillar, or from the insect to the mammal. Humans represent the highest complexity of energy transformations reached by evolution, starting from physical transformations, through thinking and consciousness, finally reaching a state of spiritual energy. Understanding that "all is energy" is one of the significant triumphs of the 21sty century. Modern physics largely contributed to understanding that "all is energy"; everything around us – objects, plants, structures and people – embodies energy systems at different states of energy aggregation.

The vertical axis of the SILVER ACE refers to a different kind of energy present at every layer without which skills and capabilities remain mere potential. Each quotient has a facet of skills, personality and energy. Energy connecting with a skill transforms it into an action quotient of success which will be expressed in that person's passion to utilize both skills and ardor to be creative and not merely be a person with creative skills.

Q - 1
EN.Q. - ENERGY & ENDURANCE
Quotient

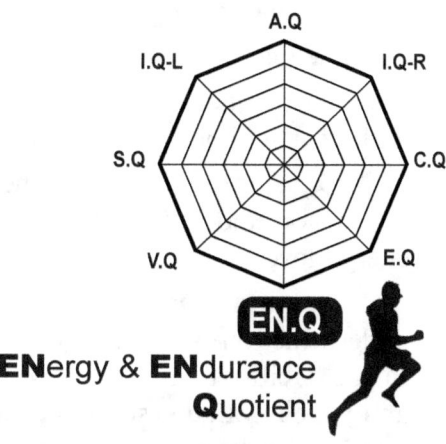

ENergy & ENdurance
Quotient

Identity

Name: Energy and Endurance Quotient

Symbol: EN.Q.

This quotient is the most important from all the 8 Q's!!

It refers to all the indexes attributed to energy creation and distribution to all the other Q's. as well as the degree of vitality, dynamism and the drive associated with it. It also refers to energy endurance and preservation facing distress and hardship and adversity.

Characteristics:

1. **Energy quotient** - the creation and management of energy;

2. **Endurance quotient** - preserving energy and preventing burnout.

Key Words:

Engine

Energy

Endurance

Expression at work: Vigor, passion for action, swift performance, dynamism, ability to handle failure in situations of defeat.

Deficiencies:	Fatigue, depression, low self-esteem.
Location in the model	**Vertical axis** – the energy level
	Horizontal axis – center
	Counterbalance – aspiration quotient (A.Q.)
Neighbors in the model	1) Emotional intelligence (E.Q.)
	2) Value quotient (V.Q.)

The energy quotient sustains relations of reciprocity with its neighbors in the model:

1) E.Q., emotional intelligence -affects optimism, depression and pessimism, which themselves affect energy levels.

2) V.Q., value quotient – a deficient value system undermines one's capacity for believing in oneself and in one's ability to take action. People of high integrity and a clear value system are known for their ability to muster the strength to complete tasks through their strong inner commitment.

The Characteristics of the Energy Quotient

"...energy is the currency of the universe..."

Professor Richard Feynman

The word "energy" derives from the word energeia, the Greek **EN**, which means **doing**. Where there is no energy, there is no action. The S.I.L.V.E.R .A.C.E model is engaged in the expression of energy in the world of action.

According to Professor Richard Feynman, 1965 Physics Nobel Prize winner (1918–1988), activities are energy transactions. There is no sale without the transfer of energy from salesman to buyer. A salesman with no energy doesn't sell. We bring our energy into our work for which we get paid in return; this fills us with various energies such as purchase, strength, happiness and security.

"Energy is the currency of the universe." = "Money is energy in a potential accumulative state."

The energy index represents all the indexes that relate to a person's energy. The vitality quotient represents the extent of internal motivation leading to activity and doing. It is the power engine that determines a person's level of dynamism and intensity. It is the fire burning within us. A person with high energy levels is known for his vitality and his strong drive to be active. In order to rise, to become the Ace that you really are, you need a reserve of constantly renewable energy and strength. When one is devoid of energy, all other quotients become irrelevant. When in that state, a person's ability to operate at his best will be extremely limited despite all his advantages.

Many studies show that the managers and leaders of successful companies are endowed with tremendous energy; they are their organization's source of energy.

Research shows that successful firms borrow their energy from their leaders and managers who are gifted with tremendous energy.

> *"If I had to choose one common, outstanding characteristic of the hidden champions, it would be their leaders…. They are as different as people in general, but all are imbued with the **power and enthusiasm** that move their companies foward… and they appear to possess nearly **inexhaustible energy**, stamina, and perseverance."*
>
> *Hermann Simon, CEO of Simon, Kucher & Partners, management consultants*
> *"**Executive EQ: Emotional Intelligence in Leadership and Organizations**" – pp.19-20*

Of all the quotients, energy is the simplest and clearest index, albeit the most revolutionary.

The energy quotient is responsible for the proper energy flow through all the quotients in the model; without energy, the various different skills we possess do not translate into practice and therefore become meaningless. The energy quotient can be seen as the heart; the engine in charge of blood flow and oxygen through all the different organs. Without blood flow, even the most sophisticated organ will degenerate and cease to function.

In the world of assessment, there are many examples of the importance of the energy quotient and the connection between it and the person's other attributes. As an example, the manager of a large industrial company took a screening test in order to be promoted to a new position. He turned out to be highly skilled and able but was nonetheless not recommended. When I presented the test results to the CEO, he disapproved of them and criticized the lack of precision of the assessment tools we had used. He knew and appreciated the manager and assumed that he was the right man for the job. As we disagreed with him, we decided to ask the manager to join the conversation. I showed him the illustration of his test results, which was that of an energy-depleted, worn-out manager. The candidate was silent at first but then suddenly burst into tears and shared with us the exhaustion he had been experiencing for quite some time and his feeling that he did not have the strength and the energy the managerial position required.

Everyone dealing with assessment intuitively relates to the energy quotient, the level of which determines the initial and principal impression of any entrepreneur, manager or salesman in any job interview. The energy quotient is no guarantee of success but is imperative for its existence. There are energetic people who are not necessarily Aces, but there are no Aces devoid of energy. An Ace lacking energy is a dead one. Even though there are no clear means with which energy can be measured it remains one of the major outstanding elements for the prediction of success. If I had to choose one single success factor it would be an abundance of energy. Given a satisfactory level of energy it is possible to successfully develop all the other factors.

The ENergy Quotient – ENgine and Fuel

Energy production in a car depends on the type of engine and suitable fuel. EN.Q. is the engine that carries a person or firm successfully to its goals, hence the letters of its name – **En**gine. Just as a sophisticated, fancy car cannot get very far with a weak engine or no fuel, by the same token a highly capable person lacking EN.Q., which determines the size of the quotient, will not succeed. Any vehicle – scooter or truck– needs the power to match the engine. Our psycho-physiological infrastructure, affected by hereditary, nutritional, hormonal and health-related factors, determines the volume of our energy.

Drive, motivation, need or ambition to do things, are driving forces like fuel. Some stem from the need to compensate for other deficiencies or past experiences. In that case, a person would be motivated by his wish to fix or restore something from his past, to compensate for feelings of inferiority and prove himself to the world. This approach contemplates that the drive could be accompanied by intense emotions bringing about creativity, but could, just the same, bring about ruination and destruction of the same magnitude.

It is important to remember that even with the best of engines and the finest fuel, the car will not move without a spark to ignite it.

EN.Q. - The 'heart' of the energy "blood system"

The EN.Q.'s task is to send energy to all the other attributes.

Energy is that which brings the potential skills to life.

"Without energy, there is nothing!" Warren Buffett

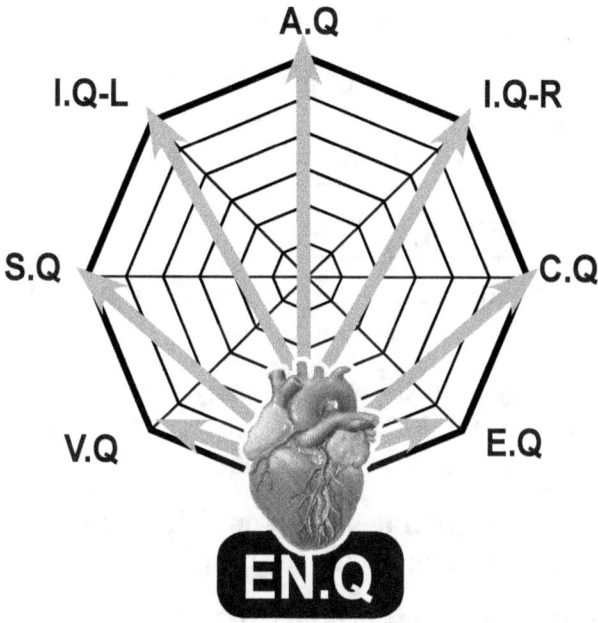

Most of the existing methods to evaluate a worker's chances to succeed are based on identifying his skills or different personality traits by means of a battery of assessment tests including dozens of subtests representing different domains of skills and aptitudes. As the chair of one of Israel's largest assessment organizations for over 35 years, I constantly developed and improved tools to identify the skills of job applicants.

We learned through experience that **skills are not enough**. Sometimes, there is a contradiction between a person's skills and the way they are actually expressed. All of a person's skills put together do not necessarily represent his abilities in action, and they do not constitute a satisfactory indication to the question of which person is worth investing in. Knowing that a lightbulb's wattage is 100 watts is not enough to make it work; we need to connect it to electric current in order for it to give light. In the same manner, I learned that we need something more that could make a skilled and capable person become a "superstar."

Many approaches to assessing skills and abilities scan and identify them but do not distinguish between potential and putting such abilities into practice. Experience has taught us that there can be a significant difference between a person who has a high I.Q. and one whose actions are intelligent and wise. Energy and passion for action are essential for drawing out an ability or talent in the occupational world; ability without passion cannot be realized. This is the difference between potential energy and kinetic energy or, more specifically, the difference between a fuel tank and a running car.

A quotient is the expression of a skill put into practice; the vector that comes from two forces that characterize the two axes of the model. One axis relates to skills and abilities and the other relates to energy.

$$\boxed{\text{Quotient}} \; = \; \boxed{\text{Energy/Passion}} \; \times \; \boxed{\text{Ability/Skills}}$$

This definition of the quotient shows the criteria for success, being the expression of human potential at its maximum:

From potential energy > to dynamic energy: When there is high energy without skills or advanced skills without energy, no high quotient will be reached because with these givens, no potential will be realized.

From a high I.Q. > to an intelligent person: High intelligence blended with energy for intellectual thinking makes an "intelligent person."

From creative aptitudes > to a productive person: Creative energy with a highly developed right brain makes a "creative person."

From motivation > to passion: The quotients consist in energy centers and skills that enable the light bulb/focus to illuminate.

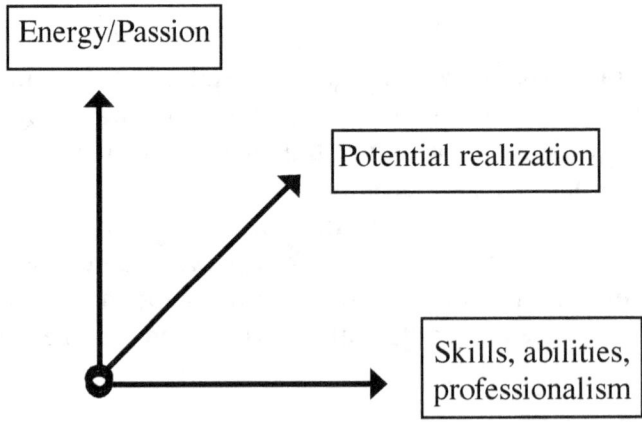

Managing Energy

Energy management deals with optimal energy production / this bring us to the law of human energy evolvement and the question:

Why do people aspire to climb the human energy ladder?

Why does a person aspire to spiritual levels and self-realization when his basic needs are met? What is that drive to climb up the ladder and evolve?

Every organism strives to make the best energy "deal." The tree grows upwards to where the sun is at its full force, thus getting the best energy "deal," which represents better energy deals, a preferred transformation and ever-growing energy coefficient.

The Law of the C.H.E. (Coefficient of Human Energy)

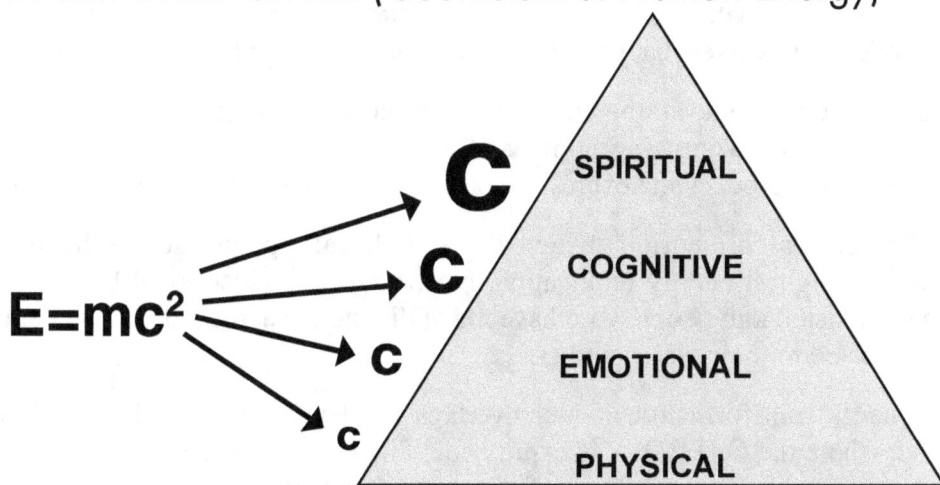

The C.H.E. law uses Einstein's energy formula to understand the ever-growing energy coefficient going up the ladder. The genius of Einstein's formula is not in the connection it makes between mass and energy (M and E), since mankind has always known that energy and mass are connected. Einstein's theory is unique in its concept of C^2 - the exponentiation of energy (the constant C in Einstein's formula refers to the speed of light). C in the equation can be referred to as a factor of variable size at different levels/strata rather than as an absolute constant, meaning that the same mass can produce different amounts of energy at different levels. For example, the paper on which these words were written has an energy value of weight. In this case, its multiplication would be utterly minimal. If we burn it, we will generate more chemical energy, and if the paper were subjected to nuclear fusion, there would be enough energy to supply the needs of an entire population.

This phenomenon is expressed on the human plain through the C.H.E. law, according to which, the higher we go on the energy evolvement ladder, the more we find ourselves in areas of ever-increasing energy coefficients. This universal law is what pushes humanity towards the best energy "deals" at the highest levels. Energy duplication occurs along the vertical axis of the SILVER ACE, as it does in Maslow's hierarchy, the chakra system and in the Kabbalah, and is set from lowest to highest. As one goes higher up the vertical axis, from matter to spirit, energy duplication increases.

1. On a physical level, energy evolvement is almost directly dependent on what we eat, namely, the calories that were in the food. In this case, the law of energy conservation applies: The energy we've got is the energy we can use.

2. On the emotional level, we see that the energy evolvement coefficient has grown. In this case, the laws of abundance apply: The more love I bestow, the more it grows within me and others. I create more energy as a result of the emotional processes that resonate between me and my object of affection.

3. On the cognitive level, the energy coefficient is even higher. Nowadays, we are witnessing a growing number of successful businesses, the energy of which is the product and expression of the development of the cognitive layer.

4. The spiritual dimension, which deals with calling and self-realization, has the highest energy duplication. No wonder that successful businesses have a vision and people who have made distinctive achievements by being connected to their vision and goals.

The energy transformation ladder overlaps the levels of the SILVER ACE model, where the C.H.E. law is expressed." The higher one goes up the Silver ace levels, the bigger the volume of energy is produced.

We produce much more energy on a spiritual level than we do on a physical one. An example illustrating this is presented in Stephen Covey's The 7 Habits of Highly Effective People (1996), where he discusses the successful person's ability to manage his energy and care for its recharge, calling it "sharpening the saw." The expression draws on the story of a wise man walking in the woods who meets a man sawing a tree. "Is this hard work?" the wise man asks, and the reply is, "It is very hard work. I've been at it for hours and I still haven't sawed even half of the trunk." "Perhaps you should sharpen the saw," suggests the wise man, to which the other man responds, "I don't have time, I'm too busy sawing." Covey further develops the concept of "sharpening the saw," which in fact deals with the question of recharging energy. He describes four levels – physical, emotional, mental and spiritual – that one should develop and nurture in order to succeed. A person who wants to act with optimal energy should know how to draw it from all levels.

The Crystal Principle – The Human Energy Reactor

The law of energy coefficient refers to the energy evolvement ladder: the higher one climbs up the ladder from physical to spiritual, the greater one's energy. What are the links between the four foci of energy evolvement?

The metaphor of the ladder is valid in demonstrating energy duplication: the ladder is a feeble structure, rather linear and unstable like a system, all the components of which have no reciprocal relations. A ladder is climbed rung by rung, leaving the lower one for the higher.

The optimal situation for the production of human energy is the synchronization of all systems, namely, when all four energy centers are active full force and directly aligned. This synchronization creates the structure of a four-vertex crystal pyramid. It is no coincidence that this structure is the strongest and most durable found in nature (see diagram). Every such structure made, regardless of composition – even those built by connecting toothpicks with small chunks of potato (a demonstration I enjoy in workshops) – results in a structure which can be thrown, turned upside down or rolled around and still retain its stability. That is the structure of the human energy reactor, the way both man and firm will produce utmost energy.

Practically speaking, every idea, initiative or activity should be weighed and checked to see how it affects the other three dimensions: Is the activity in one at the expense of the other? Is the clever idea in sync with the others and doesn't damage either the emotional or the spiritual aspect?

from **Ladder** ———➤ to **crystal**

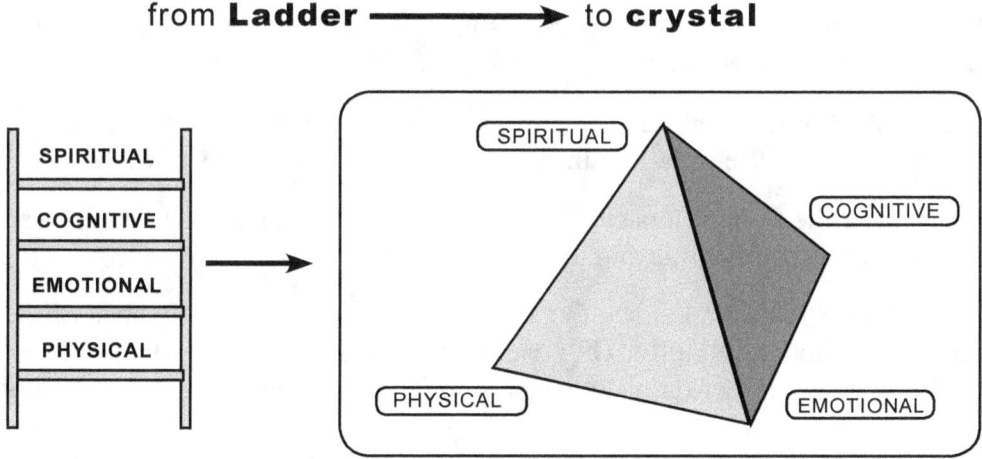

Endurance Quotient

"The Lesson of Failure is Enlightenment."

Rabbi Israel Lipkin of Salant

Martin Seligman elucidated the concept of "Learned Helplessness" some thirty years ago, adding it to the psychological lexicon following a number of experiments he conducted with dogs. The dogs received inconsistent responses to their actions, which resulted in their being apathetic and helpless. However, Seligman noticed that different dogs demonstrated varying degrees of resilience and resistance in coping with the process. The study showed that dogs displayed individual characteristics of resilience resulting in the development of the "Endurance" quotient, a concept first coined by Paul Stoltz in Adversity Quotient.

A person with a high endurance quotient is characterized by the way he handles failure and distress, which is no less significant than the way he is oriented towards success.

The EN.Q. is a central leadership component, highlighting the role of a leader as the one to efficiently deal with emergency situations. It stands to reason that a mishap will occur. The only question is how one deals with it.

Elements of the Endurance Quotient

The degree of control a person attributes to himself in a given situation – the sense of control ranging from a feeling of helplessness (bottom of the scale) to one of full control even in extreme situations (top of the scale).

The extent of responsibility a person shows when facing a problem and the extent of guilt he feels being the one caused it.

The impact limits of failure and distress – to what extent these are specifically ascribed to the cause of failure in relation to the personality as a whole.

Duration of the failure impact – is it immediate or long term, or is it focused on a relevant, specific time and locale.

People with a high Endurance Quotient will be able to feel in control of the situation without any guilt taking over and paralyzing them. Failure will not have a gnawing effect on all other parts of their personality, and it will not be accompanied by an exaggerated feeling of a disproportionately huge event requiring a long recovery period. Some claim, as Paul Stoltz does, that EN.Q. is the ultimate ingredient that predicts success. **The way people face failure**

determines their success. Teaching a person to deal effectively with failure actually teaches them how to succeed.

> *"Our business in this world is not to succeed,*
> *but to continue to fail, in good spirits."*
>
> Robert Louis Stevenson (1850–1894)

Loss of Energy

Depression is one of the most common energy drains. A person suffering from depression quickly depletes his energy reserves. Just as every level at its full capacity serves as a recharge focus, so can they turn into centers of leaking energy in cases of energy deficiency.

What are the energy "suckers" in the different levels?

At the basic physical energy level, environmental conditions can be devourers: lack of oxygen, poor lighting, and noises and such that can cause exhaustion.

At the social-moral level, loss of energy occurs in an insensitive atmosphere lacking empathy, trust, mutual respect and integrity. The energy devourers will be people who hurt, humiliate or oppress others.

At the behavioral level, energy devouring occurs in a rigid, bureaucratic environment lacking flexibility that ignores reason, logic and the heart. The opposite would have a similar effect when the environment is inefficient, chaotic, unstable and purposeless.

At the cognitive level, energy loss occurs in an environment that is stupid, unlearning, lacking creativity and humor.

At the spiritual level, one might lose energy in an environment which does not foster ambition, achievement, direction, purpose and vision; an environment devoid of existential significance and drive for action.

The Endurance Quotient serves as the protective cover against energy loss in difficult, energy-consuming situations.

Some of the energy guzzlers such as depression, fear or apathy can go viral: They spread like a plague, but people with the highest endurance quotients are less likely to become infected.

> ## The Law of Human Energy Loss – H.E.L.
> - Every person has a protective cover to prevent energy leakage.
>
> - There are "holes" through which energy trickles.
>
> - These "holes" are individual in nature and vary from one person to the next.
>
> - Childhood wounds are the source of most "holes."
>
> - Psychological treatment = "mending" the protective cover to prevent loss of energy.

The higher one climbs the ladder from the physical to the spiritual, the higher the multiplication of energy (C.H.E. law). This is a universal law applying to all human beings. Conversely, individuals' reactions differ in intensity in energy-devouring situations. For some, a shouting boss can ruin their entire existence for the next few days; for others it could be a matter of a few minutes' recovery. Dealing with red tape will drive some people crazy, but others won't even notice. Individual reactions stem from personal histories, weak spots and energy holes. Treating those will usually require private sessions.

Assessing energy

The human energy quotient is fairly new. Although many know of its existence, only a few have taken up its study, so there is limited professional literature on the subject. This may come as a surprise since of all the quotients and human characteristics, this one is closest to the physical domain, which overflows with testing and measuring tools.

As previously mentioned, the energy element is sometimes revealed in subconscious projective material dealing with the person's motivation and preparedness for action. Despite the legitimate debate about its adequacy, graphology also serves as an efficient tool relating to a person's level of energy and stamina. The person's physical condition is, in itself, already a source of information revealing the person's energy condition. Illness is energy consuming, hence it stands to reason that an ill person would be low on energy which is tested, evaluated and reliable at a specific moment and is valid only then.

Lack of energy

A basic level of energy lack testifies to the absence of crucial, existential energy, which may be the result of bodily injury, psychological causes such as depression, or a combination of the two. Low physical energy usually hinders the emotional strength needed for physical action and goal achievement. One's energy is largely innate, but environmental and physiological circumstances can both kindle or kill it.

The pathological state of a near complete lack of energy is defined by medical professionals as CFS (Chronic Fatigue Syndrome); laymen may use the pejorative term "Yuppie Flu." It is a psycho-physiological disease with symptoms that include chronic fatigue, difficulty in concentrating, requiring tremendous energy to perform even the most minor daily chores, and muscle pain which even a long rest does not alleviate.

Lack of energy and burnout

A worn-out person is not necessarily lacking in energy. Burnout refers to a process taking place in a defined field. A person may feel worn-out in one area or in a certain job but be vital in a new job or different assignment. Energy lack and being worn-out may look the same but differ vastly: the first being total and all-inclusive. Since energy is affected by simultaneous processes, chances are that a worn-out person will also be low on general energy, but this is not necessarily the case. This explains the change in the energy quotient over time. Disregarding burnout may result in more weakness and fatigue, which will eventually result in the body developing an illness just so that it gets some rest.

Lack of balance

High Energy Quotient (EN.Q.) and low Aspiration and Ambition Quotient (A.Q.) is a state of high raw energy lacking direction and the balance of the aspiration quotient.

The gap will express itself in several ways:

1. **Aimless hyperactivity** – a high, inefficient activity.

2. **Energy eruptions** – a dangerous situation caused by the gap between the two quotients is a state in which high level energy is not channeled towards the mission and is not materialized as spiritual energy. In the absence of a constructive channel, high levels of energy may eventually burst as violence, resembling a volcanic eruption that drains excessive accumulated energy, which is characterized as bending right or left on the model:

Violent energy outbursts to the Right, towards the emotional quotient (E.Q.), will have emotional components and will be characterized by outbursts of charged emotions such as hatred. This type of violence flares up quickly but calms down just as fast due to the element of empathy, allowing for the ability to reach reciprocated understanding. The proximity of emotional intelligence to the change quotient (C.Q.) encourages adaptation and problem solving in the new circumstances. Once the violence has dissipated, the cause of the dispute is not always remembered clearly. Stereotypical right-brain violence is common among relatives, close friends and couples.

Energy outbursts to the Left, towards the value quotient (V.Q.), will take the form of "wars of principle." They do not flare up easily but once in full force they are crueler by far than are energy outbursts to the right (above). In the name of "values," man has performed the most horrendous of deeds without the restraint of human empathy, which is on the right side of the model. These actions are accompanied by feelings of idealism, moral superiority and the dehumanization of the other. People who suffer from left-side energy outbursts view their violent actions as ideological commitments that oblige them to overcome the "weakness" of their human emotions.

Energy empowerment

"Recharging one's batteries," as referring to the accumulation of energy and strength, relates to our engine metaphor, namely that energy can be consciously developed through a variety of physiological and mental processes.

The growing number of people jogging or walking out in the open or in gyms is evidence of people understanding the important contribution of physical activity to increased energy. Employers understand it also and install fitness clubs on the premises or allow workers to take breaks for physical activity. These employers act through a deep understanding of how vital it is for the success of the organization.

How does one recharge one's mental energy? At the emotional level, by increasing optimism, developing self-esteem, and creating processes to prevent burnout. Workshops in relevant areas enhance the development of such characteristics. Upon returning from such focused seminars, people actually have more trust in their abilities and are more vibrant.

It is, however, essential to be cautious of an unbalanced development. Not every high level energy guarantees success without it being bound with hyperactivity, restlessness and a lack of gratification.

Developing the endurance quotient

Unlike the laws of energy empowerment, which function according to universal laws, loss of energy is individual. The holes in our energy protective wraps are individual and the result of our own personal histories. This is the why the same event may be traumatic and energy consuming for one person and insignificant for another. Therefore, the most efficient treatment for an unbalanced endurance quotient would be psychological, ontological, or cognitive therapy and the like.

Tools, mainly designed to develop self-confidence and positive thinking, generate cognitive change and teach us to relate to failure as another stage along the path to success, helping us develop our endurance and coping aptitude.

Failure as a lesson

According to game theory, there is twice as much knowledge to be gained from a move leading to failure than from one leading to success. And while it doesn't take into consideration the stinging pain of failure, the theory acknowledges that the pain is twofold when one both fails and fails to learn.

Developing the ability to learn from failure, to derive the lesson and extract the most knowledge, is the most highly recommended way to nurture one's endurance quotient. Our protective coat against a blow to our energy, that is the result of failure, is empowered by the ability to see failure as a "lesson" and yield its positive side.

A few ways to develop the endurance quotient:

1. **Listen** to your inner voices. What they are saying? Do they see the endeavor as something total and hopeless?

2. **Investigate** the causes of failure. Who truly failed, and who is responsible to rectify it?

3. **Analyze** the facts.

4. **Act**. Take control by doing something.

5. **Identify** similar dramas from other times in your life, understand their source, and limit their repercussions. Learn to minimize the impact of childhood wounds, traumas and fears.

6. **Learn to manage** the energy balance as you do every resource, such as money or investments, that expresses the depletion of the source as a result of the failure. How much was lost? What has the restoration entailed? How can you minimize failure and recovery time? And how can you bring energy up to the desired level?

EN.Q. Characteristics:

- **Drive for Action** – the need to act, promote and move things forward;

- **Consistency** – persistence in fulfilling tasks, even in situations of difficulty, while keeping a constant investment level;

- **Vigor and Energy** – an inner feeling of vigor and energy where there is an "internal engine" and "fuel";

- **Quick Performance** – the ability to perform tasks quickly and with agility;

- **Dynamics and Vitality** – the ability to operate nimbly and with vigor;

- **Work under Pressure** – the ability to function under pressure and feel satisfaction from it;

- **Effective Handling of Failure** – the level of resilience and the ability to cope with and persist in facing failure;

- **Personal Fortitude** – the ability to unwaveringly face stress situations, frustration and hardship;

- **Recovery and Rehabilitation** – the ability to recover from situations of failure and distress;

- **Determination and Resolve** – persisting in carrying out tasks up to the point of achieving the goal.

The Cognitive Level

This level comprises cognitive characteristics, modes of thinking, information processing and mental thought processes. Its function is to process information in two ways:

1. Identifying patterns and rules; understanding, learning, analyzing and drawing conclusions – **Left**.

2. Breaking patterns, stepping away from frameworks, creating novelty, originality and intuition – **Right**.

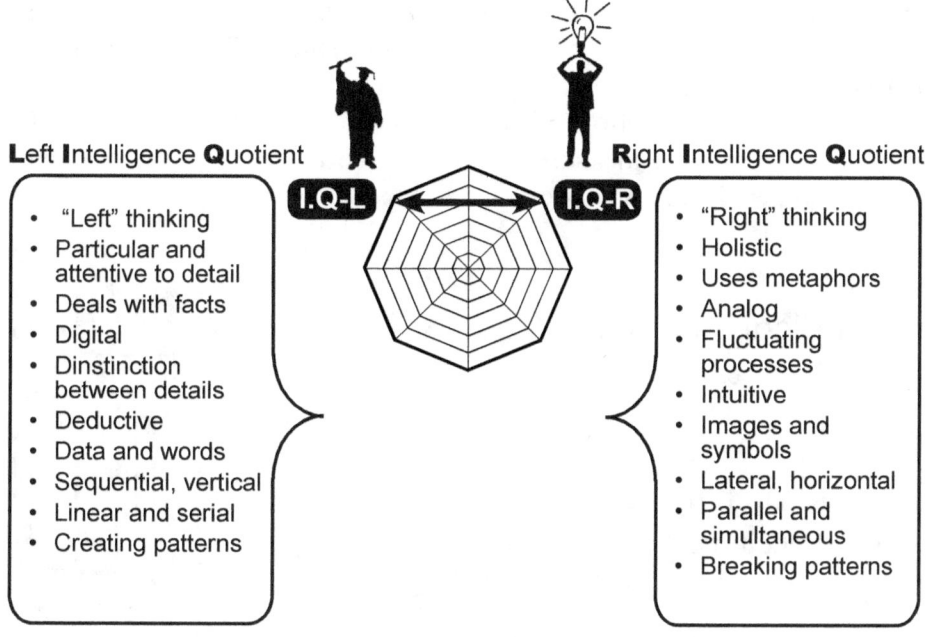

Left Intelligence Quotient   I.Q-L   I.Q-R   **Right Intelligence Quotient**

- "Left" thinking
- Particular and attentive to detail
- Deals with facts
- Digital
- Dinstinction between details
- Deductive
- Data and words
- Sequential, vertical
- Linear and serial
- Creating patterns

- "Right" thinking
- Holistic
- Uses metaphors
- Analog
- Fluctuating processes
- Intuitive
- Images and symbols
- Lateral, horizontal
- Parallel and simultaneous
- Breaking patterns

The rationalist school glorified rational thinking (I.Q.-L) and refused to recognize intuitive, illogical and non-linear (I.Q.-R) activity as thinking processes. Today, we consider both kinds of thought as two aspects of cognitive processes – different in nature but both essential and complementary. They constitute two forms of processing information and drawing conclusions that balance each other: The left side of the brain identifies patterns and rules representing understanding and learning processes, drawing conclusions and analyzing them, whereas the right side of the brain deals with dismantling patterns, changing the rules and creating novelty. The first style of thinking is based on concentration, reduction and clarity in defining and perceiving the objective; the second style of thinking is based on widening perspective up to losing the goal itself.

The characteristics of horizontal thinking (right) in contrast to those of vertical thinking (left)

The concepts of "vertical thinking" (characterizing the left side) and "lateral thinking" (characterizing the right side) were first coined by Edward de Bono (b. 1933), Maltese physician, author, inventor, consultant, professor and researcher at the Universities of Oxford and Harvard. De Bono largely influenced our present way of thinking. He has worked with many leading businesses around the world and has written over 57 books which have been translated into 34 languages, in which he analyzes modes of thinking and shows how thinking processes can be improved.

De Bono found that both rational and creative thought processes consist of cognitive processes of a different nature. According to de Bono, the right brain, which deals with intuitive thinking, is also the seat of cognitive processes, although such processes follow different laws and rules. He maintains that this type of thinking can be measured, and just like the I.Q.-L, it is affected by hereditary and environmental factors.

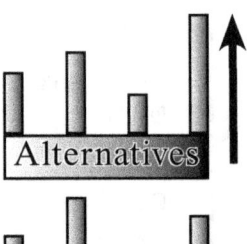

a.   Vertical thinking

    looks for the best possible alternative.

b.   Lateral thinking

    produces additional alternatives regardless of the success of the previous ones.

Vertical thinking	Lateral thinking
selects and stops	creates and moves on
as correct as possible	as much as possible
forbidding the irrelevant	encouraging the irrelevant
defined categories	no categories
the predictable way	the unpredictable way
finite process	infinite process
information is designed for finding solutions	information is designed for breaking patterns

The arch

One example of an invention based on the combination of left and right thinking is the ancient arch:

The pillars of the arch are built first with stones laid one on top of another. These stones constitute the "I.Q.-L" – a serial, sequential and logical process. It is not possible to build different layers of the pillars at the same time, and it is not possible to skip any step. This type of construction reflects the patterns and knowledge that will be built over the years. This format is also present in the conventional curriculum: A mandatory introductory course precedes advanced courses. The arched section constitutes the extraordinary process of right intelligence. The first builder of the arch probably placed the first stone half in the air and must have taken a lot of abuse as everyone expected the stone to fall. Had the builder stopped his work at that point, the structure would have collapsed since only upon completion could the arch function as such. On the other hand, the pillar construction can be stopped at any time. The arch is a metaphor for lateral thinking: Once we have laid the bedrock, we see a solid and stable structure; the whole will appear, one that is capable of supporting entire floors, if not history in its entirety.

Dominant Thinking Strategy

Most people tend to a one-side dominant thinking strategy. A true Ace is capable of moving from right to left thinking as needed. The advent of the computer in psychological diagnostics opened up a world of new possibilities for determining the dominant side of one's thinking processes. Through the absorption of processing time to each question, we can examine the strategy style of a person answering questions. For example, let's envision a test exhibiting a series of shapes facing one control shape.

The examinee is asked whether the control shape appears in any of the shapes in the series. It appears in some and it doesn't in others. All the candidate has to do is say, "Yes, it does" or "No, it doesn't."

Example:

    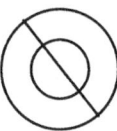 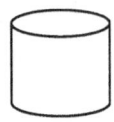

Question: Does the shape below appear in one of the shapes above?

A left-thinking-strategy person will operate in a serial and sequential manner. The examinee will go from shape to shape from right to left or from left to right until he finds the corresponding shape. A right-thinking-strategy person will operate in a simultaneous manner: view all the shapes as a whole and relate to the group as one single structure. After a general review, that examinee will reach the required conclusion.

An analysis of the average time spent on reaching an answer shows that it takes longer to reach a negative answer than a positive one for those who employ left-thinking reasoning. For those who employ right-thinking reasoning, there will be no difference in the time spent between positive and negative answers.

Balances within the cognitive level:

> *"People with high levels of personal mastery...cannot afford to choose between reason and intuition, or head and heart, any more than they would choose to walk on one leg or see with one eye."*
>
> - Peter M. Senge

The right and left thinking, or lateral and vertical thinking, as de Bono says, constitute a pair of quotients, the importance of whose balance gradually increases. The computer's rising power obliges people to enhance the expression of their special abilities: creativity, intuition, thinking out of the box. It is no surprise that in the 21st century, we find top companies capable of adopting ideas derived from inspiration, intuition and from human uniqueness, and turning them into products (Apple is a prime example, among others). Nowadays, competition is based on right-brain brands and left-brain products.

The **I.Q.-R** – The pattern-breaking "processor," representing the intuitive and creative right-hemisphere thinking, needs the **I.Q.-L** in order to implement ideas for efficient production. The **R** is creative but not efficient. The **L** is efficient but needs a balance for ideas. Developing balance enables left intelligence to realize its full potential. Einstein's violin, his imagination and sense of humor contributed to his capacity for scientific thinking.

Correct decision making – Left-right Ping-Pong

In Listening with the Third Ear (1983), Theodor Reik recounts a meeting with Freud when the question "how one should counsel a patient facing fateful questions in his life" came up. Freud said that based on his own personal experience, "When it comes to making decisions of little importance, I have found it beneficial to examine them logically and analytically according to their advantages and disadvantages. However, when it comes to decisions regarding major issues, such as choosing a profession or a life partner, the decision must come from somewhere deep inside of us, from our gut, from our subconscious…." Even Nobel laureate Professor Daniel Kahneman's research shows that the basis of our decision making regarding economic issues is generally intuitive and unmediated.

Many methodologies dealing with decision making suggest that one should weigh the possibilities logically and rationally in order to make the right decision and to clear the system of emotional noises. In reality, it isn't so. There is no unequivocal linear solution. Where we should live; what we should wear; what we should order in a restaurant; or where we should go on vacation are just a few examples of hundreds of decisions, major and minor, that cannot be resolved by relying solely on the left side.

Making the right decision is like a ping-pong game between left and right up to the point when the choice among the alternatives becomes clear and logical: We shall employ logic, and at the point where we have no clear criterion for choice, we turn to the right side. Intuitive decisions may undergo a process of rationalization through the left side. This logic is a hindsight providing an explanation for intuitive decisions. Correct decision making is based on the appropriate employment of rational and intuitive processes; the proper balance between them will ensure an efficient process without endless vacillating between alternatives.

Energy flow in the cognitive level

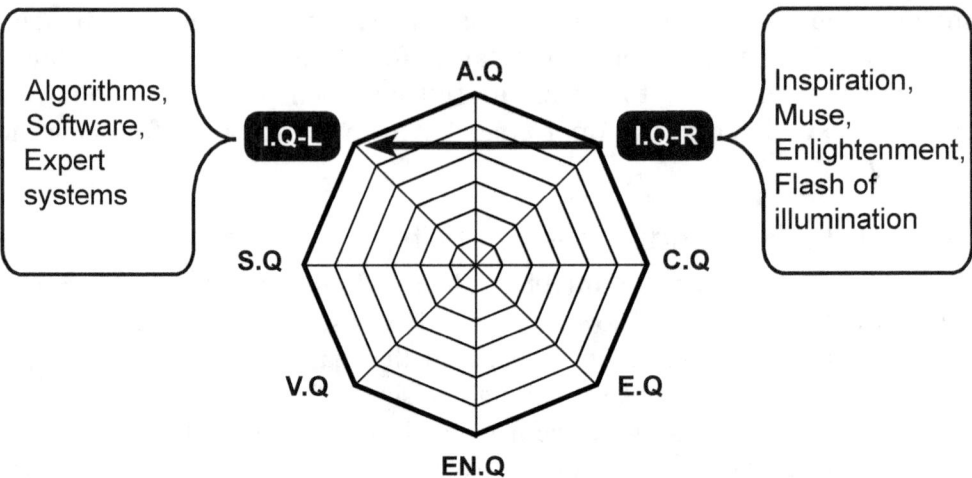

Algorithms, Software, Expert systems

I.Q-L

A.Q

I.Q-R

Inspiration, Muse, Enlightenment, Flash of illumination

S.Q

C.Q

V.Q

E.Q

EN.Q

Also, in this instance, energy is expressed in two different directions: From the left (logical rational thinking [I.Q.-L]) and from the right (intuitive, creative and holistic thinking [I.Q.-R]).

Correct energy flow is from right to left. This applies to organizations entering their creative phase that need to transform this stage into an organized and methodical performance; this also applies to mathematical and scientific inventions which may start as a kind of guess or intuition until they are proven and applied. The transition from the hypothesis to the final formula indicates the transition from right to left.

Beyond right and left in the cognitive level? Where do creativity and ideas come from as they reach **I.Q.-R**, and where does the energy go beyond **I.Q.-L**? We do not have a clear answer about the source of ideas. Some maintain they come from the world of muses, from inspiration, from divine grace; it is, however, clearer to us why they develop further. Once the idea has gone over to the left side, it develops from intuition into formulas, theories, processes and defined knowledge. Some of these formulas become algorithms, computerized systems that are completely automated. In other words, beyond the human realm of the left side of the model, there are computers and information processing systems, so that human creation has evolved in some cases to a computerized process no longer in need of any humans.

Q - 2
Intelligence Quotient - Left (I.Q.-L)

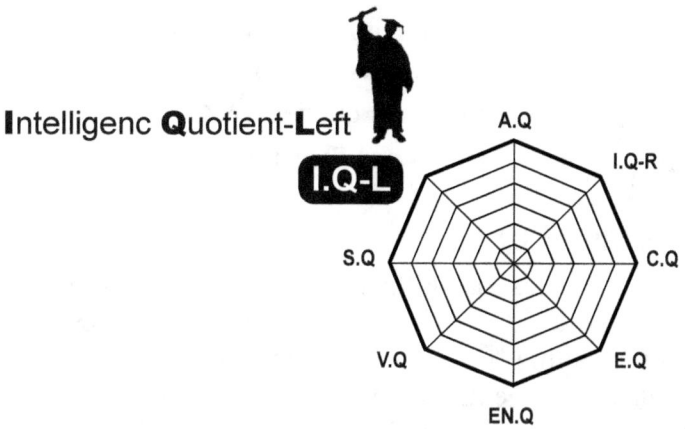

Intelligenc Quotient-Left

I.Q-L

"Wisdom and knowledge are the solid foundations of human life."

Plato

Identity	**Name**: Intelligence Quotient - Left
	Symbol: I.Q.-L
Definition:	All aspects relating to the level of intelligence: one's ability for rational thinking, ability for logical and linear thinking, how intelligently one operates, the extent of learning ability and the ability to draw conclusions.

Characteristics:		
	Intelligence quotient	**I.Q.**
	Left hemisphere thinking	Left
	Linear, vertical thinking	Linear
	Logical, analytical thinking	Logic
	Language	Linguistic
	Learning ability	Learning

Expression at work:	Facts and data, technical engineering, computing and data processing
Deficiency:	Mental retardation

Location in the model	**Vertical axis** – Cognitive level; **Horizontal axis** – Left; **Balance** – Right intelligence quotient, **I.Q.-R**; **Counterbalance** – Emotional intelligence quotient, **E.Q.**;
Neighbors in the model:	Aspiration quotient, **A.Q.**; System and Structure, **S.Q**.

The history of the I.Q.

Intelligence is a complex of skills through which we solve problems that require efficient thinking. The term "intelligence" derives from the Latin word intelligere, meaning "examine," "discern" or "decide." When we say that a person is highly intelligent, we generally refer to the left side (the I.Q.-L), which is in charge of analytical, informative and organized thinking, involved in finding rules and drawing conclusions. A person whose I.Q.-L level is high is capable of thinking logically; that person can plan, think in accordance with the rules of logic, understand and process information. That person knows how to draw the correct, logical conclusions, learn from experience and operate wisely. It is important to stress that we are not only talking about intellectual capacity and learning ability but the ability to apply thought to intelligent management.

The Intelligence Quotient is a numerical score obtained through a series of standardized tests. These tests were developed to measure the degree of intelligence according to age groups in the population. Attempts to measure intelligence began at the end of the 19th century. Francis Galton (1822-1911), Charles Darwin's half-cousin, was the first to develop tests to assess intellectual capacity, but his attempts failed. The first I.Q. tests were developed in 1905 by French researchers Alfred Binet and Théodore Simon. As France transitioned to compulsory education, the minister of education asked them to develop a tool to measure children's intelligence so they could be assigned to the appropriate educational facility. The tools were developed to examine the degree of negative deviations from the norm, that is, the intelligence indexes we know today were initially meant to diagnose mental retardation rather than the level of genius.

These tools were developed and revised many times over the years, and in 1916, the version familiar to us today was developed in collaboration with Stanford University –the Stanford-Binet Intelligence Scales. The concept of "Intelligence Quotient" was then first coined, referring to the relation between a child's mental age according to the tests and his chronological age.

It was only in 1939 that a tool for assessing adults' intelligence was developed. The version we use today, developed in 1981 by David Wechsler, is called the WAIS-R (Wechsler Adult Intelligence Scale-Revised). By means of verbal- and performance-oriented items, the test examines a variety of intellectual skills such as general knowledge, numerical memory, vocabulary, arithmetic problem solving, reading comprehension, logical comprehension and structural perception.

Intelligence quotient score distribution is normal (it generates a bell curve graph). The average I.Q. score in all age groups is 100, with a standard deviation of 15. Approximately 95% of the population obtains a score in the "normal" range – between 70 and 130. An I.Q. lower than 70 usually indicates mental retardation, a person whose I.Q. is higher than 130 is generally considered as highly intelligent, and whoever scores higher than 145 is considered a genius.

Throughout the 20th century, the I.Q. was perceived as the main factor in academic and professional success. The importance of the I.Q. grew during the industrial revolution with the rising need to test the thousands of people flocking from the countryside into the cities and the need to train them for factory work. The I.Q. was the best predictor of a person's capacity to learn and master technical material. At the end of the 20th century, as a result of the advent of the computer, which competes in logical thinking, the I.Q. lost its importance. Although still considerably important in education, the professional world recognizes the importance of other factors, such as the applicant's personality, interpersonal skills, professional experience and inclinations.

The classic I.Q. represents a person's intellectual potential, but it doesn't necessarily indicate its functioning in practice. This is precisely the distinction between I.Q. and the I.Q.-L. In order for a person to become an Ace, logical thinking capacity is undoubtedly necessary, but it alone isn't enough for operating intelligently. The I.Q.-L in the SILVER ACE focuses on the expression of such capacities in practice.

The elements of the I.Q.-L

Left hemisphere thinking

The main goal of I.Q.-L thinking is to identify and generate patterns. Once we have identified a pattern, we can predict processes, move within a defined track and reproduce certain actions. The left side of the brain seeks to solve problems and understand laws; it seeks to find and classify the patterns that control them so it can catalog and store every phenomenon in its appropriate place. Its role is to clear the "central processor" by transferring raw mental material to the right storage spaces as quickly as possible to make space for new examination processes. It can thus shorten thought processes, unlike the right side of the brain which can indulge in creating infinite connections.

Role of the left side of the brain:

1. Rapid identification of information;

2. Creation of a pattern/paradigm corresponding to this information;

3. Classification, attribution and filing the information;

4. Clearing the processor to absorb new information.

In fact, the role of thought boils down to the creation of patterns that will enable us... to not think!

Vertical thinking

The I.Q.-L is characterized by "vertical thinking," a concept which researcher de Bono introduced in his book on the differences between right-brain and left-brain thinking, between vertical and horizontal or lateral thinking. Vertical thinking is much like a multistory building. It's a type of thinking that requires order, just as there is an order in the floors of a building: It is impossible to build the fifth floor before having built the fourth; it is impossible to build the roof before the floor; it is impossible to reach a certain floor without having first gone through the ones underneath it, and similarly, it is impossible to study in university before elementary school; one cannot take a particular course if other courses were not taken first. This constitutes organized thinking in a logical and hierarchical order.

Linear

The I.Q.-L characterizes itself through linear, sequential and serial thinking of the 2+2=4 type. The necessary and inevitably chronological order in this type of thinking, as well as the factor of time more than anything else, constitute linear thinking. This type of thought pertains to technical engineering and is adequate for planning and organizing production processes and work methods. Each process implies linear reasoning – what should precede what, what happens over time. This type of engineering thinking deals with facts and data and requires precision. It is categorical thinking that enables and promotes a clear division and labeling of groups, like that required in computing and programming.

Logic

Logic is a discipline that distinguishes between the correct method of reaching conclusions and the incorrect methods and offers guidelines with which conclusions can be reached and new arguments based on previous ones. The term "logic" derives from the Greek term logos (λόγος), meaning "word," "thought," or "argument"; its Latin translation being ratio.

Logical intelligence relates to the ability to perform cognitive tasks that require rational and analytic thinking – the type of thinking based on a certain method or certain rules whose internal order can be tracked. Logical thinking makes it possible to put phenomena in some structured order, to understand the relationship between them and to identify cause and effect. Mathematics is the epitome of logic, which is why it carries so much weight; the ability to understand numbers lies at the base of the I.Q.-L.

The clearest manifestation of logical thinking is artificial intelligence. **Artificial intelligence** is basically a machine that can perform tasks such as computing, classifying, analyzing principles, and memory storage among others, based on defined logic. John McCarthy (1927-2011), one of the pioneers of artificial intelligence and inventor of the LISP programming language, defined the goal of artificial intelligence in 1955: "...to make a machine behave in a way that would have been considered intelligent had humans acted so." Humankind created its competitor. In all situations, if a computer could operate as replacement for humans, it would do so. It mustn't be deduced that the human left-brain intelligence as a commodity will become less in demand, but rather the use of computing and artificial intelligence will widen the range of our intelligence.

Linguistic ability

The development of language is one of the main factors that accelerated the development of the human brain and its division into two hemispheres. Brain research indicates that throughout evolution, linguistic processing has taken place in the left hemisphere of the brain. Language is a clear left-brain feature: It is based upon rules and laws and is linear by definition. It is impossible to write without the clear order of beginning, middle and end. Language necessarily implies movement in one clear and definite direction.

Like most other domains, language first originates in the right side of the brain as a language of visual messages, from drawings on cave walls all the way to Chinese characters. The aspiration to make processes more efficient prompted the coding of the alphabetical symbols of every language. The transition to letter-based language was an intellectual revolution that led the linguistic field towards the left side of the brain and turned it into a linear, coded process.

Learning

Human knowledge has increased at a baffling speed. The validity of an engineer's knowledge, which in the past could last decades, is now estimated at five years, hence the need to learn is now critical. Those not capable of learning and keeping up-to-date with new knowledge will not be able to cope with competition and will surely not become stars. Learning is directly connected with the I.Q.-L because, like language, it is also a linear and vertical process. Learning new material is based on prior knowledge and understanding. Studies have shown that I.Q. is directly correlated with the ability to acquire knowledge. This is the main reason for the existence of various types of intelligence assessment tests required for admittance to academic institutions, as tools predicting academic success.

Assessment and development

There are lots of diagnostic tools for the assessment of I.Q.-L, more than for any other characteristic of the model. Intelligence tests are divided into several categories: quantitative, verbal, spatial, practical, and more. The scores for all types are positively correlated with one another. Charles Spearman coined the term "General factor" (the G factor) and maintained that there is a cognitive factor at the base of all thinking processes of the left side of the brain.

One of the most popular and widespread assessment tools of the last few decades is the psychometric test, which assesses a person's mental and cognitive skills compared to the abilities of others and is used in the admissions process at institutions of higher education. The test focuses mostly on numerical, spatial and verbal thinking. In the United States colleges rely on the SAT (Scholastic Aptitude Test).

These ability assessment tests examine the potential skill but not necessarily its practical implementation, whether a person really operates intelligently in the different aspects of his life.

Pathological deficiency in left intelligence comes in the form of mental retardation, which can reach a point at which it is almost impossible to function and fit into social frameworks. Mental training is possible in less extreme cases, with the best results achieved with patients who start at an early age. Recently, there has been great progress in the development of medication for improving mental functioning. Currently, it is possible to find drugs that improve memory, concentration and the ability to cope with anxiety and stress – medication that has significantly improved academic success. I believe that medical treatment will continue to develop, but we must remember that this is about the improvement of a given psycho-genetic state, not a total transformation of a person's abilities.

The capabilities of the left side of the brain can be also developed in a non-pathological state. Mental exercises were already popular at the time of ancient Greece. In recent years, there has been tremendous development of tools to improve learning, especially in response to the widespread understanding of learning disabilities and their origins. Dr. Maria Montessori (1870-1952), among the forerunners in the field, developed an educational method aimed at nurturing the mental abilities and intelligence of kindergarten children. Over the years, countless workshops for improving memory as well as learning strategies and tactics were developed for adults. Most of these workshops function on the assumption that improvement can be achieved depending on genetic data, and "mental gymnastics" of one sort or another help to optimize the employment of one's potential.

Over the years, human physical and mental faculties have been declining as well as the I.Q.-L. In the modern age, people are no longer required to use memory or process information the way they needed to in the past thanks to the computer. But those "mental gymnastics" and cerebral exercises help slow down the deterioration. The more knowledge humans acquire, the more their intellectual fitness improves. Some cultures have sanctified the ability to learn and develop sharpness of mind. In these societies, the intelligent student is regarded as a prominent indicator of success, and youngsters' attempts to succeed lead to an especially high level of intelligence compared with other populations.

One's level of left intelligence is influenced by the processes of acquiring knowledge. The more knowledge a person acquires, the more his intellectual capacity improves both because of the knowledge itself and as a result of the exercise the brain has undergone. The more a person learns and thinks, the better thinking capacity is preserved and maintained with the ability to find solutions and develop thinking patterns. De Bono counts among the first who argued that not only should the individual's I.Q.-L be developed, it is possible and essential to develop that of the entire population. A country's wealth is directly affected by the I.Q.-L of its citizens. Therefore, raising the intelligence level of the population must be a national interest, especially in developing countries. According to de Bono, investment in raising the intelligence level of the population will yield the best return with regards to national development goals. These ideas led to the establishment of national ministries for I.Q. development in some countries.

I.Q.-L Characteristics:

- **Numerical understanding** – access and ability to work with numerical-logical material.

- **Ability to analyze and draw conclusions** – the ability to understand data, analyze it and draw conclusions.

- **Rational thinking** – rational and systematic thinking based on logic.

- **Linear thinking** – ability to think in a sequential, serial and hierarchical manner.

- **Logical thinking** – ability to analyze numerical data and draw practical and logical conclusions.

- **Learning ability** – ability to internalize new material quickly and efficiently.

- **Intelligent person** – Operates intelligently? Are actions based on intelligent decisions?

- **Quick grasp** and understanding of new material.

- **Engineering/technical thinking** – quick understanding and full knowledge of engineering and technical material.

- **Computers** – quick grasp of computers and software.

Q - 3

Intelligence Quotient - Right (I.Q.-R)

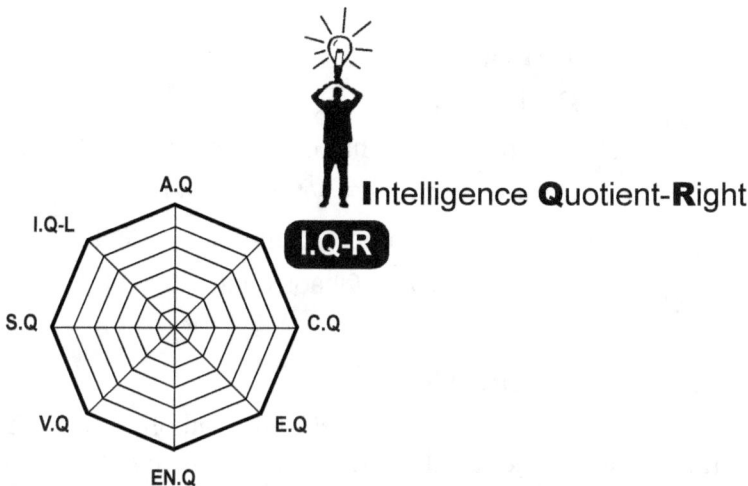

Intelligence **Q**uotient-**R**ight

I.Q-R

"The heart has its reasons of which reason knows nothing."

(Blaise Pascal)

Identity	**Name**: Intelligence Quotient - Right
	Symbol: **I.Q.-R**
Definition:	All characteristics relating to the thinking capacity of the right brain: lateral, associative, creative, intuitive and visual as well as parallel thinking.
Characteristics:	**L**ateral Thinking
	Intuition
	Innovation
	Incubation
	Imagination
	Image & **I**con
	Illumination
	Irrational
	Relative
	Ideas

Expression at work:	Creation of new patterns, breaking paradigms, invention and development.
Deficiency:	Fixation, lack of intuition, lack of humor, creative paralysis.
Location in the model	**Vertical axis** – Cognitive level; **Horizontal axis** – Right; **Balance** – Left intelligence quotient, I.Q.-L; **Counterbalance** – Value quotient, V.Q.
Neighbors in the model:	The Aspiration and Ambition quotient, A.Q.; The Change and Chaos quotient, C.Q.

Definition and Characteristics

The I.Q.-R pertains to the intellectual level and symbolizes all the thinking abilities connected with the right hemisphere. It is in charge of analog, wavelike thinking processes, as opposed to the digital-linear processes located on the opposite end of the axis. This is where conceptual thinking dealing with comprehensive ideas and the integration of information takes place. This is where creativity, art, invention and inspiration originate.

A person whose right-brain thinking is developed often refers to images, shapes and proportions, and his language uses a wealth of metaphors. This type of thinking is intuitive, associative and lateral, the muses and creativity reign here. The breadth of this vision comes at the expense of detail and precision. It is a world in which relative perspective determines meaning. It is a world of breaking patterns and rules where two apples plus two apples doesn't necessarily equal four apples.

Horizontal or lateral thinking

De Bono first introduced the concept of "lateral thinking" in his book The Use of Lateral Thinking (1967), in which he dealt with solving problems creatively through a vague form of reasoning. De Bono invested considerable energy in the subject and thanks to him the concept was included in the Oxford English Dictionary. He set creative lateral thinking in the spotlight as a form of thinking equal in value to classic rational thinking, which he referred to as vertical thinking.

The power of lateral thinking consists in breaking free from the dogmatic tyranny of paradigms. This type of decentralized, holistic and intuitive thinking does not seek answers; instead, it tries to break away from patterns and examine alternatives. This type of thinking is the basis of any creative process since it implies breaking the established order and creating a new perspective.

The Tournament Exercise

De Bono's "Tournament Exercise" is an excellent demonstration of the right and left forms of thought. The question addressed is this: In a tennis tournament with 127 contestants how many matches must be planned given that per the rules of the tournament the contestant who wins all matches plays the next until the final match, thus becoming the champion of the tournament?

How would right-brainers tackle the problem, and how would left-brainers do it?

Mr. "L," our calculus specialist, is analytical, serial and vertical, as any good engineer would be. His first step would be to divide the 127 contestants into two groups of 63, with one contestant waiting for his turn to play. Out of these contestants, 63 winners will play in the next round. The next step would be to add the contestant who was waiting during the first round, and then divide the players again into two groups of 32 contestants, out of which 16 would win and play in the next round. We divide them once again into two groups, and so on and so forth. Finally, we add up all the participants in the different rounds, and if we haven't made any mistakes along the way we should end up with the correct result.

On the other hand, Mr. "R" thinks outside the box. His first move would be to step out of the paradigm and examine the problem from a different angle. For instance, defining the tournament as a machine that produces "losers." Is this a correct definition? Absolutely! How is this done? By playing. If so, how many future tournament/machine losers will be produced? One hundred twenty-seven minus the final champion, meaning 126 matches ought to be planned!

Left – Mr. L	Right – Mr. R
Definition of the situation:	Definition of the situation:
Tournament = a competition to determine the winner in the group	Tournament = a machine that produces "losers"
Thinking steps Number of matches	How to produce losers = playing a match
1. $127/2 = 63$ (1 left) 63	How many losers the machine needs to produce = 126
2. $1+63 = 64$ $64/2 = 32$ 32	
3. $32/2 = 16$ 16	
4. $16/2 = 8$ 8	
5. $8/2 = 4$ 4	
6. $4/2 = 2$ 2	
7. $2/2 = 1$ 1	
Total matches 126	Total matches 126

In a sense, this example reflects the advantage of right intelligence to see things from a different, creative angle, which sometimes makes it possible to reach solutions in a shorter and more original way.

Breaking patterns and stepping out of paradigms can be efficient but also holds a certain moral risk that requires balancing this ability with a mature value system.

Another example that de Bono gives in his book is that of a girl whose father was seriously indebted to a cruel despot who demanded the man's daughter in compensation for the debt. The despot, understanding that the girl did not want him, offered to leave the decision up to fate. He suggested taking two pebbles from the yard, a black one and a white one. He would hold one in his left fist and the other in his right. Should the girl choose the hand holding the white pebble, he would give up his demand and cancel the debt. But if she chose the hand holding the black stone, she would have to marry him. The girl, who was forced to accept the offer, noticed that he took two black stones, meaning she could not win. In paradigm-breaking thinking, she chose one hand and the moment she touched the pebble pretended to accidentally drop it among the other pebbles in the yard. "It doesn't matter," said the girl, "let's see what is in your other hand, according to which we'll know what color the first stone was and that will determine my fate."

Innovation – the creativity of right intelligence

Under creativity, we refer to a varied complex of thinking processes that lead to an original and meaningful outcome. That outcome can be the solution to a problem, an idea, conceptualization, artistic creation or a theory. Creativity expresses itself through flexible thinking, leading to new ideas or a way of dealing with new situations. Many puzzling situations lead us to search for answers in our left brain even though left thinking is trapped in countless patterns, while the solution can quite often be found by stepping out of the paradigm or two-dimensional space.

The following is an example of solving a problem which apparently can be solved only in a creative way:

Once upon a time, there was an old farmer whose two sons were serving time in jail following a robbery. When the time came to plow the fields, the farmer wrote his eldest son, "I am ill and my horse is getting old and weak. Please ask for a special leave of a few days from jail to help me plow because if I don't plow, I will not be able to sow, and I will not have any income. Beg them to understand my predicament!" Soon afterwards, he received his son's disappointing answer, "Dear Father, because of the robbery and our behavior, they are not willing to let me out for a few days."

The farmer was saddened and turned to his younger son with the same plea. This time, however, he received a different answer, "Father, do not plow the field because that is where we hid the gold from our last robbery." As soon as he read the letter, a convoy of government officials arrived with tractors and plows to search for the gold. Having found nothing, the representatives departed, leaving the field properly plowed. Later, another note from the younger son arrived, "Father, I could do for you this much."

I.Q.-R – Breaking the patterns
Inventive thinking: Incubation, Illumination, Innovation

"Research is seeing what everybody else has seen, and thinking what nobody else has thought."

Albert Szent-Györgyi (Nobel laureate, 1937)

Invention is a new and unexpected solution to a problem or difficulty, and indeed, creative thinking consists of new ideas. Unlike I.Q.-L thinking, which searches for patterns, by way of creative thinking, we break free from existing patterns and produce new processes, like a river that suddenly flows in a new direction, thus making a new riverbed, more efficient than before and perhaps even prettier. We should remember that there is no creative thinking without breaking old patterns. Seeking a new and creative way is a delicate process rife with dangers, especially because it is unfamiliar territory.

Incubation

The stage called "incubation" is the time during which new ideas are still maturing and evolving. This is a period of subconscious mental activity that takes place while the thinker is busy doing something else. This is a delicate phase during which things should be allowed to develop without subjecting them to harsh criticism. Many studies stress the importance of the incubation phase, which needs special protective conditions and has to take as much time as it needs. Seemingly nothing happens during this time, but it is essential for things to mature.

Illumination

Incubation ends with a sensation of illumination or sudden discovery, a change of perception, a new outlook generating a new idea. This is Archimedes' "Eureka!" moment. Illumination appears precisely when one is at ease, unencumbered by focusing on the problem – in the bathtub, while driving, a moment before falling asleep or when dreaming – which points to thought processes characteristic of the right side of the model.

Graham Wallas, who studied the effects of inventive thinking, perceived them as unstructured processes of grace. Over the years, other systems developed that aimed to put some method in the process of invention. Among the most famous is the TRIZ approach developed by Genrich Altshuller in the 1940s based on a systematic way to invent creative solutions.

Intuition

"Learn to trust your gut."

Paul Pressler, Former CEO, Gap Inc.

Intuitive thinking consists of crystallizing opinions and making decisions on the basis of internal logic and sensations that are difficult to point out or to interpret in a clear, logical and structured way. There are those who regard intuition as an irrational and groundless process, not connected to thinking. This stance on intuition derives from the fact that it is difficult to track the occurrence of non-sequential thought processes along with the logic that guides them. Nonetheless, there is no doubt that this is indeed thinking whose mechanism has yet to be deciphered.

The best way to understand the significance of intuitive thinking is by being aware of its uses. Countless decisions, serious or otherwise, are the product of this mode of thinking. One such example is the case of a person who suffered injuries on the right side of his brain and lost his intuitive thinking ability. It turns out that it did not keep him from practicing as a lawyer, but his day-to-day functioning was significantly affected by the loss of "gut feelings." He found it difficult to make decisions not based on information and analysis, so he could not make up his mind what to wear, what to order in a restaurant, or what to buy at the supermarket.

In his book The Music of the Primes (2006), Marcus du Sautoy describes the creative process in mathematics and says, "The mathematical creative process starts with a guess, an inspiration, sometimes as a result of intuition." Intuition is a trait endowing humans with knowledge of reality without having anything to do with logical thinking. Intuitive knowledge is characterized by the fact that it originates very rapidly, in a split second, as though no thinking process was involved at all. A person holding to his intuitive insight cannot explain why he takes that position. Intuitive thinking crystallizes opinions and makes decisions based on internal logic and sensations difficult to elaborate or concretely interpret.

Furthermore, the very idea that our professional and business decisions are made on the basis of logical processes is utterly unfounded. Quite often, what distinguishes a successful professional from a mediocre one, especially among psychologists or physicians, is not only knowledge but a combination of particular intuitions. In a world where all the professional knowledge can be concentrated on a single computer disk, in which processing capacity is entrusted to the care of computerized systems, the principal uniqueness of an expert is his intuitive thinking. Numerous studies involving managers and leaders revealed their high capacity for intuitive thinking.

Forty years ago, Henry Mintzberg, professor at McGill University in Montreal, led a comprehensive study of managers in which he concluded as follows: "Organizational effectiveness does not lie in that narrow-minded concept called rationality. It lies in the blend of clear-headed logic and powerful intuition." If business-oriented thinking was based indeed on left-sided thought processes, that is, logically structured processes, then success in business would necessarily be directly connected with knowledge in economics and business administration. However, even though some businesspeople believe that their decisions are based on rational thinking, a considerable number of those decisions are indubitably based on intuition. Therefore, creating a system to replace the human expert is impossible.

I have met many successful businesspeople, and I have found that their distinction lies in their ability to foresee developments. When I inquired about the source of the information upon which they made decisions, they invariably pointed to their stomachs – "from here, from the gut." This also applies to stockbrokers or military leaders. One of the many studies on the subject proves that there are similar elements in the rapid decision-making processes of stockbrokers and officers during a military operation. They both employ their considered opinion together with gut feelings. Perhaps this explains why some officers make such an easy transition from the military to the stock market.

Researchers at the Newark College of Engineering in New Jersey examined the ability of managers to intuitively predict the future. They found that the CEOs of successful companies tended to use their intuition to anticipate the future and were so successful at it that they significantly exceeded random expectations. They also found high correlation between this ability and success in business.

Aigo Watson from Texas University further emphasizes the importance of intuition in the future business world: "Intuitive managers have special skills that will be essential in the future in a rapidly changing environment. They are the people who foresee new products, and they are the people capable of anticipating what the consumer wants." Therefore, when looking for candidates for a managerial position it is crucial to check their intuitive thinking.

Professor Shoshana Zuboff, in In the Age of the Smart Machine (1988), goes even further in affirming that a business organization that does not integrate the intuitive factor in its decision making will not survive. Companies that based their decisions solely on the left-sided, logical brain have not succeeded in creating an advantage over other companies or computer power.

Imagination

"Imagination is more important than information...."

Albert Einstein

When Einstein was asked how the idea of relativity based on four dimensions – which is contrary to our own sensory experience – had come to him, he explained that at a young age, he would imagine himself chasing a ray of light, and that was the basis for developing his theory. The use of imagination of this type constitutes an essential part of any new development. Imagination guides us towards visions in which we can go beyond the scope of existing experience.

One of the main elements defining the advantage humans enjoy over computers is their ability to activate their imaginations and create new situations and possibilities. Imagination doesn't belong in the artistic domain only but to any scientific or technological activity. Companies and organizations lacking in imagination are doomed since they will not be able to create a world vision to which they ought to aspire and will not be able to accomplish anything other than repeat the existing achievements.

"What is the difference between a computer creation and artistic creation?" I asked my daughter, who studied arts and worked in the field. "The mistakes," she replied confidently. "Computers don't make mistakes, and if they do, then those mistakes are programmed. An error is what's unique about human art."

Irrational Thinking

"No great mind has ever existed without a touch of madness."

Aristotle

In the past, irrational thinking was regarded as tantamount to stupidity, representative of primitive thinking or more accurately, the total absence of thinking. Today it is obvious that irrational thinking operates by different rules and laws. We may not have a reasonable explanation or the scientific ability to understand mystical or religious phenomena but there is no doubt that they have their own internal rules.

Wolfgang Pauli (1900-1958), a recipient of the Nobel Prize in Physics, was considered by Einstein as his successor; by the age of twenty, he had written a monograph on Einstein's theory of relativity for the Encyclopaedia of Mathematical Sciences. He found that many ideas and discoveries derived from the irrational realm of the soul, a domain whose existence he had denied. Pauli adopted a quantum approach and argued that rationality and irrationality were in a constant state of unity, being in fact, opposite depictions of the same reality.

That is, ideas are born from the irrational in the I.Q.-R and flow to the I.Q.-L in order to turn into scientific affirmations. That is why Pauli, the rational physicist, dabbled in such domains as the Kabbalah, numerology and mysticism.

Against this background, the events connected with his life and death take a special significance: Pauli dedicated many years of work to the question of "why the Fine-Structure Constant is in fact a constant" (a fundamental physics constant that characterizes the strength of electromagnetic interaction and serves to describe the structure of the hydrogen atom), which is the number 1:137, and how this is connected to the fact that in numerology, 137 corresponds to the word "Kabbalah." At the age of 58, he was hospitalized and died in the hospital in room 137.

Recently, many studies focused on rational thinking clearly indicate not only that the irrational isn't always erroneous – in many cases, it **is** the right thinking. Countless decisions that have changed the world were seemingly irrational. Professor Dan Ariely, one of the researchers who have made this topic their life's work, gave his popular book the title Predictably Irrational, and the next, The Upside of Irrationality to which we can add, "**Irrational - but Essential.**"

Image/Icon

Visual thinking is based on images, shapes and colors. Unlike verbal thinking, which derives from a methodical and gradual process of perception of letters, words and sentences, visual thinking makes it possible to see the big picture all at once. With the development of visual technology, visual thinking is gradually becoming dominant, from films to advanced graphics, finally taking on the internet world. In the 21st century, the image wins over the written word. Even though the computer is a product of left-sided logic, communication with the computer is controlled by right-sided, visual thinking.

Humor

"Creativity is Intelligence having fun!."

Albert Einstein

Humor emanates from right-sided thinking. The left side, devoid of humor, is deadly serious. Humor embodies something non-linear and flexible, changing direction, surprising and illogical, which is another significant difference between humans and computers. The computer may catalog and remember all the jokes that we usually forget, and there is a chance that it will be even good at telling them, but it cannot invent them because of humor's lack of algorithmic logic. Humor is childish in a way, playful (play on words), a connection to associations. Genuine stars are full of humor.

People of highly developed right-sided intelligence are full of humor and laugh frequently. When one meets an enlightened guru or a scientist like Einstein, one immediately feels their connection to humor, their laughter bubbling inside them, an almost childish irreverence combined with their wisdom and vast knowledge.

Associative Thinking

This type of thinking is simultaneous and multidirectional so that the relationship between the objects of thought does not rely on logic or any particular hierarchy but on associative connections. The brain is an associative network: Every piece of information can be considered as a central point radiating into circles of associations and connected to them; this is the basis from which Mind Mapping developed.

The mind map model made by Tony Buzan, author and educational consultant, is based on mapping by associative connections; it is an auxiliary tool for individual or group thinking processes. According to this model, thinking starts with focusing on a central idea from which associative connections originate. When direct associations are exhausted, one passes to a second cycle of association, so that each associative connection which comes up becomes a center around which additional associative connections are established, and so on. A mind-association map, about a certain topic, is received at the end of the procedure. It is a kind of map of all the interconnections in our mind associated with the specific subject.

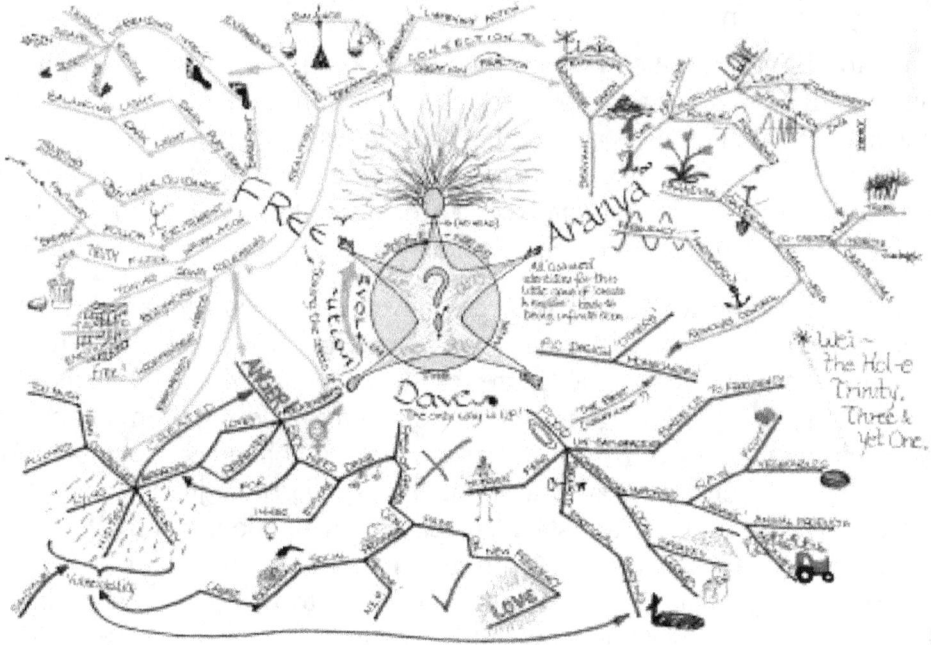

Studies of the brain's electrical activity when a person attempts to solve a problem have found two strategies:

On the left side of the brain thinking goes from a wide circle to a process of focusing; on the right side of the brain the initial point of thought develops into widening circles of associations. It's no surprise that the differences between these two strategies also represent the differences between men and women.

An association system serves as a basis for combinatorial sight or thought. The term combinatorial thought refers to the ability to notice simultaneously several factors and, in parallel, recognize the contexts between these factors as well as the new and different potential connections between them. This type of thinking is essential in the business world, and many businesspeople have a knack of viewing situations in a different light, unconventionally. They are the ones who recognize the potential which may be realized in future when others see nothing but the present, or maybe only the past. They identify possibilities, needs and opportunities that others don't see.

Despite the masculine image of the business world, combinatorial thinking in business relies on the skills of the right side of the brain, archetypically regarded as the feminine side. The amalgamation of combinatorial thinking, associative connections and gut feelings is what characterizes successful businesspeople, and the ability to see reality from a different angle makes a businessman an exceptionally successful one.

Meditative thinking

Meditation is the right-hemisphere way of thinking; it is neither logical nor sequential. It does not analyze but aspires to concentration, mental control and inner contemplation. It does not combine processes of analysis and conclusion, and it seems that in this process, the left side of the brain considers the object from outside, so to speak, uninvolved. Through meditative thinking, a person becomes both the object and the subject as one.

Meditative thinking leads one to to a kind of insight other than the logical conclusions. For years, I used to take managers on a journey of thinking differently in a center that we had established in the forest. One of the principal exercises was the "Personal Corner": Each participant was asked to find a spot in the forest in which he would stay by himself for a certain time without preoccupying himself with his personal or organizational problems, to experience just the "here" and the "now." For some, it was a first encounter with meditation, seemingly a waste of their precious time. I wasn't surprised. And so I was thrilled to hear from some of the participants that when they returned to work they succeeded in finding solutions to problems they had been stuck with for quite some time –

problems we did not directly deal with at the workshop – as if the solution were processed within them without them being aware of it.

In a world brimming with knowledge, the manager (the star) should know how to analyze data, identify trends and extensively use his analytical capacity, but he must not neglect the operation of the right side of his brain in the learning process of organizational information, where new ideas seemingly come from. I call this "meditation while facing computer data." I would recommend that managers upload all organizational databases to a computer (a marvelous product of the I.Q.-L), and gaze at them without focusing on anything in particular, play around with them, meditate on them. This activity helps discover new insights and connections that had we searched intentionally for them would never have occurred to us.

In the words of David Rock, research director of the NeuroLeadership Institute at Carnegie Mellon University in Pennsylvania, "We have to get used to letting our non-conscious brains do the work. Instead of driving ourselves crazy looking for new and improved answers, you should learn to relax, let go, and then you will find a whole world of new insights."

Meditative thinking, or thinking without thinking, thinking while gazing at data, is the key to insights which surface without thinking about them. Relaxing in the bathtub (like Archimedes) or in any other calming situation which makes it possible for the right side of our brain to start operating is the secret of enlightenment. Meditation is the way to enlightenment.

Assessment and development

There are diverse ways to diagnose creativity. It should be noted that I.Q.-R assessment relates to thinking capacity rather than its quality. Quality check belongs by definition to the left side of the brain. In order to successfully activate the right side of the brain, we must break free of our rational judgment. One of the basic creativity tests is the examination of a person's associative richness. For example: "In a given time, cite as many ideas as you can for additional uses of a paper clip; suggest new uses for a pacifier; add a few lines to the following drawings to create a new image."

All right-brain tests are involved in opening new possibilities rather than shutting them out – in the ability to move from one idea to the next rather than stopping at the answer.

Insufficient basic levels of the I.Q.-R cause pathological states in which a person finds it difficult to execute basic functions because of inflexibility, but such pathologies do not concern us here. Unfortunately, contemporary teaching methods focus mainly on developing the I.Q.-L with very little exercise and methodical development of the I.Q.-R, even though surfing the internet or channel-hopping makes an important contribution in this respect.

Creativity is a trait acquired in most cases throughout childhood and basically requires emotional and cognitive flexibility. When parents or the systems surrounding children (kindergarten, caregivers, among others) encourage creativity and thinking "out of the box," they enable their children to develop mental flexibility, denoted by the avoidance of fixation on an idea or a certain thinking pattern. Learning creativity is no different than learning mathematics, sports, or any other subject. Even in the case of natural talent, it will only improve with the right training and "space" which makes it possible to make mistakes and have "thinking adventures."

The way to improve right-sided intelligence is by experiencing, experimenting and freeing oneself from inhibitions and censure.

- Being characteristic of I.Q.-R, humor is an excellent tool to connect with and nurture I.Q.-R.

- Workshops nurturing spontaneous artistic expression in areas such as painting, games, dance and theater encourage leaving one's comfort zone and learning not to fear criticism.

- Emphasis on a different thinking pattern as opposed to the dominance of left-sided thinking instilled in us throughout each stage of formal education, such as taking the question "What's the right answer?" and changing it to "This is the answer – what are the possible questions?"

Various books and methods discuss creative development. However, the development of intuition is a more complex domain. The knowledge and information on the subject offered in professional literature is rather limited today. It is difficult to learn something that by its nature is not systematic knowledge that can be learned, especially as basic learning techniques derive from the left side of the brain, which in this case is not the desired side.

In recent years, many workshops for the development of intuition have appeared. Ned Herrmann, a professional painter, was one of the first to establish creativity development workshops for managers who relied on the left- and right-brain development model. In these right-brain development workshops, managers and engineers learned to draw, work with clay and let their creativity flow freely while accepting the irrational parts. Edward de Bono also developed tools for breaking away from the paradigms we are bound by. De Bono claimed that only with cognitive provocation is it possible to find new solutions and ideas.

The way to improve right-brain intelligence is through experience and trial and error. One of the tips I heard from Professor Shoshana Zuboff at a professional conference was that in order to develop a worker's ability to reach intuitive decisions, that person has to be as exposed to as much information and experience as possible, as opposed to the need for focus of the left brain. One of the ways to do this is to send the worker to different units of the organization. This advice is based on the assumption that intuition is some sort of unconscious thought process in which all the information collected by a certain person takes part not only as knowledge but as experience. Thus, people should be allowed to change positions and experience organizational knowledge from different angles.

The fundamental condition for the development of creative aspects is "defense" against criticism, at least in the first stages of any creative thinking process. Breaking away from familiar mind-sets is stepping away from our comfort zone towards new and undefined zones, which hold ample opportunities to make mistakes. Both the ability and permission to make mistakes are essential conditions for the development of right-brain thinking. For example, the process of brainstorming, aimed at surfacing new ideas, forbids, in essence, all forms of criticism during the process. Brainstorming is an excellent example of combinatorial and creative thinking development. The concept of brainstorming was first formulated in the 1950s by Alex F. Osborn who was a partner and founder of BBDO, the worldwide advertising agency. Brainstorming is in effect a group thinking procedure practiced to mobilize the group's creative resources in an effort to solve problems or develop ideas. The main principles of brainstorming are also an efficient way to exercise right-sided thinking: There is no room for rational judgment, and quantity is preferred over quality. Having led dozens of creative thinking and brainstorming sessions, I often saw resistance to quantity over quality as well as difficulty in understanding that opening up to new possibilities, even if they are irrational, is the only way to get out of the box. At times, the participants managed to break free and come up with new ideas only by relaxing the left brain. Then, we found the time to discuss the quality of these ideas.

In creative thinking workshops, we found that one of the strongest tools for changing one's perspectives is changing the physical visual settings. There is nothing like a change of scenery or a change in seating to affect creativity. During a discussion, changing the participants' seating arrangement is recommended: the person sitting facing you moves beside you and so on. Once, I took a group of high-tech workers to a catacomb to discuss the future of the company. Another time we had a session in a Jacuzzi in the middle of the forest with the purpose of coming up with new ideas. The debate succeeded in pulling down all the boundaries of the "right-sided box."

A study of creativity by a team of experts of the University of California at Santa Barbara under the direction of Benjamin Baird tested the most comfortable conditions for the emergence of creative thinking. The subjects were divided into four groups. Each group was given a number of tasks to perform before and after the activity in order to examine the effect of different activities on creativity. The participants who were given an undemanding assignment improved creativity more than the others. Members of that group reported, more than others, about moments of "mind wandering." Simple tasks that allow the mind to wander heighten people's creativity in problem solving.

For developing the I.Q.-R, it is highly recommended to learn meditation, to think without a specific object in mind, without any specific objective of thought. Bear in mind that this is not a waste of time any more than sleeping is a waste of time. It is very important, if not crucial, to learn how to let go of the "despotic" left side that manages, directs and leads towards goals and objectives, and to learn how to take some time for ourselves. That's where the secret of creativity lies.

I.Q.-R Characteristics:

- **Creativity** – the ability to come up with ideas that display vision, originality and innovation;

- **Integration ability** – the ability to connect different ideas or different domains;

- **Visual thinking** – thinking based on images, shapes, colors, etc.;

- **Intuitive thinking** – consolidating ideas and making decisions on the basis of internal sensations ("gut feelings");

- **Original and innovative thinking** – the ability to think "outside the box," seeing things from different angles, breaking paradigms;

- **Associative thinking** – the ability and habit of making special connections between things and ideas;

- **Combinatorial thinking** – creating special, original connections;

- **Sophistication** – unconventional, sophisticated and multidimensional thinking;

- **Imagination** – the ability to use imagination in thinking and problem solving;

- **Invention** – the ability and intense wish to invent new things.

The behavioral level represents the dimensions of action and performance.

The Behavioral Level

System & **S**tructure.**Q**

- Efficiency
- System
- Simplicity
- Consistency
- Sequential
- Specific and focused
- System
- Stability
- Planning
- Routine
- Black and white

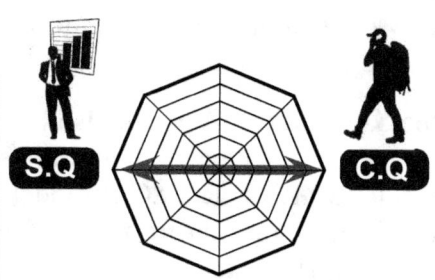

S.Q   C.Q

Change & **C**haos.**Q**

- Change
- Chaos
- Complexity
- Diversity
- Coincidence
- Uncertainty
- Conflict
- Flexibility
- Improvisation
- Curiosity
- Colorful
- Chance

Success in this level is reflected in actions. The behavioral axis, which moves between the change and chaos quotient on the right (C.Q.) and the system and structure quotient on the left (S.Q.), can also be also called the management axis.

Between the S.Q. and the C.Q.

Diversity, chaos and change versus system and structure

A picturesque example of the polarity of C.Q. and S.Q. is the difference between major American cities and major European ones. Many cities in the United States evolved from a culture of efficiency and simplicity, which is why the streets, avenues and buildings are marked with numbers and letters – as clear and effective as it can be. You can always tell where you are in relation to your destination and where every address is in relation to another, just as the system quotient should be.

On the other hand, city centers in Europe have streets named after the nation's leading figures in politics, literature and art in no discernible order. The committees in charge of naming streets may be creative, but they are not necessarily efficient. Does, say, one street named after a poet intersect with another named after a king or are they parallel? Do streets honoring saints and those recognizing special days in Paris meet? Efficient yet uninspiring is the first model, and cultured and inspiring is the second one, albeit inefficient.

Colors suggest another comparison, between the multicolor of the right side of the model and the black and white of the left side; a comparison of accuracy, order and absolute clarity in photography or graphic style, and the chaos, color and uniqueness of undefined abstract art.

The axis connecting the S.Q. and the C.Q. can also be called the management axis. The role of a manager is to navigate along the behavioral axis between change and efficiency. The S.I.L.V.E.R .A.C.E model suggests that the goal is not to turn chaos or diversity into uniformity and efficiency but to attain the maximum of both. All those systems established for the sole purpose of efficiency – the conveyor belt, the police state, central planning, and excessive workload – that didn't respect the human need for individual expression eventually proved to be less efficient.

Q - 4

Change & Chaos Quotient (C.Q.)

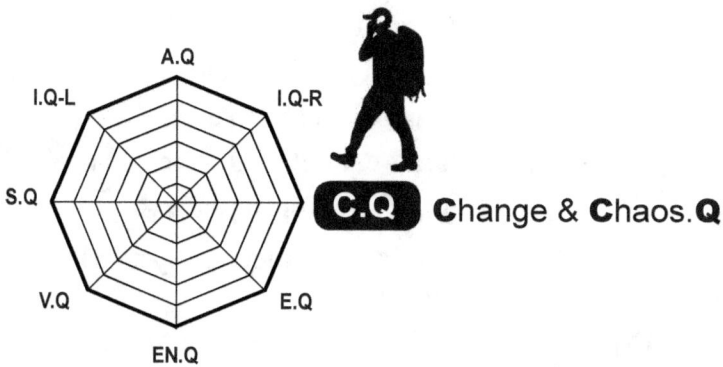

C.Q   **C**hange & **C**haos.**Q**

"It is not the strongest of the species that survives, nor the most intelligent that survives, it is the one that is the most adaptable to change."

Charles Darwin

Identity:	Name: Change and Chaos Quotient
	Symbol: **C.Q.**
Definition:	The ability to change; to operate amid conditions of uncertainty, chaos and concurrence; the ability to deal with conflict situations, complexity and crisis through flexibility, adaptation, curiosity and courage.
Characteristics:	Change
	Chaos
	Concurrence
	Conflict
	Complexity
	Crisis
	Chance
	Courage
	Curiosity

States of pathological deficiency:	Catatonia, paralysis, rigidity
Expression at work:	Flexibility and improvisation;
	Change and adaptation;
	Curiosity;
	Favorable reaction to change;
	Flexible and adaptable.
Location in the model:	**The vertical axis** – the behavioral level;
	The horizontal axis – right;
	Counterbalance – System and Structure quotient, **S.Q.**
Neighboring quotients in the model:	1) Right Intelligence Quotient, **I.Q.-R**
	2) Emotional Intelligence Quotient, **E.Q.**

1) The E.Q. (emotional intelligence) provides the required tools to emotionally cope with change. It is the form of intelligence that gives humans the optimism, personal maturity and self-confidence required to display a positive attitude towards change. A high level of E.Q. strengthens the change quotient while a low level of E.Q. weakens it.

2) The I.Q.-R (right intelligence) refers in this context to the thinking processes enabling us to activate our imagination in order to create a new reality, different from the existing one. It is what provides the ability to see things differently, the ability to break existing paradigms and patterns. A high level of I.Q.-R will bolster the change quotient while a low level will weaken it.

Change and chaos quotient (C.Q.) – definition and characterization

The change and chaos quotient is especially significant these days. We live in a period characterized by very rapid changes due to accelerated technological development. The change quotient deals with humans' attitude towards change and their ability to adapt to new situations. This is where people derive their ability to act, to improvise and deploy resourcefulness in times of ambiguity, uncertainty and chaos. The change and chaos quotient does not deal with the nature, quality and goal of change but with the ability to efficiently set the change in motion in the face of ambiguity and conflict.

Who moved my cheese?

Spencer Johnson's book Who Moved My Cheese? (1998) is about the change quotient. It is an allegorical story about two mice, Hem and Haw, each of which deals in its own way with the fact that the cheese in their maze is gone. The book became a best seller because it helped people all around the world understand the importance of coping with change.

The author was asked to write a professional introduction to the Hebrew edition of the book, an excerpt of which follows:

"Here, read this and we'll talk about it later," the publisher said as she handed me a copy of Who Moved My Cheese? Given that there is no coincidence in this world, we talked before I was to set out on a trip to the desert. I had gotten into the habit of going to the desert to see things and see myself from a different angle before heading out towards a new path, or a change of any kind. That time, I took my copy of the book preprint. There's something special and unique about the right story at the right time and at the right place.

The story of moving the cheese gave me the opportunity to encounter myself and introspect, as a way to examine what was important and to muster the courage to act. The moment I started reading, I was captivated by the metaphor. The power of a good metaphor lies in its ability to establish direct communication with the subconscious, which blends into our world of images and symbols. I found myself wandering around the desert wadis "debating" and "deliberating" on "cheese" and "labyrinths," changes and fears...

"This isn't an introduction to the book anymore," I said when I returned. "Only those who have read this book and have encountered its metaphor will understand this world of symbols and concepts, which has become part of me. So this is my introduction for someone who has read the book."

I decided to read the book during workshops intended for different groups of people. "Those are word for word, the exact terms I hear from people who consult me," said one of the career consultants in a center for the unemployed. "I hadn't paid attention that the cheese was getting more and more scarce until it was too late," said an elderly man who was forced to retire from a company where tenure was the supreme value. Career counselors meet in full force with those who ran out of cheese at their regular cheese station and were left surprised, with all the feelings of frustration and fear it aroused.

The metaphor became the language that enabled me, the consultants, as well as those who consult them, to address problems of change and emerging fears regarding management and employment a little differently. Through images, we encountered people's difficulties to understand that nobody took their cheese. The fact that the cheese was gone is no personal failure. They had to reach the understanding that the most important step is to move as quickly as possible rather than focus excessively on introspection or placing blame for the cheese disappearance. We had to identify the difficulty to get out and pursue the journey despite or because of the fact that the cheese at one station ran out.

"You know, this story has become our language, and it has got me moving," said one of the consultants a few days after the workshop. "I decided to put on my running shoes, get into sports gear and make some significant changes in my life."

This book deals with the human change quotient. As someone who studies the future, I can confidently state the one thing all futurists agree upon: The pace of change is accelerating. The cheese is moving ever so faster, not necessarily running out, but definitely moving. The importance of the ability to face change or the extent of one's ability to change is becoming a central element among the required characteristics for coping and succeeding. The C.Q. is a measure of a person's attitude towards change as well as his or her ability to change.

The change quotient consists of flexibility, the ability to emerge from fixation, the ability to move on with curiosity and optimism, and most of all, the courage to change oneself. We have wondered where the change quotient comes from, how it is acquired, whether it can be modified. The good news is that unlike the I.Q., which is harder to improve, we can learn and practice in order to expand our change quotient.

"Weren't you afraid?" I once asked a woman of vision who made extraordinary changes in her life and today is a source of inspiration to many. "I do not know what fear is," she replied. Does fear have to do with personality or character? Will the one who is afraid have no chance? It is possible to learn and practice not only in times of transition but also how to overcome fear – to have courage.

To do this, we have built "training fields" for new experiences where we encounter the fears at the edge of our comfort zones. The power of induction of the acquired knowledge gathered from climbing the training wall up and takes to the CEO chambers never ceases to amaze me. One of the executives who took part in this type of challenge told me the following day: "Now that I've managed to overcome this, nothing can stop me!"

This story is about coping with change which is based on the assumption that change is constant. There is no such thing as cheese that doesn't move. Layoffs or cutbacks occur only too often, but we should remember that the proverbial cheese can be many other things: Health, love, family, etc. That cheese moves for different reasons, sometimes even because of our own internal shifts, because we ourselves have been changing, but mainly because everything is eternally in constant change and flow.

"One cannot cross the same river twice," said Heraclitus, meaning that nothing stays the same: Everything flows and changes continuously. It is not possible to read this book twice, I reflected when reading it for the second time. I have changed, and so did the story.

The elements of the C.Q.

Change

"The future is no longer what it used to be."

As early as the beginning of the 1970s, Alvin Toffler talked of the pace of change increasing exponentially since our world itself is in an endless state of flux, which is all the more pertinent in the 21st century. The change and chaos quotient represents the notion that "the future is no longer what it used to be."

An illustration of the speed of change is the estimation that from the beginning of the 20th century until the 1970s, humankind has doubled its knowledge; by the 1990s, humankind once again doubled its knowledge, and doubled it yet again by the beginning of the 21st century. The pace at which humankind doubles its knowledge is constantly increasing so that, in the opinion of professionals, by the 2040s human knowledge will double every six weeks. This pace of change is dizzying and hard to grasp.

Until the mid-20th century, permanence was of supreme value. People wanted to buy clothing that would last for many years and a house they could grow old in; these days, we change computers, cellular phones and cars ever more frequently. With such pace of change, the ability of people and organizations to adapt to new situations has become a central factor in their chances to succeed. This reality obliges every person, especially the manager of an organization, to foresee future changes. If the map is not being read correctly, if there is no adjustment to changes, they will very quickly run aground.

The faster the pace systems and jobs change, the more complex it is to establish criteria for calculating a person's success in a certain position. In the past, evaluating suitability and forecasting success at a specific job was based on a battery of tests assessing a person's abilities. In order to validate the process and understand the measure of correlation between the success predicted and that in practice, data was gathered after the fact. However, anyone actively engaged in the occupational world knows this academic method is no longer relevant. This "scientific" process is based on the assumption that the function of time is equal to zero, as if time remains constant and unchanging all along the process.

In a validity study we conducted for a large company, managers were asked for their opinions on the success at work of applicants who had undergone assessment. In addition, they were asked about job descriptions as they were submitted at the time of assessment and the extent to which they matched the actual position in effect. We were not surprised to find out that in more dynamic companies, over 70% of job descriptions had changed dramatically in the past two or three years.

Every change holds risks as well as opportunities. Openness to change is an expression of a person's willingness to take risks and cope with anxiety about the unknown. At the same time, the ability to quit a condition of stagnation and benefit from growth opportunities is no less important. The essence of change does not lie only in the ability to adapt to new things but also in the ability to let go and give up the old. The meaning of change is to separate from what is familiar and safe, therefore it requires readiness to relinquish control. People with low change quotient struggle to let go of things, which is why they find it difficult to let go of the old to embrace the new.

Change by its own nature gives rise to tensions and crises. Successful people and organizations demonstrate their ability to cope with crisis situations and seize the opportunities they present. A person with a high change quotient is characteristically highly capable of adapting efficiently, operating in situations of change with curiosity and abundant energy. This change won't cause any paralyzing fear; on the contrary, it will act as some sort of energizing drug like adrenalin. This kind of person will find himself at his best in times of change, chaos and concurrence.

When coping with changes it is essential to recognize our fear of change, which is part of human nature, connected with the basic need of humans to feel safe and in control of their lives. The feeling that they are in control imparts the ability to choose familiar actions which seem most appropriate in a certain situation; that ability is largely based on familiarity with the situation through past experience or by a learning process. There is a large variety of cognitive factors, emotional and even physiological, at the root of resistance to and fear of change; all these contribute to the recognition of the extreme difficulty of coping with change.

Chaos

"Chaos often breeds life, when order breeds habit."

Henry Adams

Order is in fact the framework of procedures we set up against chaos. Such definition explains why there is disorder in the world. Every situation is temporary and unstable. At any given moment, laws, methods, and markets are shattered to be replaced in time by new ones. Chaos is between the eradication of the old and the making of the new.

The component "chaos" in the change quotient refers to the human ability to act in times of uncertainty and ambiguity. In this respect, we examine the nature of the response to chaos, whether it weakens and paralyzes or challenges by stimulating operation or thinking in an improved way. The ability to cope with chaos and the fear it inspires makes it possible for us not to break down when facing uncertainty and even consider this uncertainty as an opportunity to create something new. People with high change quotient perceive chaos as an opportunity waiting to be seized.

Crisis

Drastic change and chaos produce crisis, which in pathological conditions is experienced as shock. Toffler used this concept to describe the crisis that accompanies the increasing pace of change. Shock is a mental state that comes with a feeling of disorientation and loss of touch with the environment; it is a state in which the spirit calls, in a way, for time-out and steps out of the game. Studies of soldiers suffering from shell shock indicate that the likelihood of becoming shell shocked increases in direct relation to the extent of the chaotic factor and the unfamiliarity of the environment the soldier finds himself in. Soldiers who had been transferred from their original unit to a socially and geographically unfamiliar environment were found to be more prone to shell shock than those who remained in familiar territory. The external conditions of chaos and uncertainty went beyond the soldiers' control.

One of the major impairments caused by future shock, such as shell shock, is system collapse and a feeling of "this is not for me," which makes people and organizations duck the game and drop out of the competition all together.

In Oriental languages, the concepts of "crisis" and "opportunity" are identical. A high change quotient symbolizes the ability to turn a crisis into an opportunity and to perceive it as a factor making possible the very change that will necessarily improve the status quo. Static situations may be free of tension and crises, but by the same token they are lethargic and inert and do not allow any movement or progress. Crisis may be the cause of change or its consequence, but its presence is a certainty in any dynamic environment. By its nature, change entails tensions and crises. Successful people and organizations prove that they can cope with crisis situations and make the most of the opportunities they offer.

Concurrence and Diversity

A person whose change quotient is high has the ability to handle several things at the same time, as if he has a sort of split personality allowing him to concurrently watch several television series, log in to Facebook, talk on Skype, etc. The point is not to move quickly from one thing to the next but rather do several things at the same time. In a future so saturated with changes and novelties, surely one of the abilities required to succeed in the occupational world is concurrence, or multifunctioning, multitasking and multicareers.

This particular characteristic of the change quotient combines difference and concurrence, acting in parallel in several channels. Each channel is defined, distinct and abundantly eventful, just like television channels loaded with many different programs. Uniformity and standardization contribute to efficiency, but they are also the source of fixation and rigidity.

Concurrence refers not only to assignments and tasks but also to conceiving multipossibility careers. One will never have just one career with a single employer until retirement; one will not have several careers throughout an entire lifetime, but several parallel, concurrent careers without giving up other options or dreams. Market trends forecaster Faith Popcorn called this outlook "living your 99 lives."

The abilities and skills of people with a high change quotient make it possible for them to live concurrently in several domains and to be active in each of them without detriment to another.

Conflict

Rapid changes do not come about harmoniously; they generate gaps and cause conflicts. Conflict is a basic existential condition within every one of us as well as every socio-dynamic organization, including the family. For example, one of the factors which has influenced the rise of divorce rates is connected with the changes that couples go through and the conflicts that flare up when there is no coordination in the pace or style of change. Many couples who began their relationship harmoniously will find that one partner is changing pace or direction differently than the other.

The ability of the individual, the family or the organization to efficiently deal with conflict situations is one of the key aspects of the change quotient. Impeding changes will cause an organization to atrophy. The tension brought about by conflict is healthy since without it there is neither production nor progress.

Therefore, conflict is not some problem we have to solve but a blessing we should derive benefit from.

Complexity

The change and chaos quotient represents the ability to operate amid complexity. The world – with the organizational environment as a part of it – is moving towards increasingly complex situations, and complex relationships can affect our situation in any place and at any moment. Situations in China or developments in Japan should be taken into account by every manager as well as by everyone else. The internet, the media and highly accessible knowledge connect us to a world that is more complex and more complicated. In such world, there is no room for naïve, clear-cut and one-dimensional simplicity. The ability to succeed is entwined with the ability to navigate in ever-increasing complexities without being paralyzed by fear of those complexities. A person with a low C.Q. gets confused in the face of such complexity and is incapable of operating.

Curiosity and Courage

Curiosity and courage are two central characteristics of people with high C.Q. A person whose change quotient is high is not perturbed by uncertainty and complexity; in effect he is filled with curiosity, and that curiosity turns things around from negative to positive.

Researchers, such as Fuchs, have shown that situations of change and crisis are usually accompanied by a natural fear of the unknown, fear of getting out of our comfort zone and of the dangers facing us.

We need courage to cope with all that. Those who thrive in times of change are not fearless but courageous. Fearlessness by itself can be dangerous; it might lead to irresponsible actions, while courageous actions in the face of fear make it a constructive and enriching process.

Chance

"People often do not realize that they have a chance, so they miss it."

Nassim Nicholas Taleb

High C.Q means the ability and curiosity to "see" the chances in the chaos.

Chance is the unknown, a force assumed to cause events that cannot be predicted or controlled and which have an uncertain outcome. A chance event has no obvious design, form or pattern - and this is what makes it challenging to spot chance coming toward you.

Chance could be a favorable set of circumstances that presents the opportunity for good fortune and luck. It could also be an unpredictable element that results in an unfortunate accident or hazard. Examples of chance are an accidental meeting, a random phone call, an unplanned visit, the stumbling on an idea, place, picture, or even a word. Missing a flight, or a traffic light, and so forth.

After understanding the role chance plays in our lives, the question is: Do we have control over the odds?

Because of their fear of failure, people try to protect themselves against negative outcomes by creating buffers – calculations, assessments, forecasts, and evaluations – that all help avoid and reduce the risk that chance presents. By doing so, people also consistently overlook opportunities and miss out on them.

On the other hand, leaving things entirely to chance resembles the flip of a coin – that is, taking chances mindlessly, which can lead to random failure or success.

It is preferable to think of success as a contest of chance in which you have control over the odds. As you begin to master concepts in personal achievement, you increase your odds of achieving success.

Deficiencies

In *Future Shock* (1970), Alvin Toffler was among the first to assert that time intervals between one change and the next are getting ever shorter. The future, then, is approaching at increasing speed. This is along the lines of the difference between a person who goes for a walk and watches the scenery beside him pass very slowly, and a person who travels in a fast car through the same place and sees the same scenery passing at high speed. Processes that in the past took thousands of years take place in a few years, and it seems that the pace of change will only increase.

As a psychologist, I worked with the shell shocked and studied them, closely watching their reactions. Shock is accompanied by a feeling of disorientation and loss of touch with the environment. The treatment of future shock just like that of shell shock will be through increasing awareness, only this time it will not be awareness of the past but that of the future. We will try to plan what the future holds in order to be prepared for different possibilities. This is the most efficient way for preventing future shock, and it is also the duty of any person in management and leadership: The leader-manager should see himself as the ship's captain climbing to the top of the foremast in order to look far into the horizon.

A situation of deficiency in the change quotient will be reflected in an inability to carry out, implement and assimilate changes. It will be further reflected in the inability to live through situations of chaos and uncertainty, situations of conflict and complexity, especially in the inability to do several things simultaneously. Extreme deficiency is characterized by a pathological state called "catatonia" in professional jargon – rigidity of all systems, sometimes not only mental but also physical systems and the inability to tolerate any change whatsoever. In extreme cases, we can observe intense difficulty to adapt even to changes in lighting or the intonation of voices, while in less extreme cases it will be expressed as a form of anxiety and by fear of change.

An additional pathological expression of deficient change quotient is "Obsessive Compulsive Disorder (OCD)." One of the possible manifestations of such deficiency is obsessive preoccupation with having everything around in the same order, with no changes. Those diagnosed with OCD check again and again to make sure there has been no change in their world. These anxious people go through much suffering, which brings some of them to lose touch with the environment and to create an existential bubble for themselves.

Among the population defined as normal, we can observe a decline in the change quotient as people get older, just as physical systems increasingly lose their flexibility, so does the mental system. With time, the capacity to endure uncertainty gradually diminishes, and anxiety is triggered by any environmental or personal change. A person who finds it hard to cope with chaotic situations will experience intense anxiety every time the environment is unfamiliar or unstructured. Loss of control may be expressed through uncomfortable physical or psychological sensations, as the difficulty to adapt to change leads to rigidity and intransigence. This kind of person will hold on to whatever is at hand with all his strength, even when real life requires change.

Lack of the change quotient will be revealed as inability to tolerate differences and the need to generate uniformity and standardization. The pathological state is expressed by the inability to deal with several issues concurrently. Such a person is capable of doing things only sequentially; only after having completed one task will that person be capable of allocating resources to another. Such people and organizations will find it difficult to cope with the competitive environment and will soon find themselves out of the game.

Assessment and Development

Don't wait for the storm to pass - learn to dance in the rain!!!

The ability to cope with concurrence and complexity can now be measured and quantified in a simple and clear manner. In multiple-choice tests, the more options there are to choose from (distracters), the longer will be the average time to answer the question. An examination of the results will yield a graph indicating a direct relation between the number of distracters and the time required to answer the question. With people for whom coping with concurrence is difficult, it appears that above a certain number of distracters, the time graph sharply ascends. At some point, the examinee will go through a total power failure and will be incapable of performing the required multichannel processing.

There are dozens of methods for developing the ability to be flexible in new and unfamiliar situations. Typing in the words "change" or "change methods" into an internet search engine will bring up hundreds of workshops, methods and books on the subject. Most of them deal with understanding the mechanisms of resisting change while others focus on how to change a person or an organization. When an organization needs to develop its change quotient, it generally seeks the help of an external agent, such as an organizational consultant, recognizing that their particular case calls for a professional guiding hand. Those consultants use different methods and titles from organizational transformation through re-engineering to coaching but the goal is the same – reinforcement for the purpose of generating change.

Oriental cultures have the very same word for crisis and opportunity. Developing the change quotient means learning to perceive opportunity in crisis, seeing a crisis as a factor requiring the dynamism which brings about change.

Some time ago, I was invited to give a lecture to a group of senior managers and military officers. The topic was "How do managers/officers cope with the pace of change and with chaos?" They expected to be presented with a ready-made formula for coping. They were therefore surprised when I told them the formula was "not coping at all!!!" I told them how I stood trembling in line for a roller coaster ride at Disneyland, the frightening "Kamikaze." Anyone who has experienced that nightmare knows that when you get to the front of the line, there is a sign posted that says: "If you have a heart condition or if you are a pregnant woman or… you are kindly requested not to board." At that point, I had a thought, "How do you cope with the fear of such a roller coaster?" The child standing in front of me saw the sweat break out on my pale face and asked, "Are you OK, mister?" I said I was afraid and asked him how he could stand it. That's when he gave me the formula: "I love it. It's the third time I'm doing it." "So you want to know how to cope?" I asked my audience, "**One simply has to learn to enjoy it! That's the secret of coping.**"

Prepare your children for change

A few years ago, when my children were preparing for their high school graduation exams, I was amazed how they chose to study. They would sit in front of the television zapping through the channels, listening to music through their headphones with a textbook lying open on their laps. After scolding them a few times, I realized that they understood something I still did not; they were acclimating themselves to a world of intense concurrence and to change at a high speed, a sort of brain exercise in a multistimuli environment. In fact, they knew much better than I how to cope with the tremendous diversity and lack of uniformity in our world.

Many of the habits of young people today are examples of exercising the change quotient heading to a world where everything is expected to change at a terrifying speed. Anyone who has lived in close contact with children has witnessed it at close quarters. The zapping and following several programs all at once while messaging their friends actually are forms of exercise in change and chaos. The speed with which they learn how to engage in different subjects, tasks and areas and then disengage seems to us an apparent illustration of their superficiality, but maybe this is a good preparation for a world of fast transition from one video clip to the next.

The parents of less frantic children can also contribute to the development of their change quotient by providing them with proper training in situations of change. A few years ago, my wife and I decided to move from the central region of Israel to the Galilee in the north. We felt that the change would do us good. We also knew that we had to transmit a message to ourselves and to our children – that if we want to do something involving change, we have to be bold, face our fear, and then do it. As responsible parents, we worried about the difficulty we would be putting our teenage children through. We knew that the change would be tough and could be painful, and we wondered if fulfilling our dream at the cost of the children experiencing difficulties to adapt was justified. But thinking again, we understood that these children were about to live in a world of change, and we had to teach them to deal with the anticipated changes to come, not to spare them the change but experience significant change together with them. Looking back, we realized that we had done the right thing. Today, our children are thankful for the drastic move they went through.

A protective and constant environment may be important for children, providing them with the feelings of safety and stability as a basis for their own self-esteem, but when parents create for their children a "padded" environment devoid of change, they are likely to prevent them from acquiring essential C.Q. skills as well. The proper training for children is to undergo the first life changes with their parents, in the protective and supporting environment of the family, and to learn together as a family how to cope with change. A child who has experienced change and remembers it as a positive experience will know how to handle it on his own in the future.

C.Q. characteristics:

- **Improvisation** – the ability to find quick and practical solutions in stressful or unexpected situations;

- **Flexibility** – the ability to move without difficulty between different tasks and different situations;

- **Will to initiate changes** – the will not to rest on our laurels but to generate changes in our environment expecting positive results;

- **Ability to operate concurrently** – the ability to perform several different tasks at the same time;

- **Functioning in conditions of uncertainty** – the ability to operate actively in situations of ambiguity and lack of clarity;

- **Quick adaptation to changes** – the ability to accept new situations and to deal with changes rapidly and without difficulty;

- **Functioning in conflict situations** – the ability to operate well in conflict situations;

- **Curiosity** – looking forward to changes and novelty, enthusiastically expecting to carry them out;

- **Courage** – adventurous impulse towards new things;

- **Chaos** – operating efficiently in messy and chaotic situations.

Q - 5
System & Structure Quotient (S.Q.)

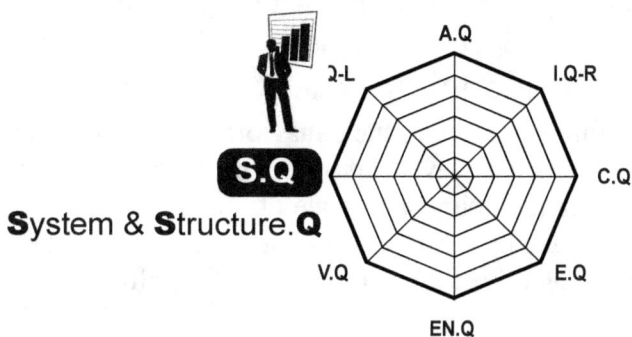

"Order and simplification are the first steps toward the mastery of a subject."

Thomas Mann

Identity:	Name: System and Structure Quotient
	Symbol: **S.Q.**
Characteristics:	**S**ystem
	Structure
	Sorting
	Sequential
	Simplicity
	Short
	Stability
	Standardization
	Specific
Pathological deficiencies:	Obsession, rigidity
Expression at work:	Organization, method and focus

Location in the model	**Vertical axis** – the behavioral level
	Horizontal axis – left
	Balance and counterbalance – Change quotient, **C.Q.**
Neighbors in the model:	1) Left Intelligence Quotient, I.Q.-L
	2) Value Quotient, V.Q.

Neighbors in the model

System and structure is located in the behavioral level, between the personality and the cognitive levels. This level personifies the nature of a person's behavioral nature as reflected in his doings and style of operation. The location indicates that behavior is affected by personality-related factors (from the value quotient, V.Q.) as well as by cognitive factors (from the left intelligence quotient, I.Q.-L).

System and Structure
and the Left Intelligence Quotient (S.Q. - I.Q.-L)

System and structure is influenced by left-sided intelligence, and in effect constitutes its behavioral expression. The ability to operate in a structured and organized way is the direct result of the ability to think this way. Planning in advance, which is one of the foundations of system and structure, is based on the ability to think things through and analyze them in a linear and methodical manner. System and structure is the counterbalance of the change quotient: It is what turns creation into an efficient process of routine production.

System and Structure
and the Value Quotient (S.Q. - V.Q.)

The value quotient blends into the behavioral aspect of system and structure. System and structure deals with organizing external space, creating an formal system of tasks, objectives and performance while the value quotient has to do with organizing internal, personal and cultural spaces; the V.Q. is the moral basis of method and structure. System and structure provides uniformity and stability, which constitute the reliability of the value system. The value quotient gives order and method their absolute shade and color.

Definition and Characterization

System and structure characterizes a person's behavior and operation in terms of method, organization, simplicity, clarity, focus, distinction between essential and trivial, and uniformity. This quotient makes it possible to define tasks on a timeline, to determine a list of priorities and clearly know one's direction and goal. The main purpose of this quotient is to make the processes more efficient and to prevent any waste of energy.

A person with a high system and structure has the ability to organize the world in an orderly manner, to separate the essential from the nonessential, to plan, to determine objectives, and to create measurable and logical structures and processes. He keeps everything organized and classified according to a logical order, aspires towards clear and organized goals, and feels fervently about efficiency and focus.

This quotient is located at the left side of the behavioral level, and it is needed to develop the thinking and action strategies of a hunter. A hunter has to choose his target within the environment and focus on it. A hunter must distinguish between the essential and the nonessential and identify the target in all the camouflage and the background noises which could distract him. In order to do this, he defines his priorities in both physical space and time. He must focus, simplify things and perceive the essential without letting changes in the environment confuse him.

The elements of the S.Q.

System & Structure

This particular factor identifies the situational pattern and makes it possible to turn chaos or a collection of data into an organized system with a defined set of rules and laws. It refers to the ability to contain data in defined structures and systems. A high system and structure quotient allows a person to identify the system within the data and act in a methodical way. Method refers to the laws, rules and algorithms according to which things operate.

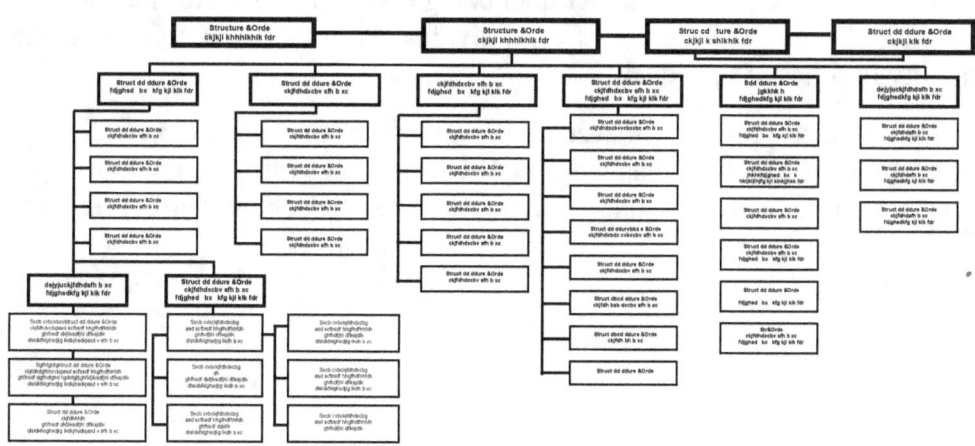

Sorting & Sequence

This element is in charge of the ability to bring order to chaos and to organize priorities. This implies sorting things out according to some form of logic, according to time, space or any other dimension. On the basis of this process, it may then be possible to outline strategies and translate them into an array of tasks to perform.

In the course of numerous observations and interviews that we conducted over the years with successful people in the business world, we found repeatedly that they have a developed internal order on the basis of which they can clearly identify the essential and focus on it. They can define their own orders of priorities in relation to the time dimension thus they operate with a clear perspective of the dimension of order.

Time is a central element of the S.Q. The dimension of time is situated on the left: It is linear, sequential in terms of past and future, unequivocal and one-dimensional. Awareness of time is one of the prominent characteristics of a star, making it possible to produce distinct processes which prevent the emergence of chaos and uncertainty. These processes make up a pattern to be used again later without having to reexamine and reshape reality.

Stability

The element of stability provides a dimension of constant routine activities and their components. It examines to what extent a person can generate stability in light of the changes taking place around him, and to what extent he is capable of enduring tempestuous times. Just as the ballast of a sailboat makes it possible for her to sail in stormy waters without being tossed from side to side, the high system and structure quotient of an individual or an organization can create stability in times of upheaval.

It is important to emphasize that stability does not mean fixation or permanence. The element of "stability" enables people to turn chaos into order and organize their lives in a routine of regular activities amid all the changes affecting them.

Standardization

"Any customer can have any car they choose in any color they want so long as the model is a T and it is black."

Henry Ford, father of the Industrial Revolution

The standard element is the opposite of difference and uniqueness, which characterize the change quotient. The principle of efficiency (which the S.Q. controls) gives priority to uniform systems operating in the form of routine processes. Standard uniform production processes increase the efficient functioning of an organization and even that of an individual. The principle of efficiency is what gave rise to the ISO standards, which themselves define standardized procedures.

The standard element affects the reliability of a product and is designed to appeal to consumers' trust and confidence. The more uniform the systems, the more efficient and reliable they are. Not only is the quality of the product determined in accordance with high standards of production but our confidence in the product is also connected to the degree of standardization of the process.

Specific

System and structure deals with clarity and focus. This element refers to the ability to characterize each part and detail in the system in a definite, focused and clear way. The objective is to create a clearly defined system and method, leaving no room for ambiguity. A person with a high system and structure quotient will be goal oriented, capable of acting with focus and clarity.

Simple and Short

In my meetings with successful people, I have always been aware of the clarity with which they perceive the complex and the intricate. They could take a complexly knotted rope and untie it methodically. A good manager or leader will succeed in clarifying things and will put what is blurry and confusing into focus so that it can be dealt with.

The S.Q. represents the "masculine management language." In structures of masculine culture, such as the army, the language of "short and simple" becomes the dominant language. Recently, the Financial Times published an article about workshops for women applying for managerial positions in Europe in which women learn the language of management. Unlike the feminine language, which indulges in adding color, embellishments and background descriptions, managerial language is brief and simplistic. An American engineer even invented a term for it: K.I.S.S.— Keep It Short and Simple.

Years ago, I met with a successful businessman who taught me a lesson on the value of simplicity. I had developed a business idea connected with human intelligence and artificial intelligence. I presented the idea, which I thought was brilliant, to an experienced businessman and enthusiastically tried to convince him to invest in the product. After listening to my explanations for half an hour, he answered decisively and without a hint of hesitation, "It doesn't seem like a good idea to me. I don't believe it will succeed in the market." I was surprised, "Why?! It's such an intelligent idea." I'll never forget his response, "The idea is indeed highly intelligent, but it took you more than five minutes to explain it to me!" In other words, it's not focused and it's not simple!

In the domain of science, it is well known that when we face several explanations for a certain scientific phenomenon or when we face alternative theories among which it is difficult to choose, the decisive criterion will be simplicity on the assumption that all other components being equal, the simplest one is always the best. The possibility of a short and simple formulation, the "half-inch" formula, like that of Einstein's formula is every scientist's dream.

The complete lack of system and structure translates into chaos, the lack of internal organization, of logic and the ability to distinguish between the essential and the nonessential. This is in fact a psychotic state in which ideas and thoughts are disorganized. People who suffer from this type of disorder can hardly bear to organize things or put them in order; any routine activity becomes a first-time event in which reality is reexamined each time. A well-known figure with this disorder is the Australian pianist David Helfgott, whose life was depicted in the film Shine. Logical sequence, order and routine to him become a stream of associations devoid of logic and purpose.

People suffering from Alzheimer's disease or dementia have great difficulty organizing their world; their logical sequence of order was cut. They want things to be orderly, but in practice everything is a constant mess to them. This inability to impose system and structure frequently causes tremendous agony and misery. We necessarily need a basic level of order to ensure we don't get lost in our complex world.

You don't need to be an experienced psychologist to diagnose a person's absence of S.Q. One look at this person's bedroom, his environment and his clothes is enough to discern that everything he is responsible for is disorderly and disorganized. Assessing a person's system and structure is based on the way in which a person performs tasks or organizes projects. In a job interview, it is also possible to perceive a person's awareness of time, objectives and priorities by the way he presents things.

Assessment and Development

System and structure is affected by personality and cognitive factors, which is why its development is based on methods that depend on the cognitive perspective and the mental perspective. Stephen Covey's book First Things First (1994) teaches the reader how to determine what is important and how to act and behave according to priorities derived from the objectives of the individual's life.

At the individual level, we have witnessed the emergence of many methods based on cognitive systems that try to deal with system and structure with the help of computerized expert systems. In recent years, dozens of computer programs were developed in an effort to help the manager or the worker plan out time, set objectives, follow-up on tasks and so on. There is no doubt that in future, many new system and structure virtual agents will be conceived to intelligently perform some of the required organizational activities.

S.Q. Characteristics:

- **Purpose** – focused and goal-oriented task execution;

- **System and Structure** – organized and orderly execution of tasks;

- **Method** – execution of tasks according to a consistent or logical method;

- **Thoroughness** – execution of tasks in a full, comprehensive manner (examining all the relevant details and so on);

- **Focus** – separation of the essential from the nonessential and working according to defined order of priorities;

- **Simplicity** – organizing a system or method in a clear and orderly fashion;

- **Planning** – detailed and precise planning prior to action;

- **Matter-of-Fact Formulation** – in a clear and concise manner;

- **Efficiency** – efficient task execution in short time spans;

- **Time Management** – efficient and methodical time management.

Balance at the Behavioral Level

The change quotient and system and structure are like the wings of an airplane. If one is larger than the other, the plane loses its stability. It takes a lot of energy to take control of a plane with uneven wings. However, the more extensive and balanced the C.Q. and the S.Q. are, the more efficiently an Ace will be able to soar towards his goals.

Unlike theories that regard order and change as two conflicting systems on the same frequency, I believe that they can coexist. These quotients are not opposed. In fact, they balance each other, and in order to bring about durable change, the process has to be structured. System and structure make it possible to control the processes, to manage and lead them towards the purpose and the objective. The change quotient balances the scope of change; in its absence, there will be perpetual movement in opposite directions, so ultimately there won't be a real, significant result. An Ace is characterized by a unique combination of these two behavioral characteristics.

Imbalance

High S.Q. with a disproportionate C.Q.

A person whose system and structure aren't sufficiently balanced by the change quotient is someone who "runs headlong into a brick wall." Such a person or organization suffers from excessive neatness, lack of functional flexibility and inability to adapt to new situations, like a hunter who focuses on his target without paying any attention to his surroundings. The way he sees it, system and structure come above all. Consequently, his perception of life will be simplistic and limited and will not reflect the complexity of the reality. This is seen in extremely bureaucratic organizations managed with excessive order and inflexibility without the ability to stop and think about change and flexibility.

High C.Q. with a disproportionate S.Q.

As far as the individual is concerned, this is a state of frantic instability and its essence is the need for change. This is the inefficient side of the scale, characterized by the inability to plan and focus, by pathological situations, even the incapacity to function. There is a strong desire to bring about changes, yet there is an inability to carry them out and make them part of a routine.

Movement along the C.Q.-S.Q. axis

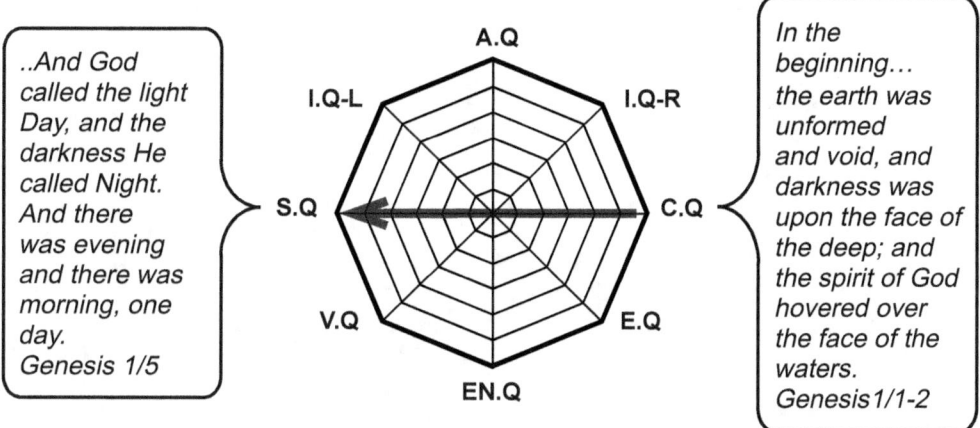

..And God called the light Day, and the darkness He called Night. And there was evening and there was morning, one day.
Genesis 1/5

In the beginning... the earth was unformed and void, and darkness was upon the face of the deep; and the spirit of God hovered over the face of the waters.
Genesis 1/1-2

The basic **story of creation** as it appears in Genesis clearly illustrates the energy flow between C.Q. and S.Q., from chaos to organized structure. All ideas and inventions are born in the right side of the model, in chaos. That is where the ocean of potential ideas lies, that is the source of inspiration and muse. The role of the left side of the brain, the I.Q.-L and the order quotient, is to find ways to realize these ideas and put them into practice, to preserve a flash of inspiration in our memory so that it will be possible to replicate it instead of having to reinvent it each time anew. This is the conceptual foundation of science and law. The easier it is to replicate a raw idea, the less dependent it is on humans, at the same time, however, the need for precise execution of the process increases.

System and structure is the complement and the equalizer of chaos and constant change; it is the basis of the organizational machine which functions efficiently in accordance with procedures, structures, rules and laws. There is no need to fear excess in the order quotient, but it is important to pay attention to the direction of its development. The right direction for energy flow is from right to left; from chaos to system and structure; from feminine to masculine. The S.Q. must not take over the C.Q. because it will produce fixation, paralysis and lack of healthy flow.

The Social Level

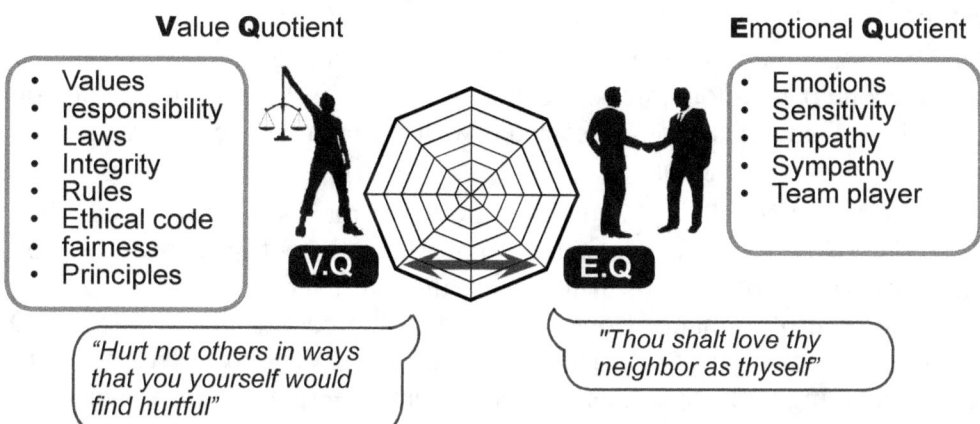

Value **Q**uotient

- Values
- responsibility
- Laws
- Integrity
- Rules
- Ethical code
- fairness
- Principles

Emotional **Q**uotient

- Emotions
- Sensitivity
- Empathy
- Sympathy
- Team player

"Hurt not others in ways that you yourself would find hurtful"

"Thou shalt love thy neighbor as thyself"

The personality level is where raw survival energy transforms to a more advanced stage, expressing personality and values. This is the point where the separation between left and right begins in the model.

This level characterizes a person's emotional and ethical maturity.

The personality-related energy axis between emotional and moral intelligence moves between:

The social, personality-related level characterizes people's emotional and moral maturity, constituting the basis for the existence of society, family, team, or any other form of association among people. This level stems from socialization processes and it makes socialization possible on the basis of emotional and moral maturity and values.

No social interaction can occur without a value system, without a certain level of mutual respect and trust, or without a consensus as to the permitted and the forbidden. No positive human activity can exist without a mature emotional system and without empathy and sympathy.

The emotional-social level presents personality-related and moral expressions essential for the creation of society. This is the separation between right and left: Right – the emotional, empathetic, personality-related aspect; left – the world of social values, laws and principles.

The proximity of the social level to the basic energy level indicates its connection to the physiological dimension.

E.Q. Emotional intelligence – emotional maturity.

Emotional health, maturity and a positive attitude directly contribute to physical resilience, while a negative emotional state is likely to undermine it. By the same token, sickness and the deterioration of health can also undermine emotional stability.

V.Q. Ethical intelligence – the maturity and readiness of the value system.

The reciprocity between the value system and the human body has been less talked about, but without this connection, lie detectors, for instance, indicating physiological manifestations associated with a threat to one's moral system, could not possibly function.

The social, personality-related level is what makes teamwork possible. It is impossible to work adequately and efficiently within a team without interpersonal empathy and sensitivity on the one hand, and without a value system on the other hand. Contrary to other approaches that consider E.Q. the sole key to team-performance processes, the SILVER ACE sees the entire level combining both aspects as the component directing good teamwork.

This symbolic expression of duality can be seen in the following phrases: "Thou shalt love thy neighbor as thyself" and "Hurt not others in ways that you yourself would find hurtful." On the one hand, we have emotional intelligence – love, empathy, sympathy – "Thou shalt love thy neighbor as thyself"; on the other hand, there is the moral principle – the rule, the law – "Hurt not others in ways that you yourself would find hurtful."

Energy and its flow within the level

Healthy energy channels flow from right to left, from the emotional quotient to the value quotient. On the right side, personal and social emotions originate and this energy transits towards the formulation of rules and laws in the value quotient. The value quotient is what puts emotional chaos, the E.Q., in order.

Principles and rules help us preserve our energy, know what to do and how to act without wasting energy examining the situation each time.

Balances at the Social Level
The value quotient and emotional intelligence: E.Q. - V.Q.

The E.Q. makes it possible for us to be aware of all the emotions within us and cope with them, whereas the V.Q. puts emotional chaos in order, implementing rules, laws, fundamentals and values. It is the moral rulebook that brings control over emotions. When the intensity of emotion increases, the need for a clear and organized value system grows. A person with a high value quotient whose emotional intelligence quotient is not on par will rigidly and resolutely fight for principles without the required interpersonal sensitivity. In such cases, there is a risk of crossing moral boundaries when identification, empathy and sensitivity turn into sentimentality. The balance of the V.Q. is what stops and guides us when emotional identification becomes a dangerous driving force.

Q - 6
Emotional Quotient (E.Q.)

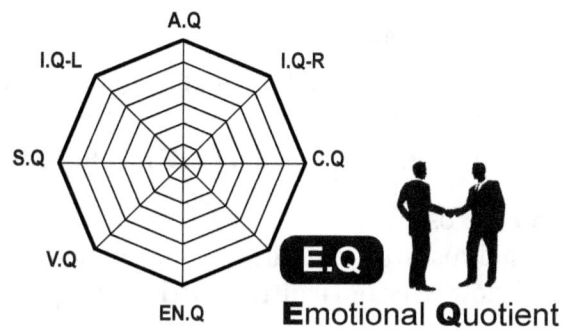

Emotional Quotient

"Thou shalt love thy neighbor as thyself."

Leviticus 19:18

Identity	**Name**: Emotional Quotient
	Symbol: **E.Q.**
Definition:	**Emotional maturity**
Key words:	**E**motion
	Empathy
Characteristics:	Emotional awareness and control
	Empathy for the feelings of others
	Emotional communication and sympathy
	Interpersonal sensitivity and awareness
	Sensitivity – to others/to the market/to the client/ to cultures
Expression at work:	Teamwork
	Human relations
	Sensitivity to clients
	Good communication
	Networking
Deficiencies:	Autism

Location in the model:	**Vertical axis**	Social level
	Horizontal axis	Right
	Balance in the level	Value Quotient, V.Q.
	Counterbalance	Left Intelligence Quotient, I.Q.-L
Neighbors in the model	1) Change and Chaos Quotient, C.Q. 2) Energy and Resilience Quotient, EN.Q.	

Emotional intelligence is influenced by both above mentioned quotients:

1) C.Q. – change and chaos quotient: There is a link between emotional intelligence, emotional maturity, and the change quotient. A person whose emotional maturity is low will find it difficult to have a high change quotient.

2) EN.Q. – energy and resilience quotient: The energy state of a person influences his degree of sensitivity and his emotional readiness and maturity. Those with low energy levels may fall into emotional regression.

Definition and Characterization

Emotional intelligence refers to a person's ability to identify, access and manage his emotions and those of others; that is one's emotional maturity.

With the decline in importance of the classic I.Q. in light of the computing revolution, the importance of emotional intelligence has increased. The first use of the term "emotional intelligence" is usually attributed to Wayne Payne, in his "Study of Emotion: Developing Emotional Intelligence" (1985). The term also appears in scientific literature, in articles by psychologists John Mayer and Peter Salovey (1990), who studied the existing differences among individuals' ability to identify their own emotions as well as those of others and to overcome emotional problems. Mayer and Salovey defined emotional intelligence as "the ability to monitor one's own and others' feelings and emotions, to discriminate among them and to use this information to guide one's thinking and actions." In 1995, the term received widespread publicity with the publication of a book by journalist and psychologist Dr. Daniel Goleman, Emotional Intelligence (1997), which is mainly an interpretation of Mayer and Salovey's work. The book became a best seller and made emotional intelligence a familiar concept.

Emotional intelligence in the SILVER ACE model indicates the extent to which a person displays emotional maturity. It has to do with the world of emotions – our consciousness of our emotions and our control over them as well as our consciousness of our sensitivity to the emotions of others. By sensitivity to others the model refers to our ability to sense others through empathy, to show sympathy on an emotional level. We should emphasize that the definition of emotional intelligence as emotional maturity highlights the difference between emotional maturity and sentimentality. "Sentimentality comes where there is no authentic emotion," said the Hebrew-language author Yosef Chaim Brenner. Sentimentality lacks the element of control that exists in the E.Q.

The concept of "Emotional Intelligence" is made up of four recognized abilities:

1. **Perception of emotions** – this is the most fundamental facet enabling emotional information processing. Accurate assessment of our emotions allows us to use emotional information in our decision making. The ability to understand and experience the emotions of the other (empathy) is an important social skill for the maintaining of positive interpersonal relations.

2. **Use of emotions** – the ability to harness emotions in favor of different processes. An individual whose emotional intelligence is high can make use of his changing emotions in aid of a task. The ability to imagine how we will feel when a certain event occurs enables us to make the best choice from multiple options.

3. **Understanding emotions and emotional wisdom** – the ability to understand the "language of emotion" and notice fine distinctions, such as the difference between happy and enthusiastic.

4. **Managing emotions** – the ability to regulate our own emotions and those of others, namely, controlling our emotions in accordance with the situation, harnessing emotions, even negative ones, in order to attain desired objectives. Managing others' emotions refers to the ability to impact and to inspire and motivate as means of social influence.

In his aforementioned book, Daniel Goleman argues that emotional intelligence is as important as intellect, and those lacking emotional intelligence will face great difficulties in their environmental adaptation and, most probably, will experience social functioning difficulties and career handicaps. In their book Executive EQ: Emotional Intelligence in Leadership & Organizations, Cooper and Sawaf (1998) describe emotions on a continuum moving from negative to positive, where every emotion can develop, escalate and become more negatively powerful or vice versa. The wider our knowledge of emotions, the wider our reservoir of reactions and emotions will be in facing certain situations. Similarly, the more sensitive we are towards others, the better we will be able to identify their emotional states and show them empathy. In due course, we must learn to transmit our own feelings to others and make them aware of those feelings through the expression of sympathy or any other emotion appropriate to the situation.

The elements of the E.Q.

Man's emotional maturity and mellowness is expressed on two axes:

1. Awareness and Control

a. The extent to which a person is aware of his emotions' internal world.

b. The extent to which he is capable of controlling and activating his own emotions.

For a person to be characterized as highly emotionally intelligent, awareness by itself is not enough. An individual can be aware of his fears and anxiety and still be paralyzed by them. Emotional intelligence means the ability to control and maneuver in the emotional world, to initiate and be emotionally active rather than be externally activated.

2. Relationship Circles: From Self to Other

The other facet of emotional intelligence is **empathy**, being aware of the other's emotions, the ability to identify the other's emotional state, feel and identify with the other. Psychoanalyst Heinz Kohut defined empathy as "The ability to *feel and think of oneself* as being part of the other's *internal life*," not out of attachment and identification but rather seeing them without relinquishing oneself.

The term "empathy" derives from the Greek word empatheia (ἐμπάθεια), which means "physical intimacy." Empathy is the central concept in emotional maturity and mellowness and its main meaning today is mental identification. I remember a conversation I once had with my daughter, who overwhelmed me with problems that tormented her at the time. As a parent, I immediately tried to find a solution to every one of the problems she shared with me. I will always remember what she told me: "Dad, don't solve my problems, all I want is that you listen to me." Indeed, the aim of sympathetic listening is to give the other the feeling of understanding and togetherness.

In *The 7 Habits of Highly Effective People*, Stephen Covey defines emotional maturity as the basis of sympathetic communication, which he defines this way: "Ask initially to understand and only then to be understood." As Covey sees it, mellowness and maturity are the balance between the power of the ego and empathy, which employment tests focus on.

However, just as in the domain of private emotions, where awareness is only part of the equation, and the need to control emotions is also there, being sympathetic with the other is not enough. There is the need to know how to transfer our emotions to them, how to share their emotions and make them feel what we do – that is sympathy. Daniel Goleman describes this in his book as "The ability to discern other people's moods, temperament, motivation and desires and respond appropriately." The stronger our acquaintance with emotions, the wider our response repertoire will be in any given situation.

Love Thy...

In addition to empathy, there is the concept of **love**. The ability to love is one of the characteristics of emotional mellowness and maturity. Emotional intelligence is the ability to connect with the other through love: clients, workers, suppliers and managers, and sometimes even for a specific issue, action and a product itself. As society climbs the Maslow Scale away from survival and physical needs, positive emotional ties increase. Therefore, one mustn't be surprised that organizational work and processes express their approach in terms of love, such as love for the client, love for the workers, the environment and the community.

Organizations that report a high feeling of love within them operate efficiently and well. Love impacts the individual who feels it. People in a loving relationship differ in essence from those who are in an alienated one. In terms of the "I and Thou," Martin Buber's concepts from the book of the same name (1923), "The 'I' in the 'I-Thou' relationship is not the same as the 'I' that is not part of such a relationship." The ability to be in love, which changes the individual himself, is a unique human ability, non-existent in computers!

The importance of emotional intelligence for teamwork

Theoretically, the Ace is realized in all eight dimensions and maintains the balances between them. But reality is neither theoretical nor optimal: Most people have their own unique profile, which includes aspects in which they are stronger and others in which they are weaker. Most of us have only some "Ace quality," which is why one of the most efficient ways to attain being an Ace is by creating teams in which synergy will compensate for individual weaknesses.

Take, for example, a creative person – that individual will need the orderly person beside him to make work plans and define objectives, and both of them together will need a person with highly developed human sensitivity in order to hold the team together. A good team is one which sustains balance among all the different quotients. A dominant trait that isn't balanced may make the system less efficient. The need to create a team that will compensate for the weaknesses of its members makes E.Q. indispensable to every one of the team's members; it's the glue holding them together and making them a team.

As the story goes, a chairman of a famous firm's board of directors fired a CEO despite his flawless business record. When asked why, he replied, "Because he was incapable of being a team player." Modern organizations have replaced their one-dimensional hierarchical structure with a complex and flexible one.

Emotional intelligence assessment uses a wide range of tools, among them many questionnaires put together specifically towards that end. Relating to E.Q. as one would to a characteristic that isn't necessarily present at the time of testing entails the use of self-evaluation papers. Over time, many self-reported questionnaires have been developed, including the TEIQue (Trait Emotional Intelligence Questionnaire). In 2006, Reuven Bar-On developed the first emotional intelligence measurement that used the term "Emotional Quotient," called the Bar-On Emotional Quotient Inventory (1997) (EQ-i). It is a self-reported measure that assesses the elements suggested by the theoretical model.

Mayer and Salovey developed the MSCEIT (Mayer-Salovey-Caruso Emotional Intelligence Test), a battery of tests taking forty minutes to complete, at the basis of which lies the assumption that emotion is information that requires processing, so the assessment methodology must be based on performance or ability quotients, similar to spatial or quantitative intelligence measurements. In order to correct for the problem of self-reporting manifested in most E.Q. tests, this test is based on problem solving and not merely on introspection. Unlike intelligence tests, answers are not classified objectively, and there is a significant element of social convention influencing the MSCEIT.

Group simulations and individual interviews are also valuable ways to examine how a person handles interpersonal interactions.

Lack of E.Q.

Lack of emotional intelligence is expressed in clinical conditions as autism, which is the inability to experience the full range of emotions. Such a deficiency causes a high degree of difficulty in communication. Professor Baron-Cohen, one of the directors of the Autism Research Institute at Cambridge University, defines autism as the inability to feel empathy, express emotions and use language.

Without E.Q., life is lived in a bubble with few connections to one's surroundings. Due to their communication difficulties, autistic people were usually considered mentally retarded and thus were treated in institutions caring for people who were mentally handicapped. Needless to say, their functioning did not improve. Mental retardation is the lack of I.Q.-L, which is the E.Q.'s counterbalance. Today, it is common knowledge that many autistic individuals have adequate and sometimes even particularly high I.Q.s.

One of the most efficient ways to deal with the lack of emotional intelligence is by separating the two quotients= I.Q-l and E.Q. Through their intellectual intelligence, people lacking in E.Q. can learn to draw conclusions about the emotional world. They do not feel, but they understand the other with their brain just as a blind person gets to know his environment through the use of his other senses.

Developing E.Q.

The good news is that although common **I.Q.** is affected essentially by genetic factors and is difficult to change once it has set, emotional intelligence can be developed and grow continuously throughout one's life. The development of emotional intelligence can be done on both aspects that define it:

Awareness and Self-Control – the basis for developing emotional intelligence is development of the ability to establish contact with one's own emotional world. Without awareness, it is not possible to develop genuine emotional intelligence. Emotional intelligence can be developed through individual processes or group workshops in which it is examined how a person deals with emotions and whether they move him.

The Interpersonal Aspect – the second part of developing emotional intelligence has to do with empathy and sympathy: awareness of the emotions of others and the ability to express that awareness. Here, the main tool is feedback from others (another person, group or a life partner) through responses to questions such as: Was the message received as intended? How did others feel? What does the person feel? And so on. It is difficult to develop emotional intelligence without live feedback from the other party to the relationship, which is why dynamic workshops, where a person either observes or takes part, are efficient tools.

The "Imago method" developed by Harville Hendrix, PhD and his wife Helen LaKelly Hunt, PhD in the 1980s, is an interesting tool for developing emotional intelligence. The main part of this development process is exercising and practicing empathetic communication and sympathetic expression through awareness of one's own emotions and those of the other. There are two stages to the process:

- First, two people sit facing each other. One of them expresses how he feels and the other has to respond by reporting what he heard and how he understand it. If the speaker feels he wasn't properly understood, he can repeat the process until he feels that the message has been fully received and understood.

- At the second stage, the receiver tries to experience both what the speaker has felt and the meaning of the message, even if he does not agree with the partner's perception. Finally, everyone practices engaging in expression aimed at understanding the other's feelings.

This is a highly effective practice, if tiring. It is customarily used in treating couples, but may be just as effectively used with managers and staff with the intention of improving dialogue and communication between them and as a tool for resolving conflicts.

E.Q. Characteristics:

- **Interpersonal communication** – the ability to establish a communication flow through listening and understanding the other.

- **Sensitivity to the other** – the ability to listen and show understanding to the needs of the other.

- **Emotional self-awareness** – the ability to be attentive to oneself and identify the emotional state one is in.

- **Emotional maturity and control** – self-control in different emotional situations, even if powerful, and the ability to respond to them appropriately and maturely.

- **Absence of feelings of deprivation** – high frustration threshold, lack of a tendency to feel deprived and exploited.

- **Teamwork** – the ability to integrate into a group and perform cooperative tasks while providing mutual assistance to that end.

- **Recruitment** – encouraging others to cooperate, establishing positive personal ties with people.

- **Positive human relations** – helping others, lending a favorable ear to others.

- **Sympathy** – transferring emotional support to others.

Q - 7
Value Quotient (V.Q.)

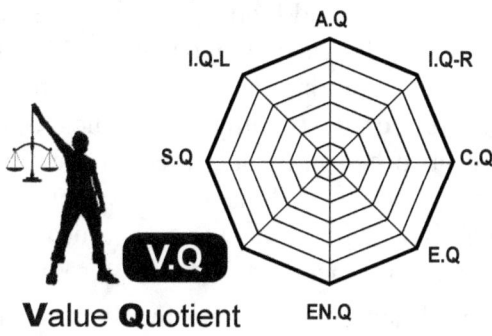

Value Quotient

"Morality grew from life within society, and has become the condition of such life."

Max Nordau

Identity:	**Name**: Value Quotient
	Symbol: V.Q.
Definition:	**Moral development and maturity**
Characteristics:	Value system
	Virtue and ethics
	Accountability and reliability
	Loyalty and commitment
	Fairness
	Integrity and credibility
	Ethics
	MTR – Mutual Trust and Respect
Expression at work:	Commitment, loyalty, responsibility and resistance to temptation
Deficiencies:	Psychopathology, sociopathology

Location in the model	**Vertical axis** – the social level

Horizontal axis – left

The location of the value system on the left side of the model emphasizes its tight association with logic, order and laws and its absence of dependence on emotions and feelings. Due to the fact that this system belongs to the behavioral level, knowing right from wrong does not derive from mental or spiritual understanding. The values in this quotient are absorbed and integrated in the foundation of our personality. This is the system upon which man lives without having to ask himself how to act at every moment.

Level balance – emotional intelligence quotient, E.Q.

Counterbalance – right intelligence quotient, I.Q.-R

Neighbors in the model

1) Energy quotient, EN.Q.

2) System and Structure, S.Q.

1. The Value Quotient and the Energy Dimension: V.Q.-EN.Q.

The value system is adjacent to the energy quotient and as such, it also has physical manifestations. The act of blushing is a physical manifestation of a mental state connected with moral judgment. It's not by chance that we say, "He flushed with shame." A person whose value quotient is healthy will react to moral offense through his body when he deviates from his value system. For example in the case of lying, he feels his inner tension increase, which is physically manifested as sweating or a quickened heartbeat. On the basis of such reactions, a polygraph can establish if a person is lying or telling the truth.

2. The Value Quotient and System and Structure: V.Q.-S.Q.

The value quotient is strongly affected by its neighbor, system and structure. The essence of the term "system" derives from the world of system and structure. A high value quotient is not merely a list of values but a sort of logical network organized according to general preference and the capacity to choose in situations of conflict or contradiction. System and structure contributes to all of these situations, enabling the value system to be reliable and integrative.

Definition and characterization

The value quotient represents the level of a person's moral development and maturity. It is something of an inner compass by which people judge themselves, their actions and attitudes as well as those of others. This is the order that maintains our inner moral world. The V.Q. allows us to know how people behave in different situations and who can be relied on.

The concept of V.Q., first developed by Maslow's students, who defined three elementary concepts on which it is based, has appeared in professional literature to mean the value index (**Value Q**uotient):

1. The existence of an arranged system of values;

2. The mellowness and maturity of that system;

3. The set of values itself.

The value quotient refers mainly to the system itself, the existence of method, order and hierarchy and its maturity. A mature value system encompasses any area in life, like an organized treatise on good and evil or right and wrong. There is a hierarchical division within the value system according to degree of importance. This division assists in decision making even in situations of conflict between the values themselves. It is important to note that uncompromising moral rigidity does not constitute a mature system but represents an underdeveloped moral world. A person with exceptionally high value standards who behaves with extreme rigidity without taking reality into account becomes a prisoner of his own value system. A mature, considered value system has the right amount of realistic flexibility, enabling effective functioning.

Cultural and personal factors may affect values; they are not absolute. An extreme example is the Mafia, based on a clear and organized value system with clear "do and don't" rules, even though we see them as immoral values. Its success undoubtedly lies at least partly with the existence of a coherent and well-publicized value system.

The elements of the V.Q.

Values are at the basis of social behavior, determining good and evil, and make it possible for us to choose between right and wrong. There can be no connection between two people or between a person and a community without a certain common value system. A high V.Q. represents the existence of a clear and coherent value system which dictates the "do's and don'ts" in light of which a person judges himself and the other.

Virtues

Virtues are rules, values and laws that allow us to sustain reciprocal relationships. This refers to the nature of the value system, referring generally to qualities such as consideration for others, sharing and participating, as well as putting personal egoism aside for the benefit of family or society. In his impressive book The Origins of Virtue (2000), Matt Ridley analyzes the development of good qualities in human society and finds that it is the result of the selective genetic evolution of humankind, like a natural moral choice. Evolution has proved that in order to survive and develop, values of cooperation as well as virtues are necessary.

Anthropologist Richard Leaky describes, in his famous book The Origin of Humankind (1998), two branches that developed in the evolution of apes which took different physical appearances derived from different value systems. Males of the first branch struggle and fight for dominance in the group; the banished loser does not get to have offspring. The losers then fight in an effort to win a position in another group. Consequently, males developed into gigantic sizes compared with the females and looked as though they belonged to another species.

The second branch developed a sense of fraternity. The weaker male is not expelled from the group but rather enjoys the stronger apes' protection. This is the beginning of a value system. No significant changes between males and females occurred in this group since genetic survival did not result from killing the weak but through family fraternity. Nature chose the second branch in its evolutionary process, the one more closely founded on family values, thus the first branch became extinct.

Ethics

Ethics, the doctrine of measures, refers to the question: What is the right deed based on the philosophy of morality? An ethical code refers to a system of rules and laws accepted by group members, the purpose of which is to regulate the relationship systems between them to enable them to act knowing that all adhere to the same rules.

The ethical code is the fundamental and indispensable basis for the existence of a society. Ethical rules also regulate emotions, impulses and urges. The knowledge that I, as well as others, follow certain ethical rules contributes to a sense of trust which makes it possible to cooperate and take responsibility within the team.

The term "ethics" comes from the Greek word ethos, which means "character." Morality is a system of conventions or ideals that apply to the individual or a group of people in society. The meaning of the word "ethics" is "a document defining moral standards and codes of conduct people abide by."

Every nation, since the dawn of history, has sought to establish values and principles it could take pride in and strives to preserve and modify them in accordance with evolving changes. These values and principles are ingrained, taught and acquired, and one is advised not to deviate from them in terms of customs and laws.

With regard to social aspects, morality is the effort to regulate the deeds and relationships between individuals, the individual and society and, to speak in a more abstract form, between man and his conscience and his awareness (Ring, Morals for What? (1999)). Cognitive psychologist Jean Piaget, who studied moral development, argues that morality develops as a result of children's cognitive development together with their learning through social experiences. According to him, morality develops in three stages:

1. Up to age 7 – The stage of absence of morality.

2. From ages 7 to 12 – The stage of moral realism; morality is perceived as concrete, absolute and total; there is no room for any considered opinion with relation to laws.

From age 12 throughout adolescence – The stage of autonomous morality in which the teenager develops his own abstract judgment, therefore attention is paid to intentions underlying the action and different positions towards it are examined.

Lawrence Kohlberg (1927-1987) pursued Piaget's work, both expanding and rendering the early stages of development flexible. He related moral development to interaction with peers and the participation in social organizations as well as parenting style.

Moral responsibility is triggered by the internal power connected to a person's conscience, the supreme authority, thus it is broad, permanent and unchanging, as opposed to law which is external.

Integrity

Integrity is one of the most important virtues. The term comes from Latin in (the negative prefix) and tengere (touch), which when combined means "untouchable," "incorruptible" – he who will not be bribed. The dictionary definition of "integrity" (according to Webster's English dictionary) is the "firm adherence to a code of especially moral values, incorruptibility." This definition tends towards the denial of the right side (the emotional side) which is entirely based on everything connected with "me." The Hebrew definition of integrity refers more to the left side of the V.Q. It is no coincidence that we say "straight as an arrow"; both straight and keeping up one's standards. Personal integrity represents the ability to act out of self-commitment, not because one wishes to avoid punishment or sanctions.

Trust

Trust is the basis of all proper interpersonal communication. It is an important stage in children's development which enables them to develop basic self-confidence. Trust is fairly easy to break, but much harder to restore. Barbara Misztal, in Trust in Modern Societies: The Search for the Bases of Social Order (1996), points out three basic elements set off by trust:

• Social life is predictable thanks to trust.

• Trust generates a sense of belonging to the community.

• Trust makes it easier for people to work together.

When there is no trust, it is impossible to cheat. Only those who trust can be cheated. Former financier, stockbroker and businessman Bernard Madoff was chairman of the securities trading firm Bernard L. Madoff Investment Securities LLC and chairman of the Nasdaq board of directors. His incredible story is perfect proof of this. His meteoric rise and fall, following his conviction for defrauding about $65 billion, could not have occurred had he not gained the trust of so many people. The downfall of the Enron Corporation, the bankrupt energy company, is another instance of breaking all the rules of ethics and morality. "It's a Big Bang in business ethics," said one of the many newspaper articles on the subject. When the company's total lack of V.Q. became apparent, it collapsed with a loud bang despite its formidable size.

How do V.Q. and high career dynamics in the modern era co-exist?

There is no longer any tenure in the workplace. The relationship between worker and organization is temporary and devoid of the commitment typical of previous decades. This new relationship calls into question the importance of a value system of commitment and responsibility.

The commitment we are talking about is not of a legal nature, but a personal one the worker undertakes. A person with a high V.Q. will feel committed to meeting his obligations and will therefore refrain from committing to any obligation he is not sure he can fulfill.

I met a young man recently, the CEO of a high-tech company taking its first steps. He is highly successful at his job and has lately been approached by tempting offers from other firms. Even though he was performing his job with dedication, he had been feeling the need for change for quite some time. Since the company he led was going public a few months later, he continued his service knowing that if he left it would have a devastating impact on the company's chances of success. He turned down the flattering offers and stayed until after the stock was issued, which was no easy decision. It was consistent with his values and moral code of loyalty and commitment to obligations. I have no doubt that in the long run, such value systems are rewarded. A value system doesn't hinder advancement but rather enhances it, standing as its foundation.

Assessment and development

The need to assess workers' value systems is particularly important for organizations that require high reliability, such as businesses in the diamond industry or the intelligence services. Due to the difficulty of assessing a person's genuine value system, these types of businesses tend to hire workers based on their social connections or on prior acquaintance.

Over the years, there have been many attempts to develop diagnostic tools to assess the level of a value system but most of them have low validity. The main need for diagnosis deals with the low ends of the scale, more specifically those ends that endanger the firm. Therefore, most tools do not check credibility but whether or not there are any red flags. A person's inner code of values can be analyzed by means of self-reporting questionnaires or interview questions. Checking reliability, however, is more complex, but there are some tools of varying validity available now, based on questionnaires, personality and behavioral tests.

The absence of a system of values

People with a low V.Q. did not go through proper socialization processes. Those people are referred to in our daily language as having no scruples. One of the classic forms of a pathological condition, in which a mature value system is absent, is psychopathology or sociopathology, as defined in psychiatric literature.

The sociopath knows right from wrong on the cognitive level, but his value system (V.Q.) is not imprinted in his personality. This is an extremely intricate personality flaw, which, unlike other pathologies, is not revealed at first glance to the observer. Sociopaths are endowed with the rare ability to adapt to the other's expectation, impress and charm them. They know how to wear a mask of emotional intelligence (the balancing dimension at the same layer) and consequently charm their way into the hearts of others. Their lack of a value system enables them to adapt to the situation as a chameleon, without any feelings of guilt or shame for the absence of authenticity and trustworthiness, making their identification rather difficult. Even a lie detector cannot always tell the difference since sociopaths do not feel guilty about the lies they tell and their bodies do not react to lies with excessive perspiration or accelerated heartbeat the way others do.

Developing V.Q.

There are very few efficient ways to treat the absence of a value system. Clinically speaking, we know of very few successes with psychopaths and sociopaths. When they are caught, society generally tries to punish them or instill fear of sanctions in them for non-compliance with the conventional value system. In other words, we don't try to change them; we only warn them of the punishment. Developing and instilling values should start at a very early age. Religion is a very powerful system for bestowing values, addressing all parts of the personality in the process of value modeling – mind, emotions, fears, logic, love and awe – for which it has rituals, stories, myths and characters to identify with. Another approach for the assimilation of new values in society is the connection between values and the individual subconscious. An example of such technique is the persistent advertisements and slogan attacks on people designed to influence them and their attitudes at the less conscious level.

A salient example for the assimilation of a principles system within a large group of people is the practice of brainwashing in totalitarian regimes that managed to assimilate commitment to a political party and an idea to the point of loss of individuality. Since the value system is influenced by its proximity to the physical one, it was understood that breaking a subject was more easily achieved with a threat to existence. As indeed brainwashing was most effective in conditions of hunger, imprisonment or torture.

V.Q. Characteristics:

- **Taking on responsibility** – readiness to commit to a trustworthy task performance and responsibility for results;
- **Integrity** – functioning through compliance to clear, professional and human norms and values;
- **Concern and dedication** – involvement, loyalty to and identification with the settings a person belongs to;
- **Commitment** – taking personal obligations upon oneself and fulfilling them;
- **Decency** – bestowing a fair and proper treatment on others;
- **Respect and trust in others** – conducting oneself in light of these values;
- **Reliability and authenticity** – resisting temptations; reporting reliably;
- **Methodical, clear and organized** – system of values and principles;
- **Clearly defined inner book of law** – according to which one operates;
- **Mature value system** – a clear, devoid of inner conflict value system.

Counterbalances

The Diagonals- Between Left and Right

There are two 180° diagonal balances in the model that indicate a system of two-way relationships, level balances and diagonal balances.

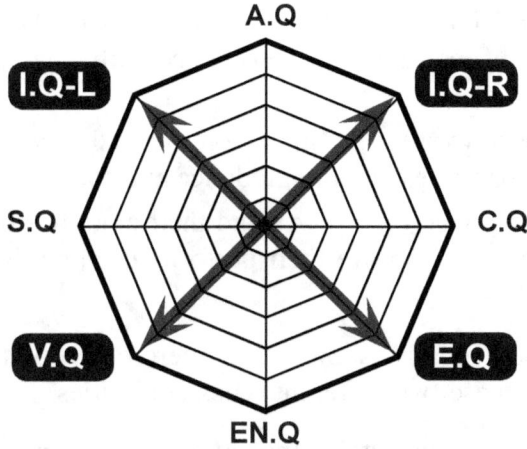

1. The Value Quotient (V.Q.) and the Right Intelligence Quotient (I.Q.-R)

The I.Q.-R, right intelligence quotient, specializes in breaking patterns, breaking through boundaries as well as in intellectual and creative "anarchy." It is not limited by rules and laws, and as such, with all its splendor and extraordinary qualities, it could become dangerous if it were not properly balanced out.

The more we encourage people to step outside the box and break past boundaries, the more we have to make sure that they have a V.Q. to balance this freedom. Scientific creativity is increasing along with options that can be dangerous if those involved do not have a mature value system; the lack of which is likely to become more acute over the years. The V.Q. is the counterbalance that responds to the act of breaking patterns and noncompliance to rules, stabilizing unbalanced, unconventional creativity thus preventing the emergence of such dangers.

2. Left intelligence quotient (I.Q.-L) and its diagonal counterbalance – emotional intelligence (E.Q.)

Researchers Cote and Miners offered a "compensatory model" of emotional intelligence and cognitive intelligence postulating that the relationship between work performance and emotional intelligence becomes more positive so long as a person's cognitive intelligence decreases. Their research results showed that there is in fact a compensatory relationship: Workers with lower I.Q. will reveal themselves as all the more efficient, the higher their E.Q.

These results can be explained in several ways:

1. People with high E.Q. but lower I.Q. "read" the behavior of their group better than others. This type of skill contributes to their adjustment and their interpersonal functioning in accordance with what is expected by the organization.

2. Those workers who express feelings more honestly than others will build strong relationships and earn more guidance and social support than others.

3. They are able to manage themselves and their emotions better than others, and in this sense, they improve their performance and their ability to deal with difficulties.

This research unequivocally shows that there are complex relations of reciprocity between these two different types of abilities.

Disparity between emotional intelligence and intellect, namely when intellect is developed out of bounds, is what generates cases of "infantile genius, or the "idiot savant" " or variations of Asperger syndrome, intellectual genius in an underdeveloped person, a gap between a person's emotional maturity and his mental capacity.

Because socialization takes place during different stages of childhood, more attention should be given to emotional preparedness rather than just development of the intellectual muscle or else a lack of balance on this diagonal axis will result.

The Spiritual Level

The spiritual level corresponds to the top level of Maslow's Scale of needs, namely, the crown chakra, the connecting point where a person goes beyond his personal thinking and psychology and exhibits the highest energy coefficient. When a person is connected to his vision and calling, he creates the highest energy. This is a basic requirement of an Ace, to have an energy coefficient of vision and calling. These Aces can create these coefficients, with which they move people. At the spiritual level, energy is translated into just that – self-realization and goal reaching.

Separation between right and left, that had reached its peak on the behavioral level, disappears here, returning to a uniform state. This is how it had been on the raw energy level, which explains why there is energy flow only along the vertical axis and no energy flow between right and left on the spiritual level. Of all levels, the spiritual level is the one pointing beyond day-to-day existence towards mission, purpose and the future.

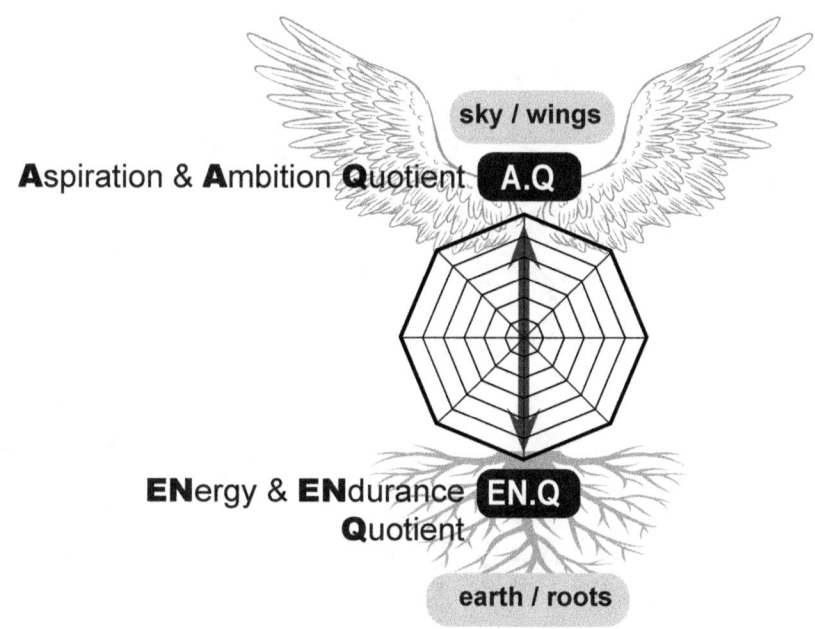

Q - 8

The Aspiration
and Ambition Quotient (A.Q.)

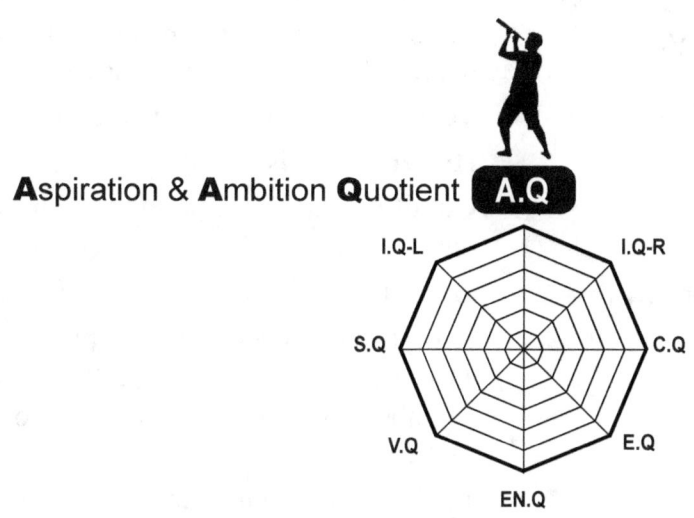

"If you want to build a ship, don't drum up people to collect wood and don't assign them tasks and work, but rather teach them to long for the endless immensity of the sea."

Antoine de Saint Exupéry

Identity:

Name: Aspiration and Ambition Quotient

Symbol: A.Q.

Definition:

All the factors relating to the level of aspirations and the need to reach above and beyond. The drive to set challenges and to achieve objectives.

Key words:

Spiritual intelligence

Aspiration

Ambition

Achievement

Assurance

Aim

Actualization

Expression at work:	Ambition and purposefulness,
	Aspiring to self-realization
	A sense of mission, direction and meaning
	Self-confidence
	Vision and purpose
Deficiency:	Living a life with no meaning, existential depression, and a sense of insecurity.
Location on the model:	**Vertical axis** – the spiritual level
	Horizontal axis – center
	Counterbalance – the energy and endurance quotient, EN.Q.
Neighbors in the model:	1) Right Intelligence Quotient, I.Q.-R
	2) Left Intelligence Quotient, I.Q.-L

The aspiration quotient is influenced by its neighbors with a tendency either to the left or to the right.

1) With a tendency to the left, towards the I.Q.-L, ambition and aspiration will take a rational, practical and logical direction with measured objectives. This is the result of analytical thinking based on information and data. A conservative and conventional person is, by definition, a doer who is highly capable of meeting deadlines and functioning efficiently, who usually strives to move logically and rationally beyond defined, structured objectives.

2) With a tendency to the right, towards the I.Q.-R, vision and aspirations will take an intuitive, visual and imaginative direction, breaking patterns and building a new world and a new reality. That person is creative and inventive, able to picture his mission in a visual manner based on a world rich with images and imagination.

Definition and characterization

The A.Q., the aspiration quotient, is the principal quotient affecting an Ace's existence. It represents the entire set of quotients connected with the level of aspiration, need for accomplishment, level of self-confidence, adherence to mission and commitment to one's purpose.

A person whose aspiration quotient is high acts in commitment to his vision, out of a sense of personal purpose. He generates the highest multiplied energy and radiates active, vision-oriented energy to his entire environment.

Spiritual intelligence

The concept of "spiritual intelligence" was coined by Danah Zohar and her spouse, Ian Marshall, in their book Spiritual Intelligence (2001). To them, ultimate intelligence is "the intelligence with which we address and solve problems of meaning and value," they explain in their book. Through it, "we can place our actions and our lives in a wider, richer, meaning-giving context [and] assess that one course of action or one life-path is more meaningful than another."

Spiritual intelligence deals with the meaning of the activities one undertakes and answers questions like what the meaning of life is, what the purpose and mission of an individual is – namely the contents beyond goals, aspirations and achievements. Thus it is placed at the very top of the model, which is where the process of self-expansion starts (see chapter on the Vertical Level). Spiritual intelligence is that which pushes us to go in search of meaning and the creation of vision. Vision is born of the wish of the individual to leave his mark beyond physical existence. Stephen Covey's *The 7 Habits of Highly Effective People* and Rebecca Maddox's *Inc. Your Dreams* (1995) largely deal with the human need to make a difference; both books are used in various workshops aiming at creating Aces. Other related questions, derived from spiritual intelligence and the understanding that it is the source of the Ace's ability to turn into a mission-driven shining one, are: What mark would you like to make? What is the meaning of your existence?

As Maslow predicted, the more we satisfy our existential needs, the higher we climb up the ladder towards the top of the pyramid as indeed, during the last decades, following economic Western abundance, practicing spirituality is on the rise. Individuals, organizations and companies are engaged in personal and human development, in search of theories and methods that combine science with spirituality, in what is referred to as "New Age." The current intensive involvement in these domains is paramount at the personal level as much as at the level of humanity in general, investigating the direction and destiny of mankind and the coming stages of evolution. Many are occupied with finding the path from handling a career to that of calling and mission.

The elements of the A.Q.

Ambition

"Soul is measured by the size of its ambition."

Gustave Flaubert (1821 – 1880)

Success does not happen by itself; one must deliberately strive towards it. Don't believe those who pretend to be modest and claim, "I got lucky." Without the will to reach the top, nobody manages to muster the strength needed to overcome the hardships and failures along the way.

To understand the concept of ambition we use dieting as a metaphor. Many studies have tried to explain the well-known phenomenon in which many dieters tended to regain the precise weight they had lost shortly after having achieved their goal. This may be a surprise, as if the body "remembers" the former weight and sets it as a goal to be reached. Being lighter than that weight makes the body "feel" hungry, but being above it the body feels "satisfied." It turns out that the process that leads the body to this balance is neither weight nor amount of food but rather "body image," as if the body has a mechanism that constantly examines the amount of space our body takes up and compares it with the space we occupied prior to dieting and is vividly alive in one's inner perceptions, which is relatively unchanged and at which our body feels comfortable.

Ambition is the gap between one's current place and size and one's inner size. Ambition resembles hunger created within us and expresses the gap between our current state and our internal image in all areas. The initials of "**M**y **B**ody **I**mage" are in the middle of the term **Ambi**tion, which is no coincidence. It is the very mechanism that will cause a certain person to feel hunger while another will feel satiety; one will be content with climbing a hill while another will seek higher peaks. Just as they do for the physical body, people have a certain perception of their financial bulk or the scope of their success. Salespeople have shown, in research, that a certain level of income causes "satiety" in some people, and "hunger" and "desire for more" in others. The height a person feels the need to "climb" from base camp up to the peak determines the level of his aspiration and ambition quotient. Therefore, a child from a poor neighborhood who aspires to be the president of the United States has a higher aspiration quotient than the president's child, aspiring to become the president.

Achievement

The ambition quotient represents the scope of aspiration, the gap between one's self-perception and the reality, whereas the achievement quotient represents the extent of commitment to close that gap. Ambition by itself does not suffice in order to attain the objective; the driving force leading to action is the achievement quotient.

The need for achievement is among the most central in the hierarchy of needs. People's need to achieve, to lead and to leave their marks varies greatly from one person to another; this aspect is significant in defining one's A.Q. I have often encountered people with high ambitions who did not feel the need for achievement, that is, all ambitions remained on their drawing boards and did not motivate them to action, sort of "wanting but doing nothing about it."

Assurance

In some languages, the term "assurance" means "confidence," "security," "permission" and "daring," which are the materials one needs and is exemplified by the assurance quotient, which explains what gives a person strength and confidence in his chosen path, hence the audacity to act. These are basic requirements for ambition to materialize. Without confidence and faith, ambition will not last for long and will not yield results.

A high achievement quotient reflects faith in our strengths and optimism regarding our ability. Although it may have some of the characteristics of religious belief, it is instead about the ability to believe beyond reality – "Yes, it can be achieved!" "Where there's a will, there's a way."

Many studies have shown that faith in desired results increases the probability of their actual occurrence; therefore, such faith is capable of changing statistical probabilities or to affect them. This is the ability to change probability.

Faith, somewhat like love, changes the one demonstrating it. Someone who believes in his abilities will obtain better results than another person with equal aptitudes but no faith in them. Studies investigating children's special achievements in music and other areas show that in every case, there was a parent who had unequivocal faith in his child which brought about these above average results.

A person who believes in his way, in his potential and destiny soars high. People with a high A.Q. have a solid faith in their path which empowers their ability to materialize their mission.

People suffering from serious ailments who believed wholeheartedly in successful treatments prior to getting them were more likely to be cured, as is the case with alternative treatments.

As a Chinese legend has it: A wise man asked, "What is genuine faith in a teacher?" His answer: "When the teacher says he will tell a joke and the believer is already laughing even before the joke is told."

Meaning

The aspiration quotient follows Viktor Frankl's concept stating that meaning in human existence is central to survival. As a psychiatrist and neurologist and the founder of logotherapy, Frankl claimed that those who survived the horrors of the Holocaust did not succumb to despair and suffering thanks to their faith that their lives had meaning. "He who has a 'Why' to live for can bear almost any 'How,'" said Frankl, quoting Nietzsche.

Aim oriented

Aim oriented, is a person's ability and passion not to give up despite temptation or hardship and is the expression of the endurance quotient at the spiritual level.

It is also the ability to be goal oriented and goal focused. Many Oriental teachings use archery to practice control and connecting with the target, as Eugen Herrigel wrote in Zen in the Art of Archery (1990), "The archer should not aim at the target but becomes one with it. He focuses his whole being on the target not allowing for any distraction, be it internal or external, until he becomes one with it."

How does one focus on the target and what can be learned from these professional sharpshooters?

Many people I met were highly capable but lacked the ability to correctly aim for their targets. This inability was caused by the dispersion between goals. An experiment in marksmanship, which examined the capacity of sharpshooters to hit the target, teaches a most basic lesson in aiming and focusing on a target. One target was placed at point A, for which shot accuracy was tested. Then, another target was placed at point B, where again shot accuracy was tested. The level of accuracy obtained was almost the same. At the following stage, sharpshooters were given the choice between two targets set for them, at A and B. A strange phenomenon occurred: Accuracy dropped, as if the presence of the second target prevented them from focusing the way they did when there was only one target.

In life, an individual may have the choice of several options. To get results, it is imperative to focus on one specific target as though the others do not actually exist, just like the sharpshooter who must focus on one target without being distracted by the other. The ability to focus and aim at the target in a way that one's whole being is concentrated solely on it is one of the characteristics of the A.Q.

Aspiration & Vision

"If you have built castles in the air,
your work need not be lost; that is where they should be.
Now put the foundations under them."

Henry David Thoreau (1817- 1862)

The aspiration quotient reflects a person's mission, vision and level of dedication to his mission. Mountaineers, those who don't quit or stop halfway up, are almost magnetically attracted to the top. As many studies suggest, the main force helping an organization to advance and succeed is the pull of mission and vision, which is a powerful tool for change. It can be imagined as a vector coming out of a future vision connecting with a present situation, thus pulling one towards it. This is why any organizational change begins with creating the organization's vision; every release from impasse at the individual level begins with clarifying one's personal mission. A clear vision allows for deriving strategic objectives and even a change of direction en route, knowing that one is well on the way towards the target.

My professional and personal experience has taught me that a vision's "pull" is much stronger than the "push" of reality, even the harshest one.

"Where there is a will and a vision, there's a way...." (Theodor Herzl)

Connection to vision is generally accompanied by future sense, which is a clear feeling of what the future looks like. Leaders and innovators have foresight and see the vision of the mission clearly and most vividly. This entails the ability to see in which direction the market is developing and the needs that may emerge, all before consumers are aware of them. Inspiring leaders like Steve Jobs saw and sensed the future.

Being an Ace

Aspiration to become an Ace, a winner, is an A.Q. characteristic. As previously mentioned, Ace is defined by Webster's English dictionary as "outstanding, champion, extraordinary, excellent." It is also connected with the term "winner," someone who comes in first in a competition.

Dr. de Bono distinguishes between "competition" and "sur/petition," which he coined. The former refers to victory over competitors and others' achievements. In the latter there are no external competitors and all competition is against oneself. In this case, the aspiration is to attain one's ultimate optimum and fulfill one's potential or that of the organization. The ultimate Ace wins over others and himself.

Vision, mission and purpose

Vision derives from an inner sense of purpose and mission and is the tangible expression of the inner mission. Connecting with one's mission is neither a logical thinking process nor a product of an emotional and creative one. It is instead a process of connecting with a higher point, which requires one to overlook both ego and logic.

A sense of purpose has two sources:

1. Reasons connected with the past – the need to compensate for and cure feelings of inferiority and childhood wounds. This approach, based on Freudian theories, was predominant and agreed upon by most theoreticians until the second half of the 20th century. It maintains that the main driving force is the power of compensation. Therefore, people whose achievements are exceptional gave it their best because the investment and achievements cured their childhood wounds. The deeper one's wound and formidable personality, the greater the success and achievement. Many clinical psychologists still see it as the main driving force, implying that a normative person is unlikely to reach extraordinary achievements because he has no reason to make such an effort. This approach always raises questions about the way we raise our children. On the one hand, we want our children to have a comfortable and easy life; we try to make as few mistakes as possible so as not to inflict any scars, the way our parents did. We want normal and happy children. On the other hand, there are parents who wish their children to achieve greatness, which requires a special drive and hunger that comes from want needing to be filled.

2. Reasons connected with the future – the driving force in this case is the need to leave a significant mark on the world. This explanation has it that an individual wanders about the world not only to finally get their late father's approval or overcome some sense of inferiority but to fulfill their mission. In other words, the emphasis in this case is not on the past but on future aims, which set an existential goal.

Objects and bodies move in nature as a result of gravity or pushing forces. The past is the pushing force, while the future is the pulling force. This also applies to social and organizational processes. They come about as a result of changing circumstances that induce change (push) or by wishing to reach an objective (pull). "Imagining myself enjoying new cheese even before I find it is what leads me to it," says Scurry the mouse in Who Moved My Cheese?

Actualization

The need for self-actualization is a concept coined by Kurt Goldstein and later adopted by Maslow as the highest step in the hierarchy of needs. This concept articulates the need to express one's personal potential or that of an organization. That is, to operate with maximal energy and realize one's full "stardom" potential in accordance with Maslow's maxim: "A musician cannot but make music."

This reference to self-actualization is on the borderline of religious spirituality, like a person's purpose in this incarnation. When reading Maslow's writings, one can see that when he brings up the issue of self-actualization, the language he employs changes and becomes more like that of a pious preacher than that of a man of science.

The need and the drive to fulfill all the different aspects of the SILVER ACE including ambition, aspiration, vision and mission, make the A.Q. in general, and the need for self-actualization in particular, the energy producer with the highest coefficients.

The connection between human happiness and self-actualization

Is an Ace happier than other people? Is this model of self-actualization the model for happiness? The relationship between success and a feeling of happiness bothered me for a long time. Is our search for happiness the main factor that motivates us? One of the best answers to that question was given by Maslow, who studied the connection between satisfying needs, attaining objectives, personal actualization and happiness. In one of his articles published in 1966, Maslow wrote:

"It seems that human pursuit of permanent and stable happiness is not possible to achieve. Great happiness is by definition episodic and can't go on endlessly. Happiness is a feeling pertaining to emotion. The pursuit of happiness is part of our driving force, but we have to accept the fact that it is only temporary. The constant element in this regard is the fact that the ambition to pursue happiness always comes back afresh, with a feeling of longing for happiness vis-à-vis a feeling of dissatisfaction."

I was very surprised to find that Maslow's approach resembled that of Rabbi Abraham Isaac Kook, who defined happiness as "the memory of struggle and the sensation of achievement."

In other words, happiness is the side effect of achieving objectives and satisfying needs, thus it is also temporary. After a period of happiness and fulfillment, achievement becomes routine, which calls for the next challenge.

This approach is very different from other idealistic approaches which consider "The Garden of Eden" as permanent, attainable happiness. This goes not only for the biblical Garden of Eden, but also for social methodologies based on the belief that there is some state one should aspire to in which everyone will be happy. Consequently, the meaning of life is not about attaining happiness but in realizing one's purpose and potential. Happiness may just be the reward for this effort.

Yet happiness is more than a side effect. It is the catalyst directing us to action, the "carrot" we are given for having achieved something. Knowing happiness teaches us about nature and the Creator, and through happiness we can understand our purpose. If nature, God or true knowledge (choose by your own personal beliefs) wishes to direct us towards certain actions, it brings us happiness in exchange for performance. Take, for example, the decision to have children. This seemingly irrational step is accompanied at times by suffering and existential risk, but the happiness in raising children alongside the suffering is the reward. Actualization is accompanied by happiness as intense as the happiness involved in raising children.

Beyond actualization and self-expression

Is there anything beyond actualization? Is it just the very end of Maslow's hierarchy? What about the people who have realized their dreams? Do they just sit at the top of the pyramid doing nothing? These questions were not addressed by Maslow himself, perhaps because they were not relevant at the time. Nowadays, one can easily meet successful people who face a dilemma of this sort, wondering what they can do now, having accomplished their purpose.

Following the stage of **self-actualization** there appears a new ladder to climb, devoted to **self-expansion**. A person thus expands his boundaries from his private self to the community, to humanity as a whole, to all creatures, to the planet as it is today and to the next generations. This explains the increasing engagement in ecology, contribution to society, and similar trends.

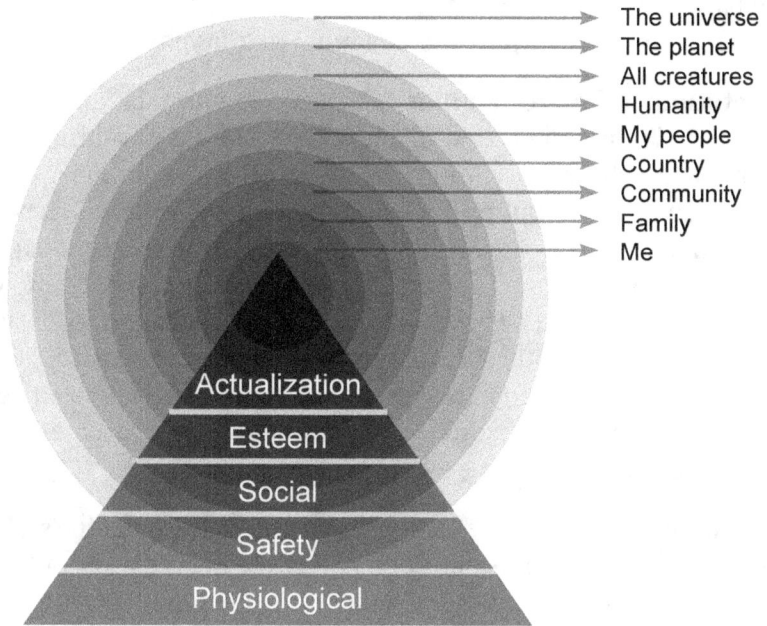

The universe
The planet
All creatures
Humanity
My people
Country
Community
Family
Me

Deficiency and treatment methods

"Without vision, people will loosen restraint…."

Proverbs 29:18

A modern person, gradually freeing himself from his existential physical problems, is confronted with the highest level of needs in Maslow's hierarchy. **Lack of a mission and vision quotient** deeply troubles some people, while a sense that their lives have no significance and that they don't matter haunts those people who have a low, if not pathological, level of this quotient. In his book Nausea, Jean-Paul Sartre shrewdly describes perturbing feelings due to lack of the mission and vision quotient – the sensation that everything is nauseating and enormously frustrating, which may lead to depression and even to suicide.

Lack of self-actualization – as a component of A.Q., is very costly for the individual. A person who feels he is "missing out" on his life and cannot realize his potential lives a life of frustration and acute pain. This issue increasingly comes up in consulting sessions, and it is the main cause of people's pain and suffering. There are many treatment methods that can assist in finding meaning and purpose: individual logotherapy, philosophical guidance, spiritual methods, or personal and group coaching. Numerous coaches and consultants use expressions such as "finding one's path" or "journey" on the assumption that all people or organizations need to do to connect with their vision is to remove the barriers impeding them from connecting with their purpose, since the need to accomplish one's purpose is natural and human.

Lack of ambition – We are familiar with people who lack ambition or the drive to achieve. "I'm not interested in anything," they say. Nothing apparently motivates them to achieve anything, "Why bother?" Sometimes, the source of these statements is a crippling fear of failure or of success. These people set their goals at an easily achievable level so that they don't get disappointed. Lack of ambition could happen to someone who was pushed at a very young age towards achieving goals above his capabilities; it can also derive from the frustrated ambition quotient of parents attempting to realize themselves through their children. In such cases, the child activates a defense mechanism which eliminates or diminishes his ambition quotient. In extreme cases, lack of ambition can even become an existential agenda.

Human nature pushes to achieve self-realization. Achieving one's goals is a fundamental part of human existence and one of the main causes of happiness. Preventing happiness is a pathological condition. Therapy should then aim to break through the barriers impeding fulfillment of this fundamental need.

Obstruction could also be caused by fear of success, in which case accomplishing ambitions is perceived as a threat. When for various reasons an individual does not permit himself to realize his full potential, treatment should concentrate on removing fears and anxiety. We must help that person do away with those fears and anxiety and expose him to an environment that will encourage him to express himself and his purpose.

When an organization looks for people who want to climb Mount Everest, it should not let them climb hills. Aces need a sense of purpose. They need far-reaching goals, the feeling that the task is part of a meaningful vision and mission. It is important for a person to experience a certain distance between what he does and what can be done so that he does not get "too" satisfied, so that he remains "hungry" regarding his MBI (**M**y **B**ody **I**mage); an Ace who attains his full inner body image no longer has ambition! Sophisticated organizations increase the motivation of their workers by connecting them with large successful groups – like popular clubs, such as the "Millionaires' Club," a golf club or volunteering and cultural activities – as part of a process of identity and self-image expansion to feed the "hunger" and the motivation to succeed.

Pathological conditions caused by lack of A.Q. – Pathological conditions, such as life feeling meaningless, lacking significance and ambition, vision and purpose lead to pathological depression and suicidal thoughts. The emergence of suicidal thoughts depends on the counterbalance quotient, the energy quotient:

- A depressive condition is accompanied by absence of energy and lack of strength; there is no desire to go out into the world and one wishes only to passively stay in bed. When a person has no energy at all there is a reasonable chance that suicide will not ensue, but a situation of "passive suicide" could develop: an inability to initiate any form of action to the point of existential apathy, like that which is often displayed by frail, worn-out, exhausted people.

- However, pathological absence of A.Q. or of the zest for life combined with a high level of energy might make those people put those suicidal thoughts into action. In those cases where drug therapy increases energy, there is sometimes an increase in the danger of actual suicide, therefore some preventative treatments actually reduce energy.

Lack of balance

Low energy quotient (EN.Q.), high ambition quotient (A.Q.)

When the level of ambition and vision goes beyond one's basic energetic capacity, the spirit has no adequate body. Such a person might just burn himself out simply because the degree of his aspirations is higher than that of his energies and his abilities to perform and contain. He is in danger of physically collapsing. This is why different spiritual approaches attribute so much importance to the physical training of the spiritual man, so that the body can be an adequate receptacle for the high spiritual levels.

The healing powers of vision A.Q.

Organizations and individuals who find themselves helpless and hopeless are stuck in a vicious circle of energy loss. This is what happened to the dogs in Seligman's notorious experiment, a feeling of helplessness causing inability to function. Organizations often get stuck in this situation in times of financial problems and existential crisis.

Result: Lack of confidence and self-esteem reflected in fear of action, poor self-image and feelings of unworthiness. Maslow elaborates on the heavy price people suffering from poor self-esteem and lack of confidence have to pay. Most "underachievers" can be characterized as lacking confidence. When working as consultant for the Wisconsin Project, a government initiative designed to re-insert chronically unemployed people into a normal employment cycle, I came across populations for whom the inability to go to work had become pathological. Those people suffer from a pathological absence of A.Q., and the feeling that "I don't have anything to offer." There is no doubt that this also involves lack of motivation and the absence of any need to achieve, but the central factor affecting their condition is lack of self-esteem. Work is giving; consequently, a person who feels worthless will have great difficulty in giving to others.

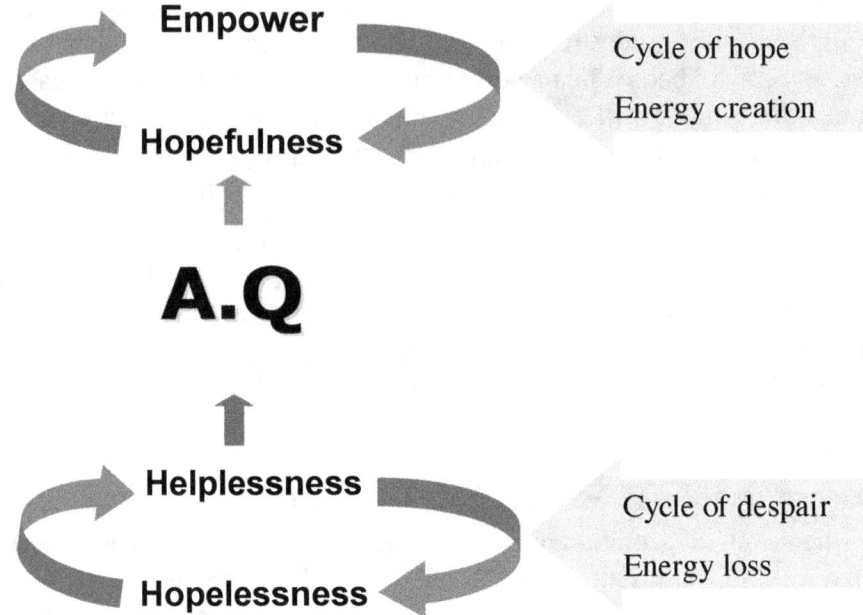

A.Q. Characteristics:

- **Achievement and ambition** – the drive to reach considerable accomplishments and get to the top, far above and beyond;

- **Competitiveness** – the will to make remarkable achievements in comparison with those of others nearby;

- **Dominance** – the aspiration to occupy positions of influence and power;

- **Vision and mission** – the passion to act with vision and purpose;

- **Leadership** – the ability and the will to lead to objectives;

- **Need for challenge** – challenges enliven me;

- **Need to leave one's mark** – the will to leave a meaningful mark;

- **Influence** – the aspiration to influence others' lives in a meaningful way;

- **Self-actualization** – a sense of purpose and meaning with the need to act for self-realization;

- **Self-confidence** – having faith and confidence in our capacity, our goal and our path.

Summary:

The Eight SILVER ACE Quotients

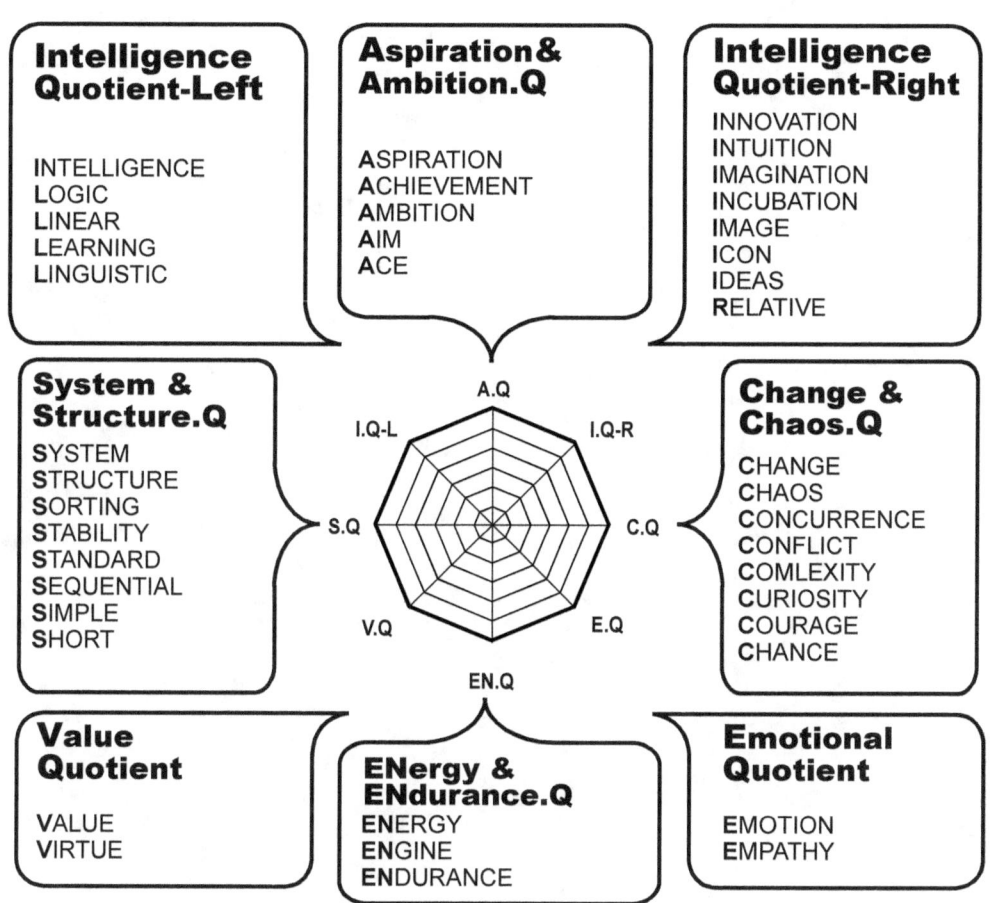

Intelligence Quotient-Left

INTELLIGENCE
LOGIC
LINEAR
LEARNING
LINGUISTIC

Aspiration& Ambition.Q

ASPIRATION
ACHIEVEMENT
AMBITION
AIM
ACE

Intelligence Quotient-Right

INNOVATION
INTUITION
IMAGINATION
INCUBATION
IMAGE
ICON
IDEAS
RELATIVE

System & Structure.Q

SYSTEM
STRUCTURE
SORTING
STABILITY
STANDARD
SEQUENTIAL
SIMPLE
SHORT

Change & Chaos.Q

CHANGE
CHAOS
CONCURRENCE
CONFLICT
COMLEXITY
CURIOSITY
COURAGE
CHANCE

Value Quotient

VALUE
VIRTUE

ENergy & ENdurance.Q

ENERGY
ENGINE
ENDURANCE

Emotional Quotient

EMOTION
EMPATHY

Are Humans Superior to Computers?

This is the central question employees and employers have to face in the 21st century.

The SILVER ACE model, in its overview of human skills in the world of employment, indicates those unique human skills that will directly influence the professional world and the professions of the future.

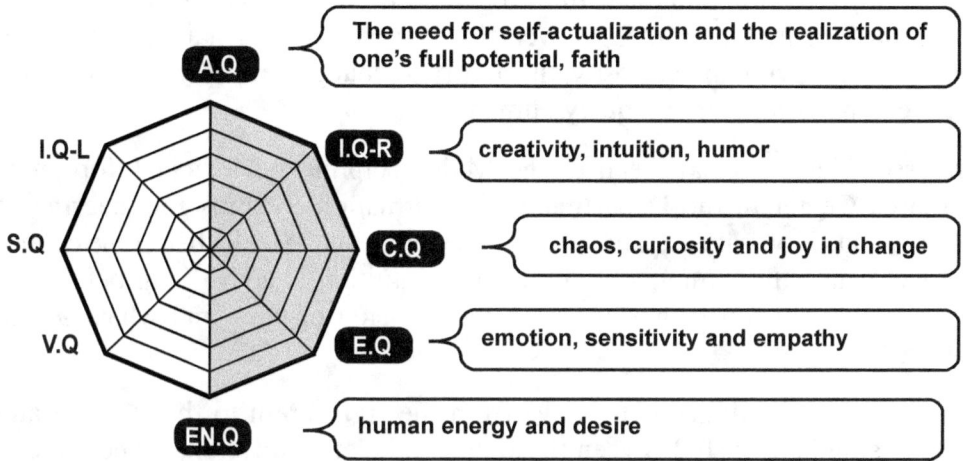

1. The vertical axis – energy and passion

Human need and ability to climb up the ladder towards the spiritual level, the stage of self-actualization, are what make humans unique. Thus, a human becomes an interface between the earth and the sky, between the world of survival and the world of spirituality. It is the ability to bring "knowledge of the higher worlds," as Rudolf Steiner put it, and to apply it to flesh and blood. There is nothing a person needs more than self-realization and to express his potential, both bringing about great happiness. Computers have no need for self-actualization or the desire to express potential; computers cannot expand their circuits beyond their individual selves towards the community and humankind in general.

Human energy operates at the emotional, intellectual and spiritual level, not according to the law of energy conservation but according to the law of abundance. Investing more energy in these levels does not create an energy shortage but an energy increase, for the giver as well as the recipient. These laws of abundance do not exist in the world of computers.

The special connection between skills and energy generates the desire to express skill. This combination we call **quotient** is a human characteristic. Computers have no passion, so the expression of their skills will be in a different form. Furthermore, computers lack the ability that only humans are endowed with, that of believing, which makes it possible to change the probability that certain things will occur.

2. Right brain; left brain

The main processor of a computer is the left brain. It is based on logic, algorithms and computational thinking. The right brain is presumably what constitutes man's preeminence over the computer. Imagination, invention, intuition, creativity and curiosity, the ability to change, empathy and love – all these characteristics are uniquely human.

Professor Yuval Shahar, head of the Multidisciplinary Medical Informatics Research Center in the Department of Information Systems Engineering at Ben Gurion University, explains in an interview with the Calcalist: "One cannot analyze data with computers only. Human intuition is active long before the stage of information gathering, as in the decision on how and what data to collect."

A unique human ability is to move from the right brain to the left one and operate simultaneously between these two completely different processors. A human acts as an interface connecting the worlds on the right that are beyond him, with the worlds on the left which are beyond human existence; connecting the muses and chaos, with expert systems, virtual agents and the law.

3. Aspirations to fulfill one's potential

The vertical axis, representing the aspiration to fulfill potential and self-actualization, characterizes human uniqueness. Computers obviously cannot aspire, have no need for self-realization and are certainly incapable of connecting with the spiritual world. Humans connect the worlds of action with those beyond humanity. Only humans can bridge worlds which are not directly connected.

4. Energy interface and flow

The ability of humans to act as interfaces and channels of communication between different worlds is unique – humans as hubs, as intersections between worlds inaccessible to computers. This is not a passive interface but an interface enabling and sustaining processes of energy flow between different worlds and realities. A healthy flow of human energy takes place from the right to the left, from the physical to the spiritual (see the diagram below).

Humans as interface between "worlds"

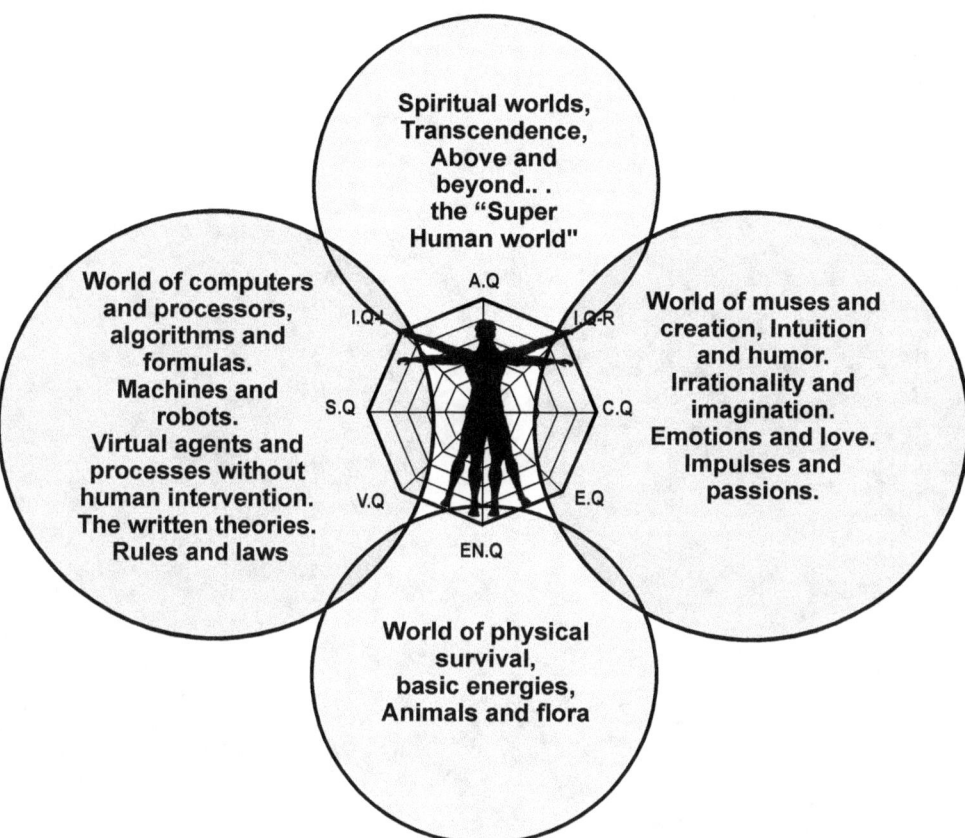

Types and Profiles

In this section, we shall try to illustrate the theoretical SILVER ACE model by applying and examining it using types and images we are familiar with. These types are in fact stereotypes, images present within all of us, in our collective subconscious, which embody part of our perception of the world. Like all stereotypes, they are one-dimensional and each represents a certain aspect of the model, but they are an efficient means for employing the model which is why we chose to use them.

Prototypes

Just like with any other type, as well as in the context of organization, we are dealing with stereotyping, though clearly no position holder fully responds with their stereotype. A stereotype is a basic generalization of a large group, characterizing the main skills required for the job.

During different periods in the life of an organization, different skills and different types of people are required for the same job. For example, the CEO of a newborn start-up will not be the same as the CEO of a mature and established organization.

The SILVER ACE model characterizes the archetypes according to the skills and quotients required of them.

The following are some of the figures leading an organization's life in different stages, with reference to a fictitious, modern, theoretical, high-tech start-up company:

The climbers - entrepreneurs

- VISION, MISSIOM
- AMBITION
- NEED OF ACHIEVEMENT
- AIM, GOAL
- ENDURANCE
- POWER, ENERGY

The climbers

As a psychologist who happens to be a mountaineer, Paul Stoltz discerns three types of mountain climbers which, according to his thesis, personify a metaphor representing the entire population:

Types of "climbers"

1. **The quitters** are those who showed up, saw the escarpment of the mountain and preferred to give up on the climb and turn back.

2. **The campers** climb the mountain only until a certain point where they stay. They do not leave their "comfort zone."

3. **The climbers** constitute 10% of the population. They are endowed with a drive that will lead them to the highest peak and different capabilities than others.

Stoltz related the differences between the three groups to their levels of endurance in situations of distress and failure – the higher the mountain, the harder it gets to climb – and coined the concept of "adversity quotient," the ability to overcome obstacles and turn them into opportunities.

The climbers, as Paul Stoltz described them, are endowed with a high adversity quotient – they are able to absorb failure and situations of distress. The climber's ability to preserve energy despite difficulties and failure makes it possible for him to keep scaling peaks. Thus, it is no wonder that most of the world's political leaders have extremely high adversity and resilience quotients. In order to cope with extreme situations of threat, frustration and blame, one has to be highly capable of handling rejection and hardship. In 1915, Winston Churchill was removed from his post as First Lord of the Admiralty and at the age of forty found himself alone and exhausted. Only his mental strength and his mission preservation made it possible for him to finally reach leadership.

Paul Stoltz perceived the adversity quotient as the principal distinction between entrepreneurs and climbers and the other two groups (campers and quitters). According to him, the ability to handle obstacles is a must but cannot suffice on its own. Those who climb to the top of the mountain are endowed not only with the adequate ability to handle failure but also with immense inner passion, vision and drive, which give them the required strength and energy and motivate them to reach the top. Without the urgent need to reach the peak, they won't harness the right aptitudes and won't invest the required efforts to overcome the expected hardships and failures along the way.

According to the SILVER ACE model, the endurance quotient is indispensable for characterizing climbers, yet it is insufficient on its own. A mountaineer needs a high level of energy but must also strive to reach the top and preserve his mission. The ultimate mountaineer perceives reaching the summit as his "life's mission."

The energy quotient EN.Q. is not enough on its own; one also needs a strong passion to achieve and a sense of self-actualization – A.Q.

The entrepreneur is the progenitor, the creator, and the organization starts with him. One should distinguish between "entrepreneurship" and "initiative" – the two concepts may seem similar yet represent different issues. No entrepreneur can do without initiative, but displaying initiative won't necessarily make you an entrepreneur. The entrepreneur is the parent of the organization/enterprise and as such he provides the organization with what a good parent provides his children – roots and wings. An entrepreneur is not only a man of vision (wings) and he is not only a man of initiative and execution (roots); his uniqueness is in the connection between the two aspects. He can be compared to an entirely goal-oriented missile with tremendous energy capacity.

Supporters and recruiters

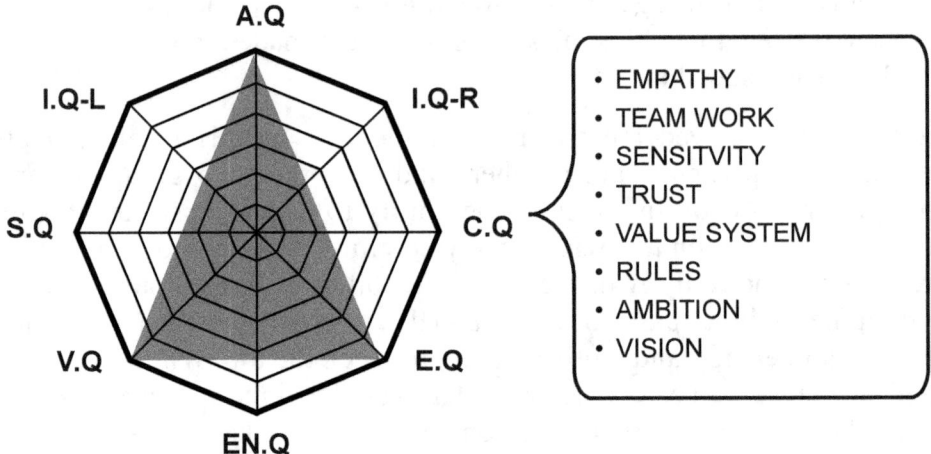

If an entrepreneur is likened to a missile, the next step in establishing an organization requires a passenger airplane which will be capable of finding the right people and leading them to the objective. In the transition from the enterprise to forming the organization, people who know how to build teams and determine a system of rules and action methods will be needed, which is why the "stars" base has to be broadened for launching with E.Q and V.Q points. People will not join an organization that doesn't display values as well as a certain level of emotional maturity.

The entrepreneur sweeps people with his enthusiasm, but he does not dedicate himself to conserving and developing them. The talent scouts, recruiters and supporters handle this task. In the modern start-up; they are a group of founders that joins the original entrepreneur. The founders constitute the top "family", without whose support the enterprise remains barren. A value system and emotional intelligence are required not only in recruiting workers but also in finding suppliers, banks, funds and other agents, and of course, clientele.

The preservation and development stage is hard on the egocentric entrepreneurial leader. If he cannot move to the level of emotional and moral maturity, ensuing quarrels over values, loyalty and friendship could cause the organization to collapse. Considering the S.I.L.V.E.R .A.C.E model, it is clear that an organization needs the entrepreneur's energy and vision, which is the combination of a rocket engine and broad wings enabling the liftoff.

Creators, planners, developers

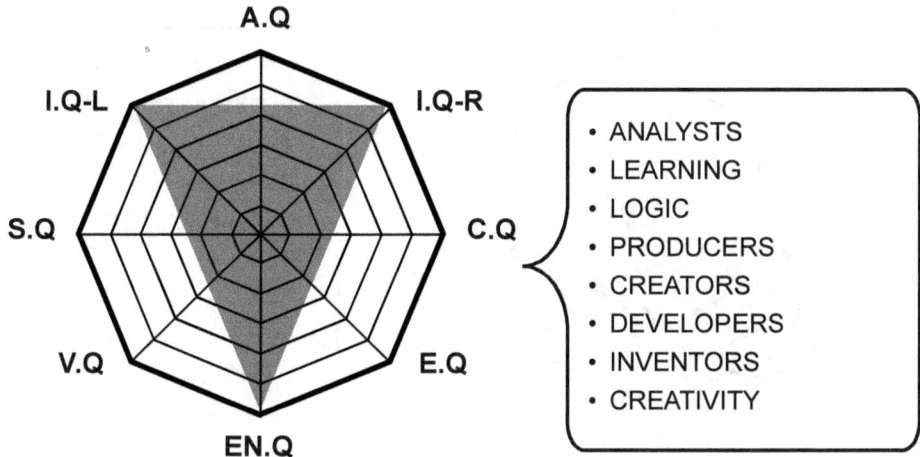

Results start to run the organization at this point, and professionals, like engineers, technicians, production and development staff are most significant. In terms of the missile metaphor, a wide-winged transportation aircraft which is the organization's performance and organizational mass and the purpose of which is to analyze, study, improve and bring results is already there. The I.Q.-R and the I.Q.-L are the metaphoric "eyes" of the instrument; an eye to the right, another to the left both connected to information, processing and thinking systems.

The integration between energy flowing to the brain and development, marketing, creativity and performance with end results propels the organization forward as a constantly improving and thriving body.

The CEOs – The Navigators
The "Navigating Managers"

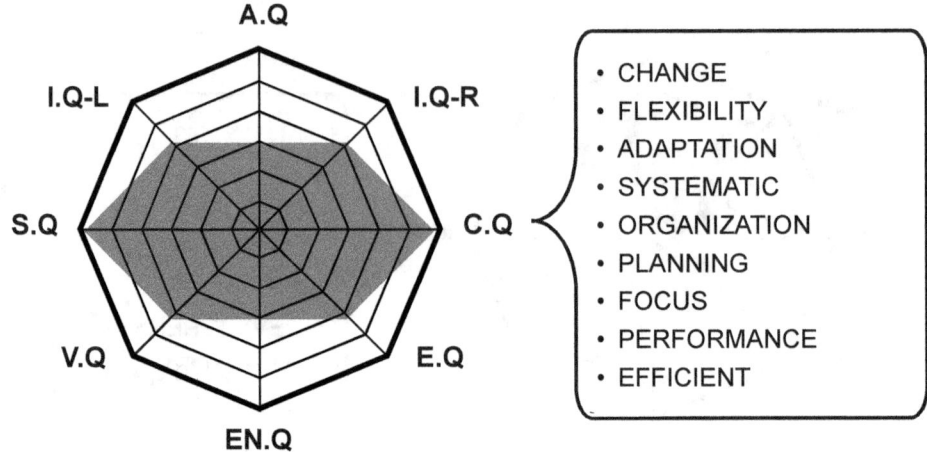

With its ongoing development the organization needs wider wings, heavier than those of a fighter plane that can change direction depending on the map. At this stage, the entrepreneur develops his own wide wings or alternately makes room for the professional CEO who brings with him the management approaches, work methods, strategies and tools to manage information. The CEO works along the C.Q.-S.Q. axis (the management axis), which is characterized by the transition from change, chaos and conflict, to organization, method and purposefulness. His job is to react to a constantly changing reality and navigate the organization towards its goals. He specializes in balancing right and left; between creativity and change and efficiency and organization; between creating conflicts and tensions, and coordination and conciliation; between changing processes and process setting. All these are evidence of his power and success.

A Synergetic Team Creating an Ace Organization

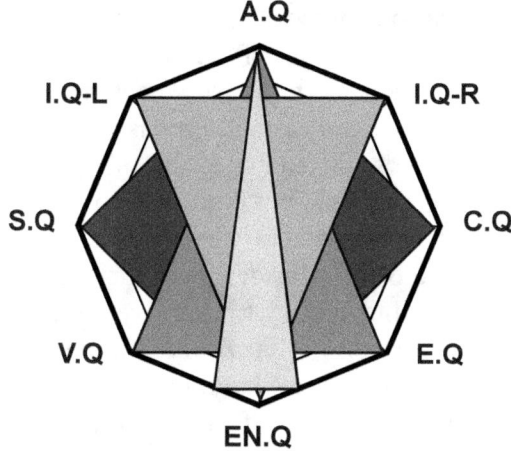

The organizational staff can be likened to a sophisticated and functional spaceship capable of organizing itself and adapting to different situations. At this stage, all the elements of stardom are fully realized. When the organization is properly structured, its staff can be considered as a synergetic team that generates a star possessing all the characteristics of a SILVER ACE: The **entrepreneur** brings tremendous energy, power, resilience, ambition and vision; **recruiters and supporters** provide workers and customers with emotional maturity, empathy, and sensitivity; **creators and developers** are in charge of production, thinking, learning, and creativity; **managers** are responsible for change and conflict management, appropriate and efficient organization, and methodically planning out work. Building a team which makes one complete star is the secret as well as the recipe for success, but it is also the root of tensions, conflicts and difficulties in communication.

The SILVER ACE model allows one to know what is there and what is missing in order to attain a full Ace team.

Placing all team members on the model accurately allows for everyone's importance and contribution to be acknowledged and clarifies possible communication failures between them.

Profiles

At this point, we will describe some real people, since no one is one-dimensional, and analyze their star maps as illustrations of the model. The characters to follow are real people who have undergone certain assessment processes through which the different combinations emerging in various dimensions will become apparent. We also recommend studying those different types in the spirit of the model itself: Start with a general intuitive impression stemming from the right brain, then elaborate and organize the information, a process carried out in the left brain.

First, take a look at the shape of the star denoting the character in the model, his strong points and weak points and try to intuitively relate to the character, to bring it to life. Those who have internalized the model will sense that they are able to feel the character even before having learned any detail about that person, then they can go into more detail if they wish to do so.

The "results-oriented producer"

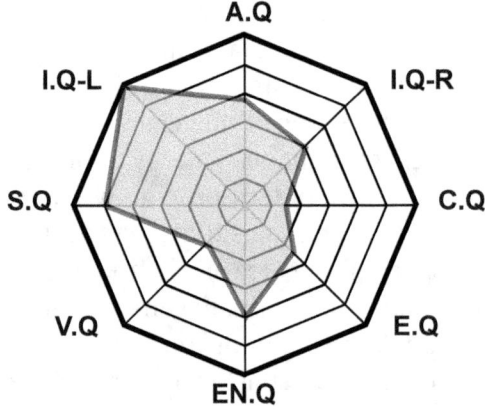

This is a "bottom line" and results-oriented person. His left intelligence quotient is predominant and as such, he operates logically and takes results and data very seriously. What cannot be measured is irrelevant as far as that person is concerned. His energy is directed at obtaining quantitative results, paying less attention to quality processes. He is an organized person and therefore has difficulties in dealing with situations of chaos, uncertainty and change. He lacks flexibility and finds it difficult to get out of stalemates or change course. If there is a wall, he will go through it if he can avoid changing course this way. He relates to conflicts as issues that require solutions but has trouble containing prolonged conflict situations. He operates methodically step-by-step.

Thinking as an engineer, he relates to people in the organization as a resource no different from any other. He does not cultivate human relations and he does not pay attention to the emotional needs of his co-workers. He learns from mistakes and improves himself constantly. In order to make him change his mind, one must adopt a logical approach. He will have difficulties communicating with his counterbalance quotients (I.Q.-R, C.Q., E.Q. and V.Q.) which he perceives as insufficiently results oriented. As such, they deal with principles or interpersonal processes, which he therefore perceives as stirring up chaos and disorder.

The "Rigid Bureaucrat"

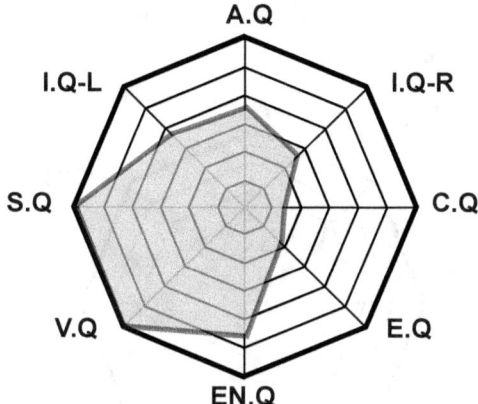

The dominant quotients for this person are the system and structure, and the value quotients. This is a man of principles and rules who operates in an orderly and organized manner. He is guided by a highly developed moral system of "do's and don'ts," so he is always clear about what is right or wrong. He is a reasonably intelligent person with reasonable learning capacities, but not particularly brilliant. He is clearly not the creative type and has great difficulty coping with any change whatsoever. His abundant energy is directed at dealing with procedures and arrangements.

This image illustrates the classic administrator, a person of control, regulations and accounting. As such, he struggles to communicate with others since he is not a team player. Being rigidly principled, his interpersonal relations are equally harsh, extremely non-empathetic towards the needs of others as he is incapable of displaying empathy. He is highly likely to encounter antagonism resulting from his work relations and inflexibility in interpersonal relations. He will always be undoubtedly right but unwise in many cases as well. He will stand on his principles even at the cost of his co-workers' cooperation. He can detect failures and gray areas and will prove to be an excellent bureaucrat, but he is also incapable of sophistication when expressing criticism.

This kind of person is more suitable for formulating procedures than setting elaborate processes in motion. He will not be able to identify unconventional methods for violating such procedures and will not be able to prevent them; therefore he will be less suitable for positions which require handling complex delinquency. Some will see him as a "square," whereas he will be "an uncompromising man of principle" to others. This sort of person finds it very difficult to cope with changes in the organization or his personal life, and he cannot function in situations of chaos and uncertainty. He therefore tends to object to creative initiatives for change and hold on to existing paradigms. He will have difficulty in communicating with people who have right-sided characteristics, those who break conventions and generate chaos and with those who bring human elements undefined in tables of procedures and order.

The "Social worker"

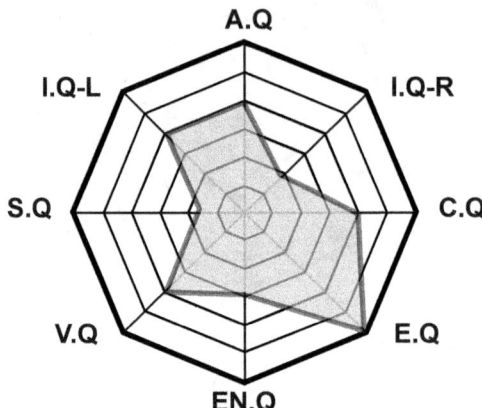

This individual's strength lies in his emotional intelligence and his way of relating to others, balanced only partly by the value quotient. He has a certain visionary passion although unaccompanied by a particularly fervent ambition. He has a reasonable level of energy and acts through learning and logic. His weaknesses are in his system and structure. He is not focused and sometimes cannot make the distinction between the essential and the superfluous. He is not deterred by conflict situations and knows how to contain interpersonal conflicts, but because he isn't especially creative at finding solutions, he is not highly capable of dealing with severe conflict situations and chaos.

This character type corresponds to professionals in various fields such as social work, psychology, consulting, education and human resources. This kind of person is dedicated to people and is attentive to "who said what." He involves members of the group in the process, and becomes the glue that holds the group together. He is an excellent team player, supporting and encouraging group processes. He will take action to consolidate the group and make room for each participant. Even if he doesn't officially work as a psychologist or in human resources, he will be considered the group's "soul," and its members will come to him for empathy and sympathy. This character type will have difculties communicating with the counterbalance quotients (the I.Q.-L and the S.Q.) which put emphasis on getting results and efficiency, leaving less room for interpersonal sensitivity.

The "Master of Development"

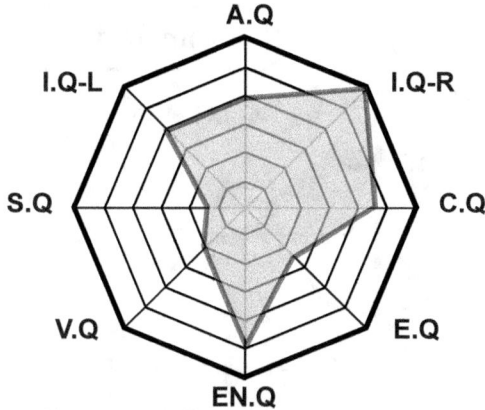

This is the creative thinker, and the laboratory serves as his studio. He is a creative thinker but not a team player, generally radiating loneliness. He operates with his gut and his head in parallel, is highly intuitive and capable of working in conditions of chaos and uncertainty.

One of his strong points is his high change quotient and his ability to change directions without getting stuck in a course incompatible with changing reality. He has an excellent capacity for "thinking outside the box" and coming up with new ideas. When faced with a riddle or a challenge, he looks for the solution obsessively, stopping at nothing. He is flexible at thinking and operation but disorganized and disorderly. He is bursting with energy but not sufficiently focused. It is difficult to keep up with him because of the wealth of his ideas and because he feels comfortable in situations of chaos and uncertainty, whereas others tend to recoil. He is the one who pulls the organization or the team out of ideological paralysis by offering original solutions, but it would be difficult to work alongside him as a team member. He is essentially a loner. People will turn to him when in need of an original idea, but they will have to be very selective faced with his innumerable ideas. He will experience difficulties in communicating with rigid, procedural people (V.Q., S.Q.).

The Salesman Profile – The Bow and Arrow Model

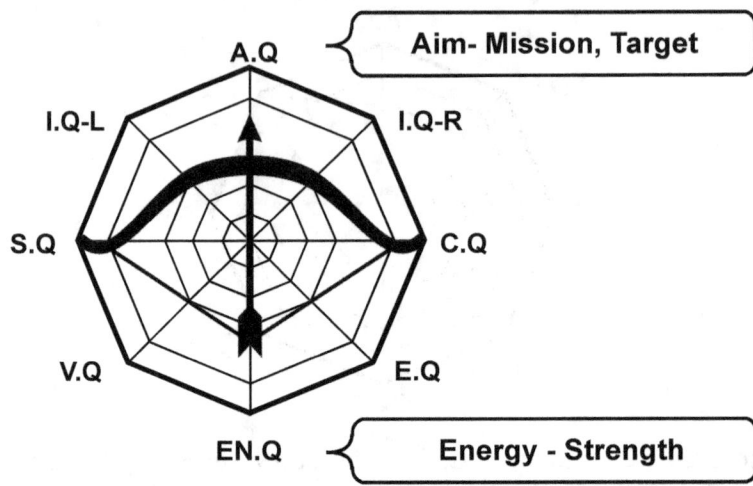

A sales star will shoot an arrow loaded with energy straight at his target with a powerfully balanced bow.

In this chapter, we will examine salespeople and study how the eight dimensions of the SILVER ACE model are expressed in the case of sales stars. The world of sales tends to use hunting metaphors: "hunting down the customer," "hitting the target," "capturing," "attacking the market" – these are but a few examples of expressions that salespeople and sales managers use, which is why we have chosen to use the bow and arrow analogy to name this model.

Just as in the general SILVER ACE model, there are two axes here:

The vertical axis – the energy axis represented by the arrow aiming at the target.

The horizontal axis – the behavioral axis represented by the bow resting upon the two ends of relationships and results.

The Arrow – The Energy Axis

This is the central axis in the sales domain. It is made up of two types of energy: the energy quotient at its base and the aspiration quotient at its top. This is also an energy model, where sales and purchases represent the classic processes of energy transformation: material energy turning into emotional energy.

Buying and selling is a classic process of energy exchange, where the salesman is the one putting the process in motion. A salesman lacking energy, or worse, one who robs the customer's energy, will not manage to complete a sale, certainly not when the buyer has an alternative in which he receives energy. After many workshops for salespeople, I learned that if they do not have the correct energy, no sales theory or vital sales expressions will be of any help. It is no coincidence that the typical salesman is teeming with energy especially when it comes getting potential buyers' attention on the street or in shopping malls.

Many years ago, when I hitchhiked my way around the world, I quickly learned that I was dealing with sales. I only had a few seconds to "sell" a passing car the idea of taking me along. I saw it clearly. When I prepared myself in the morning like a salesman off to work, recharging my energy reserves and passing it on to the drivers – smiling, establishing eye contact, wishing them "Good Day" – the results were amazing. By transferring positive human energy, unlike the laws of material energy, not only do we ensure positive results for ourselves but the 'salesman' himself is filled with positive energy. A proper sales process re-energizes both sides.

The energy quotient (EN.Q.) – Energy is what gives the arrow its strength and power, enabling it to soar towards its target. Sales, just like purchases, are energy-saturated and energy-recharging processes. The fact that people enjoy shopping illustrates this. In addition, when depressed people find solace in shopping, there is a conversion of one form of energy (money) into a different form of energy. In order to be a sales star, one needs intense energy that will successfully stimulate the potential buyer and recharge him or her with energy.

Sales can also cause a process of energy depletion due to failure and rejection. Negative statements such as, "I didn't manage to close this deal," can be voiced without the expression of frustration, but they could also resonate with many past childhood echoes: "You are no good," "Nobody wants you," and the like. A good salesperson possesses a high endurance quotient that will not wear out but at the same time will be attentive to the customers' feelings.

Improving selling techniques has been the focus of salespersons' training for many years. Good salespeople complete sales, and after some intensive training their sales rate will rise to some extent.

This principle of training and increasing the level of endurance quotient is simply by training to deal with more customers without any improvement in their skills.

Based on the understanding that every salesperson has his personal barrier which is the result of the number of letdowns the salesperson can handle. It's as if he physically suffers from every disappointment, which results in his inability to initiate an additional sale. Such an accumulation of failures causes fatigue upon hearing the simple and legitimate answer, "I am not interested in buying this product just yet," which automatically translates into, "You are no good." Being worn-out as a result prevents the person from looking for a solution by creating additional requests for his product.

We therefore conclude that a good salesman is one who is able to handle rejection and set failure aside. He is capable of seeing rejection as a single incident that does not imply anything about his personality, ability or future, and is not a personal failure. This approach prevents the experience of failure to spread like a cancer towards the other "limbs," to bring about burnout and eventually, a feeling of helplessness. The energy quotient preserves the good salesperson from draining out all his energy when sales are down, which is an inseparable part of the sales process.

The aspiration quotient (A.Q.) – the head of the arrow is made of ambition, accomplishment, connection and adherence to goals. Ambition and accomplishment are the forces pushing the arrow to the target. The size of the target derives from "body image" (MBI), which is the central part of the ambition: What is my financial image? What sales volume suits me?

Any sales star needs to be "hungry" for more than he has at any given moment. This "hunger" results from the gap between self-image and body size, the way we are, in effect. One of the most common mistakes is to take the claims of salespeople seriously, satisfy their demands and produce satiated sales people. A successful sales star must continue to feel this "insatiable hunger."

The arrowhead is an internal connection to the objective and is also one's sense of purpose. The more a sale is connected with the individual's identity and purpose, the more energy will be allocated to it and, as a result, the more powerful the sale.

Shooting a bow and arrow is not a technical process of aiming and coordination but a mental process in which all parts of one's body and personality participate, with intention in the lead.

The Bow – the behavioral axis

Results
Data
Focus

Connections
Flexibility
Creativity

The bow makes it possible to direct the arrow at the target and hit it exactly. According to the axes of the SILVER ACE model, the bow corresponds to the horizontal axis moving from right to left. According to the spirit of the model, the bow is made of connections and results: The right end reflects the ability to generate connections, and the left end reflects the ability to translate these connections into practical results.

At the right end of the bow are the connections, changes and creativity – E.Q., C.Q. and I.Q.-R.

E.Q. – the ability to make connections based on emotional intelligence (E.Q.) which derives from the ability to sense the other, to identify with him, and communicate through emotions. The emotional intelligence quotient is of vital significance in the sales process, and the ability to emotionally communicate with the customer is one of the key capacities of a good salesperson. In recent years, this skill has become ever more significant. A good salesperson is no longer the person who "sells ice to an Eskimo." The new salesperson relates to the customer's need, understands him and finds the most suitable response to that need. The new salesperson manages to connect with the customer with empathy and sympathy, a connection that can be sustained over time, and eventually the customer will reward him.

C.Q. – a salesperson needs a high change quotient in order to create multiple connections and to constantly move from one connection to the next so as to ensure he can quickly read the new map and change direction if need be.

I.Q.-R – creativity, intuition, unconventional solutions, originality, the ability to concretize, and humor are characteristics of right-sided intelligence that an excellent salesperson needs.

At the left end of the bow are **results and values.**

V.Q. – today's customer is sophisticated, he is not taken easily: He knows exactly what his options are and is unforgiving to those who don't show him enough consideration. Therefore, a salesman with a low value quotient (V.Q.) could find himself soon enough without any customers.

The snake that tempted Eve in the Garden of Eden is the metaphor for the old-school salesman, the seduction artist. In the biblical story, when God asks Eve why she ate from the forbidden Tree of Knowledge, she justifies herself saying, "The snake tricked me." It is understood from the biblical text as well that a sale based on temptation comes at a price. In addition to being ineffective, it arouses hatred.

"And I will put enmity between thee and the woman, and between thy seed and her seed ...." (Genesis 3:15).

S.Q. – a salesman once told me, summarizing the importance of system and structure (S.Q.): "Already in the first few minutes of a meeting, when I'm building up the initial connection with the client, I already know what the chances of closing the deal are as well as its scope." This means that a sales Ace has to be focused, efficient and methodical, one who can very quickly distinguish between the essential and the insignificant, between investing in the right place and wasting time.

I.Q.-L – represents the measurement of results and sticking to objectives. What cannot be measured doesn't exist for a salesperson. One of the great dangers he faces is getting carried away with enthusiasm without controlling reality. A sales superstar employs logic, moderation and applies lessons of experience.

Balancing the two ends of the bow

Many years ago, I went to buy furniture in a small town. There were two furniture stores on either side of the main street. I started at the shop to my right and spoke to the owner who was a very pleasant and professional salesman and who was fully engaged in establishing a connection. We talked about my needs and my taste, and he was happy to show me around his shop. There were too many options, and I was unable to decide, so I left the shop, promising to come back. I crossed the street to the other shop, where the salesman approached and asked me what I needed. He listened, and then said, "Forget everything you have seen here. This is the only thing you need," pointing at a set of furniture that indeed matched my needs and my taste.

The second salesman used the left side of the bow and displayed purposefulness and efficiency, distinguishing between the essential and the minor very quickly. Each salesman had a bow with a certain bend. The first one created a purposeless connection, and the second demonstrated purposefulness disregarding connection altogether. As with a bow that bends to one side making it impossible to hit the target, I ended up buying furniture from neither. A genuine sales Ace would hold the bow at balance between the two ends: both establishing a connection and striving for results.

Assessment - Interview
According to the SILVER ACE

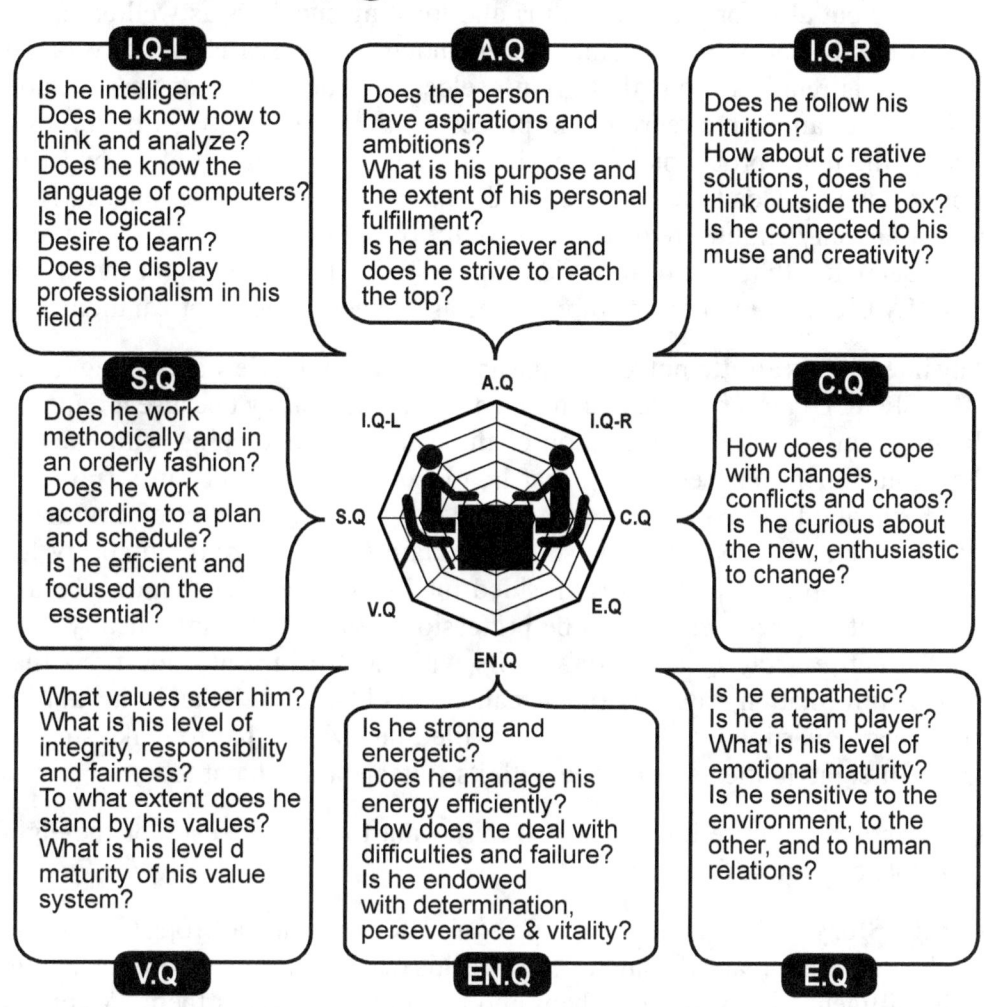

I.Q-L
Is he intelligent?
Does he know how to think and analyze?
Does he know the language of computers?
Is he logical?
Desire to learn?
Does he display professionalism in his field?

A.Q
Does the person have aspirations and ambitions?
What is his purpose and the extent of his personal fulfillment?
Is he an achiever and does he strive to reach the top?

I.Q-R
Does he follow his intuition?
How about c reative solutions, does he think outside the box?
Is he connected to his muse and creativity?

S.Q
Does he work methodically and in an orderly fashion?
Does he work according to a plan and schedule?
Is he efficient and focused on the essential?

C.Q
How does he cope with changes, conflicts and chaos?
Is he curious about the new, enthusiastic to change?

V.Q
What values steer him?
What is his level of integrity, responsibility and fairness?
To what extent does he stand by his values?
What is his level d maturity of his value system?

EN.Q
Is he strong and energetic?
Does he manage his energy efficiently?
How does he deal with difficulties and failure?
Is he endowed with determination, perseverance & vitality?

E.Q
Is he empathetic?
Is he a team player?
What is his level of emotional maturity?
Is he sensitive to the environment, to the other, and to human relations?

"But he made such a good impression during the interview..." this is often said of workers who had been hired on the basis of enthusiastic yet unprofessional interviews and proved to be a disappointment. Quite often, all we know about someone who made such a good impression in an interview is that he or she knows how to make a good impression. Although this is a very important qualification for certain jobs, it is not enough to ensure one's aptness for every position. The general impression given by the candidate is one of the main biases in an interview, what we call the "halo effect," whereby one aspect of the candidate paints the picture but doesn't allow us to see all the other skills required for the job.

An interview is one of the most popular tools for getting acquainted with the interviewee. We use interviews as a tool not only for work recruitment processes but also for building teams and locating suppliers as well as in the framework of social relationships. Even though the research validity of an interview is relatively low, there is no selection process that doesn't include this method, and some recruitment processes are based solely on interviews. One of the main problems in interviews is the lack of clarity about what to look for, what needs to be assessed and what we are really assessing. In fact, such ambiguity slightly reduces the validity of the interview. We do not aim to go deep into the issue of interviews in this book but to highlight the use of the SILVER ACE in order to improve the assessment process of candidates.

Any interview is an attempt to map out a person. The interview according to the SILVER ACE can serve as a map for an assessment journey because it requires the interviewer to form an opinion of the candidate in keeping with each of the eight dimensions separately, that is, to examine the candidate's frame of mind, his ability to cope with change and uncertainty, his level of emotional intelligence and so on. If we wish to ascertain someone's full suitability for a job, our impressions of his right-sided intelligence or of his eloquence are insufficient. Interviewers should be professional enough to methodically map out the entire array of a person's skills without drifting into questions that provide information, say, only on the candidate's I.Q.-L level, that is, his ability to answer a question intelligently. The skilled interviewer has to make sure he scans all eight quotients, each one with its suitable assessment tool.

Throughout the entire interview, you may want to examine each of the eight quotients on four different levels:

1. **Life Story** – A résumé tells a person's life story. It's a projection of the choices he has made throughout his life, his maneuvers, his spheres of action, his diligence in examining them and his attitude towards them. A correct reading of the map surfacing and emerging while reading a résumé enables us to grasp his personality, study him and his experiences in different life situations. It is advisable to enter "his life's movie" to understand how he acted, what happened, how he reached his decision and more, all intended to fully comprehend the person in front of us.

2. **The interview as a situational simulation** – At this level, the interviewer focuses on the dimension of the "here and now" of the interview and investigates what goes on between himself and the interviewee, how the interviewee responds to him and to the surroundings and what he

is feeling. This is a separate and essential communication channel that either underpins or refutes the assumptions that came up in the previous channel. This is where a discrepancy can be seen between what the candidate says about himself and his reactions in practice and real time during the interview. For example, the candidate maintains he is flexible towards change but cannot adapt to "surprises" during the interview. It is essential to discern different levels of energies throughout the interview. For example, whether and to what extent the interviewee gets excited when describing a change initiated by him, or if he is just answering the question mechanically.

3. **The behavioral interview** – The SILVER ACE relates to quotients that translate into actual abilities, skills and characteristics; it is recommended to find a way to examine the candidate's actual behavior. There is no point in asking questions that go on about how the interviewee would act in different theoretical situations; he should be asked to describe how he handled a certain situation in the past. There are sample questions for this aspect of the interview for each quotient.

4. **The interviewer as a "seismograph"** – A good interviewer will use his subconscious as an assessment tool. As a seismograph, the interviewer's subconscious constitutes a powerful tool of great sensitivity. The interviewer has to sense the candidate throughout the interview and account for what he is feeling as the interviewer. What associations have come up in his mind? What do they mean to him? Does he feel enthusiasm, attachment or dislike? When do such feelings appear and as a result of what? It is essential to identify the associations that come up within you, the interviewer, during the interview, and understand their significance in your inner world. In order to analyze the interviewee, you have to know yourself well. My advice to interviewers is to devote one column throughout the interview for noting all subconscious messages they receive concurrently with the accumulated information.

The SILVER ACE quotients in the interview process
The energy (EN.Q.)

The energy factor is made of the energy quotient and its managing capacity as well as the endurance quotient; the interviewer should relate to both aspects. The first question should relate to the interviewee's level of energy. Does he have sufficient power and drive for activity? Does he have the mental and physical strength required for the job? An interview is an extraordinarily effective tool for this dimension.

Energy is expressed in the very meeting itself, from the handshake to the atmosphere created in the room. It is interesting to note the intensity of energy along the interview timeline: Does the candidate sustain the same level of energy or does he tire quickly? Does he start weakly and gain momentum during the conversation? The interviewer should act as an instrument that absorbs energy and checks whether the interviewee makes him drowsy. An energetic person stimulates the people around him whereas one who lacks energy puts them to sleep.

Energy reading – I have developed the ability to read a person's energy map during the interview and derive information of utmost importance. Throughout the interview, discussing various topics and bringing up certain points, one actually intercepts the energy level that accompanies each topic. A person may talk of four or five subjects; in fact, these are different levels of energy: One consumes energy, another has a low energy level, the third has positive energy, while the last is full of energetic enthusiasm. An energy map points to the energy flow in the direction of different areas, just like a medical instrument which measures the flow of blood and oxygen in different organs of the body. Energy will be expressed to a considerable extent in a person's biography and the chronicle of his performance. An energetic person cannot conceal his energy; it will appear in nearly all aspects of his life: at work, in his studies, in the military and the community.

The endurance quotient relates to the ability to withstand frustration, to get back on one's feet. To determine the level of the endurance quotient we will examine how the candidate copes with situations of distress and failure. The interviewer can use the candidate's résumé as a starting point. What happened when he was fired or failed? How did he encourage himself and did he manage to restore himself? We should note if he took control of the situation, demonstrating responsibility, or if he put the blame on someone else and gave up. Did failure affect him adversely for a long time, and did it impact other parts of his life?

Quite often, the candidate will attempt to conceal his failures, but how he copes with hardship can be validated against the "here and now." Asking a candidate, "How do you deal with failure and rejection?" is not sufficient because an intelligent answer would do. Alternately, one can create a situation of frustration or criticism during the interview to see how the interviewee reacts. When training interviewers, I once tried to demonstrate this by asking an interviewee to tell me of an instance in which an idea he tried to promote was rejected. He talked of the rejection of one good proposal he had submitted and eloquently explained that it hadn't upset him and that he took the rejection with understanding. I reacted with deliberate hostility, "They were right to reject it, it was a stupid idea. It seems out of character that an intelligent person like you would submit such an idea." He tried to explain, and I obstinately rejected all of his arguments. Then I actually saw him fuming; he glared at me and erupted aggressively. His inability to deal with failure and rejection was demonstrated on the spot.

Points for referral during an interview:

- The interviewee's energy level;

- Vitality, vigor and strength;

- Level of dynamism, drive for action;

- Resilience when faced with distress and failure;

- Wise energy management;

- Ability to replenish energy;

- Burnout and energy loss prevention;

- The interviewer's sensation regarding the energy level throughout the interview: Did energy flow from the interviewee, or was the interviewer drained and tired?

The emotional intelligence (E.Q.)

Let us proceed to examine the candidate's emotional maturity, his ability to feel and display empathy, and the type of interpersonal communication he maintains – all these aspects will impact the prediction of his behavior within the team, facing the customer, and in the framework of the corporate culture.

Emotional intelligence is one of the easiest aptitudes to examine in an interview assuming we are able to correctly read the candidate's résumé as well as what occurs in the interview itself. It is impossible to learn about a person's emotional intelligence through direct questions such as, "Are you a team player?" One should note the connections made between the interviewer and the interviewee as well as between the interviewee and his surroundings and ask for examples that illustrate how the interviewee acted in different interpersonal situations. The candidate's emotional intelligence will come to the fore when allowed to connect with his emotions. At times, it may be easier to do through conversation about family and friends. When the interview is conducted by a team of interviewers, we can also get a sense of the candidate's capacity to act facing a heterogeneous team with different opinions.

Points for referral during an interview:

- How did the candidate act when required to work with a difficult team?

- Who are those with whom he can't get along with and how does he cope?

- How did he handle a sensitive interpersonal issue?

- How did he manage to rally people towards action?

- Is he capable of turning a group into a team?

- How did he manage a problematic member of the team?

- How does he conduct himself in an unfamiliar environment?

- Is he sensitive towards the interviewer? Is he empathetic towards him?

- What emotional sensation did he stir in the interviewer?

The value system (V.Q.)

As employers we should know that a worker can be trusted since we entrust parts of the organization to him. This factor enables us to refer to moral and ethical maturity, and determine if the candidate operates by an ethical code, if he is committed to the organization, if he publicly identifies with it, and whether he takes responsibility for his actions and his environment.

The V.Q. is a key issue in the assessment agenda but it is also one of the most difficult to evaluate by interview alone. As detailed in the chapter on value quotient, strangely enough sociopaths have the rare ability to charm during an interview. Those who lack a value system can adjust chameleon-like to different situations and people. How can we hone our abilities to identify an impostor or a fraud? In this case, the interviewee's life story is an efficient tool. We shall look for those moments in the interviewee's life when his value system was supposed to intervene: cases of compliance with contracts, reneging on commitments or quitting a job. We will try to identify the person's behavioral norms and their essential values.

A sensitive interviewer should be attuned to his gut feelings, and if he feels that something needs to be looked into carefully he has to act on it with utmost sensitivity but without discrediting the candidate. After the interview, it is always recommended to talk with the interviewee's previous employers who can either corroborate or refute the interviewer's gut feeling.

Points for referral during an interview:

- Situations in which the candidate remained loyal in spite of temptation;

- Situations in which the candidate's ethics and sense of fairness were challenged;

- Instances in which the candidate conflicted with a policy he disagreed with;

- Situations in which the candidate did not follow procedures;

- Examples of respect and trust the candidate gained.

Change quotient (C.Q.)

In this channel of the interview we try to examine the person's ability to adapt to changes and take action in situations of chaos, uncertainty and concurrence. The résumé is the first tool that can show us if a person needs frequent change or seeks stability and permanence as well as what gives him a sense of security and satisfaction. We'll ask him about the different transitions in his life: How did he adapt when transferred to a new location or to a new job? Did he experience these events as opportunities or as crises? How long did it take him to adjust and understand the culture of the new place? At the same time, we'll sensitively check what is going on in the interview itself. A change of atmosphere, response or attention will show how the interviewee reacts. How long it takes for him to notice that something has changed, and how long it takes for him to adjust to the change. We'll also examine what gives him a sense of control and how he reacts to change and uncertainty. Through all of these indicators, the interviewer will be able to form an opinion on the level of this person's change quotient.

Points to refer to during an interview:

- Instances in which the candidate was required to adapt to new situations;

- Initiatives for change he took in previous workplaces and in his private life;

- Incidents in which priorities were changed;

- Activity in situations of chaos and uncertainty;

- Simultaneous operation on several levels;

- Working conditions and methods which pose difficulties for him;

- His reactions to changes during the interview. Does he display flexibility?

System and Structure (S.Q.)

In this channel, the candidate's working style and behavior will be examined. How organized and orderly is his work? How methodical and attentive to small details is he? We will examine if he is a planner, if he takes action to achieve his goals. We'll check if his life story as a whole, and the way he functions in particular, attests to an organizational and methodical ability. How he handled tasks, and what kind of student he was, and so on.

At this stage, we'll also pay attention to what occurs during the interview: how the candidate conducts himself during the interview; how he relates to the time limit; whether he presents things in a structured and organized manner; if he cares to be understood and if he manages it; whether he is conscious of the task at hand; and whether he is able to make efficient use of the time at his disposal to achieve this task. An organized and efficient person will act this way during the interview.

Points for referral during an interview:

- The interviewee's handling of a project to be executed;

- Examples of plans made and executed by the interviewee;

- Awareness and attention to efficiency;

- Distinction between the essential and the superfluous;

- Follow-up on processes;

- Time management at work and after working hours;

- The interviewee's handling of the interview in terms of planning and efficiency;

- Clarity and focus during the interview;

- The interviewee's time management during the interview – Is he efficient? Is he focused?

Right intelligence quotient (I.Q.-R)

In this channel, we'll examine the extent of the interviewee's creativity and originality. How he perceives things – Is it based on banal paradigms and patterns or on originality and innovation? These aspects will be reflected in the candidate's style both in his résumé and in the way he conducts himself in the interview. It will be reflected in his enthusiasm for novelty, in the way he relates to the interviewer and the choices he has made throughout his life.

People endowed with a developed I.Q.-R tend to rely on intuition. When interviewing a successful businessman, I asked him what he relied on in his decision making. He pointed down to his stomach and said, "I can feel it in my gut whether a deal is good or not." People possessing a developed I.Q.-R will have many examples demonstrating their creativity and inventiveness. They will be able to talk about innovative solutions to crisis situations and original reactions. Just like any other channel, it is a good idea to see how the interviewee handles questions requiring creativity and humor.

Points for referral during an interview:

- Situations that require finding new ideas quickly;

- An example of a new process conducted by the interviewee;

- Examples of original solutions to problems;

- Ideas for improvement suggested by the interviewee;

- An idea introduced or implemented by the interviewee;

- Use of humor, witticism;

- Creativity in extricating himself from embarrassing situations;

- The interviewee's capacity to stimulate creative thinking.

Left intelligence quotient (I.Q.-L)

This is classic intelligence, the intelligence quotient. It is very important but, in fact, we can frequently learn about it from sources outside the interview. Cognitive intelligence is highly correlated with a person's learning capacity and knowledge, and it is the sine qua non for admission to many academic programs. Therefore, getting a degree, achieving academic excellence and gaining admission to special programs are important indicators that demonstrate the candidate's level of cognitive intelligence.

During the interview we try to ascertain not only if the candidate is intellectually capable but also whether he operates smartly. Does he learn from experience? How does he analyze situations and draw conclusions? Does he keep up-to-date with innovations and advanced techniques? Many interviewers tend to focus on questions about this quotient, wasting precious time. "How would you have dealt with situation X?" or "What do you think about Y?" are questions to which the answer only shows the interviewee's ability to give an intelligent answer, without providing any further information about him. It is therefore worthwhile to invest energy in probing other channels to find out if the interviewee acts smartly.

Points for referral during an interview:

- The interviewee's level of professionalism ;

- Situations in which the interviewee received positive feedback and those in which he received negative feedback;

- What action he took to improve his performance;

- How he coped with a weak spot in his knowledge;

- Situations requiring that he learned something new in a short time;

- The kind of student he was in school and in college;

- The way he analyzes and draws conclusions: Is he open with the interviewer?

Aspiration quotient (A.Q.)

In this channel, we examine the candidate's level of ambition and his need for achievement. What motivates, satisfies and pushes him into action? We study "body image" in terms of success and the lowest threshold he is willing to reach.

At an advanced stage of the process, when we are better acquainted, we shall ask the candidate if he is driven by a sense of mission and aims at his goal. Whether he acts to accomplish his vision and calling, and if he is connected to the spiritual meaning of intelligence. We can talk to someone about his vision, the meaning he ascribes to his existence and his purpose in life, but we have to remember that in this dimension, it is not the right answer or an intellectual one but the sparkle in the person's eyes.

Points for referral during an interview:

- The candidate's level of ambition and competitiveness;
- Whether or not the candidate aspires to achievement;
- The candidate's body image;
- The interviewee's confidence – or lack thereof – in his abilities and his path;
- The extent to which he adheres to his goal;
- Does the interviewee have a sense of vision and purpose?
- Is he driven by his desire to leave his mark?
- Does he feel the need to be a star?
- Whether he leaves the interviewer enthusiastic and inspired by his vision and ambition.

Integration, energy and balances

Once we have formulated our assessment according to each dimension, we'll next examine the meaning of the relationships emerging from the map we have drawn: Is there an insufficiency severe enough to become pathological? Are there unbalanced gaps? Is there high cognitive intelligence firmly based upon emotional maturity and understanding? Is there is a gap between unconventional creativity which shatters patterns and a stabilizing value system? And so on. Through these questions and aspects, a complete picture of the person as a whole begins to take shape, woven in the SILVER ACE map.

In the second stage, we check the relationship between the complete picture and the characteristics of the job in question. Is the candidate qualified for the job as previously defined? What gaps have come to light? What are his weak points in relation to the required profile? Would it be possible to have them adequately developed?

The focus will be on the **energy** totality of a person in each quotient and at each level. Is there energy and passion for system and structure other than the person's knowledge of methods, organization and planning? Is there a passion for emotional intelligence? I am aware that there are no structured questions that lead to this type of assessment, but a skilled, open-minded interviewer can act as an energy seismograph and ascribe the energy that he **feels** and **experiences** to the corresponding quotient. Absorption of energy is done subliminally. The interviewer has to be attentive to himself and to his sensations: when he gets tired and starts dozing off, when he loses interest, when he is charmed and fascinated, and when he is "mobilized" by the interviewee. Furthermore, he must remember what the conversation was about when eyes sparkled and the voice was full of enthusiasm and passion.

The S.I.L.V.E.R .A.C.E
in Organizations

I.Q-L

Is the organization intelligent, analytical & learning-oriented, think logically, professional & knowledgeable?

A.Q

The ambition level of the organization. The organization's vision, purposes & mission.

I.Q-R

Creativity in the organization: innovation, thinking outside the box, using intuition & imagination.

S.Q

Method & efficiency, work according to plan, focus, & clear priorities

C.Q

Flexibility, adjustment, relating to change coping with change, conflicts & complexity

V.Q

Clear & defined organizational value system, the degree of mutual trust and respect, level of integrity & fairness

EN.Q

Vitality, strength, profit, power, dynamism & resilience in coping with difficulties

E.Q

Sensitivity towards the employee, team work, general atmosphere & customer-relations.

The Organization

The SILVER ACE model makes it possible to define the elements required to turn the organization into an Ace. The work is done by the "engines" of the eight success factors when operating at their full potential:

1. **I.Q.-L** an intelligent, analytical, rational and logical organization that learns from its experience.

2. **I.Q.-R** a creative organization which places a high value on intuition, thinking outside the box, and sophisticated thinking.

3. **C.Q.** a flexible organization which is curious and courageous, can change, adjust and operate concurrently on several levels.

4. **S.Q.** an organized and orderly organization, clear and sharp, methodical and efficient in which processes are structured and focused on the essence.

5. **E.Q.** a social organization, sensitive to its people, customers and suppliers, displaying empathy, excellent teamwork and good communication.

6. **V.Q.** an organization which upholds values, principles and ethics based on a coherent belief system of rules and laws of fairness and integrity.

7. **EN.Q.** a strong, energetic and dynamic organization with a profitable "blood flow," stable, solid, and resilient that copes with adversity and restores itself quickly after having fallen.

8. **A.Q.** an organization with lofty vision and ambition, achievement driven, with a sense of mission and perseverance.

Every organization has its own unique SILVER ACE organizational map that illustrates its strengths as well as the domains in which it should invest to increase its success. It is also a tool for an external investor who wishes to determine if investing in the organization would be profitable.

The organizational SILVER ACE is not the sum of its people's SILVER ACE characteristics.

An organization made of individuals who are stars by themselves will not necessarily become a star organization. In some cases, the result is the opposite – just try to imagine an organization made up solely of entrepreneurs. There are quite a few examples of "foolish" organizations composed of some very intelligent individuals. A university for example, even though it is a reservoir of wise people, is not necessarily an intelligent organization (in some cases, it is a stupid organization). There are uncreative organizations in whose ranks are some very creative people and organizations without any emotional intelligence even though their people have highly developed emotional intelligence.

Just like a human being, an organization does not operate as a chain but as a network. A chain is linear, serial and one-dimensional, and its apparent strength is that of its weakest link. In contrast, a network is multidimensional and non-linear, therefore it is not equal since its strength is reinforced. The network is stronger than all of its components put together, and this is its power. The neural network, for example, makes it possible to engender a wise brain, even though each neuron acts simply without any sophistication.

Anyone who has ever worked with organizations is familiar with the phenomenon of a most intelligent organization made up of a collection of the most mediocre managers. The organization's wisdom is not its managers' I.Q. but that of the organization. In general, responsibility for different quotients lies with those who fill different functions, and the classic division is as follows:

The human resources department is in charge of the emotional intelligence (E.Q.) domain and sometimes the value system (V.Q.).

Marketing is in charge of the right intelligence quotient (I.Q.-R) and the change quotient (C.Q.).

Operations is in charge of the left intelligence quotient (I.Q.-L) and

system and structure (S.Q.).

Administration is in charge of system and structure (S.Q.).

The entrepreneurs, the owners and the board of directors are responsible for the aspiration quotient (A.Q.) and the energy quotient (EN.Q.).

Although this classic division has been gradually changing, the organization team has to take charge of all the elements of the S.I.L.V.E.R .A.C.E. Any domain not taken care of in its entirety will become the organization's vulnerability.

The SILVER ACE model changes with the organization

Each stage in the organization's life needs its own SILVER ACE profile since at each stage there are critical requirements without which the organization won't be able to survive. For example, the SILVER ACE of an organization at its outset should be more of an entrepreneur's profile than that of an organization that has reached its stage of consolidation and expansion.

After the first stage of entrepreneurship, especially in start-up companies, the need for system and structure arises. At this stage in other organizations, the need for creative thinking and breakthroughs arises in order to break into the market and get out of routine. In some organizations, even at this stage, the need arises to change their initial strategy as it did not work out due to environmental or other changes. The new emerging need can be resolved in a variety of ways, from taking on new partners who have the needed characteristic to working with external consultants in order to implement change or restructuring the organization's management.

Characterizing the SILVER ACE components of the organization

Below is a description of the different quotients as reflected within the organization. The organization, just like an individual, encounters situations of insufficiency which at the extreme can cause organizational pathology.

Organizational EN.Q.

As previously mentioned, the energy quotient is made up of the following key elements:

1. The energy quotient = the level of energy it produces;

2. The endurance quotient = conservation of energy.

Energy is the foundation of the organization's existence. Although this is a clear given, to this day little thought has been dedicated to organizations as energy systems.

Over the years, I have realized the crucial importance of organizational energy. I found that it is possible to observe an organization and precisely "feel" its energy state. It is difficult to scientifically measure such a criterion, but a professional consultant will be able to identify that feeling with certainty. If ten professionals join the organization, it is probable that the "energy marks" each of them contributes will be similar to those of his colleagues. In a burnt-out organization that lacks energy, the importance of all other dimensions becomes secondary. Conversely, when the organization is bubbling with energy, we can feel it in the air right away. Often, start-up organizations are good examples since their atmospheres are imbued with dynamism and activity.

The C.H.E. law – The Organizational Energy Ladder

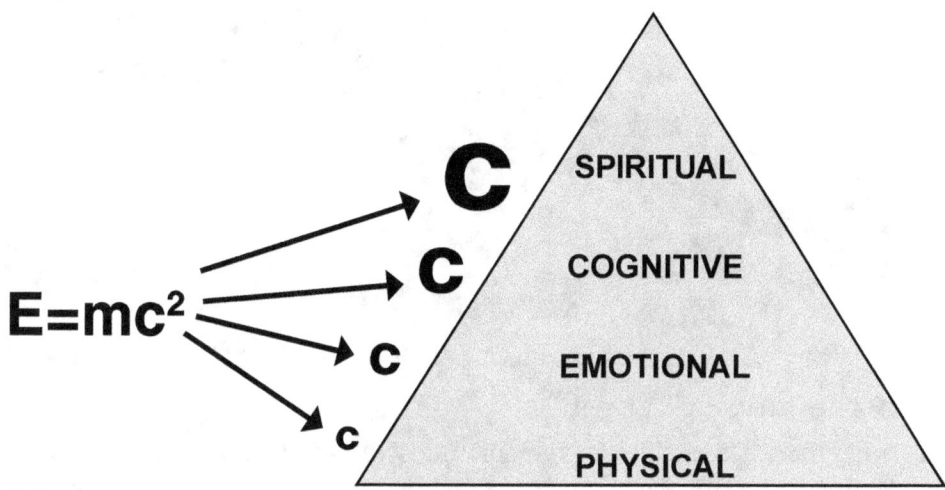

The slave ship parable serves as a good example for understanding the law of human energy coefficients within the organization (The Law of the CHE) at its four stages. The ship is commonly viewed as an organization, but according to the spirit of the model it can also be viewed as an individual.

The Parable of the Slave Ship

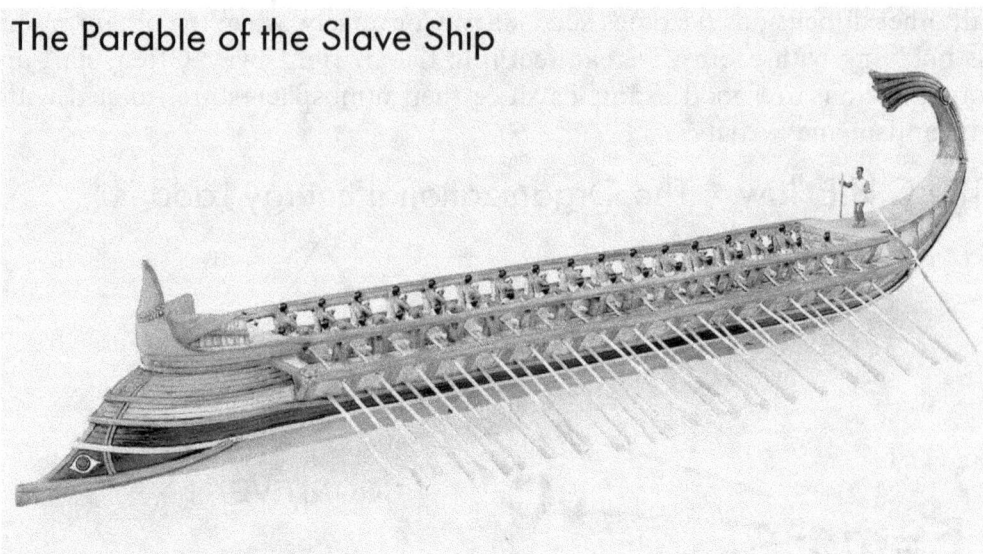

1. The Physical Level

Let's imagine a slave ship of ancient times in which the slaves' role is to row, chained to their places and oars, while slave drivers tower over them with their whips at the ready. When the rowers get food, it converts from potential energy to kinetic energy (energy of movement). The movement of their hands on the oars passes from their muscles to the ship and makes it move in accordance with the quantity of food they consumed. This stage is the lowest rung on the human energy scale and the lowest level of raw energy transformation. If we divide the distance the ship travelled by the number of rowers, we will get the quantity of energy we produced out of every one of them. History has proved that companies and organizations based on coercion and repression obtained the lowest energy benefit from their workers.

2. The Emotional-Social Level

This is the second step on the energy transformation scale. The slaves will be released from their chains, their tormentors wielding the whips will be dismissed, the slaves will be given their freedom, they will be able to form teams, and we shall allow the development of emotions and empathy, love and poetry. This is how a company with values and a code of conduct that provides support and a sense of security will come into being. Team spirit and support on the ship will make the atmosphere joyful. Suddenly the ship will sail at a much higher speed and will travel longer distances. In this situation, one produces higher energy coefficients.

3.   The Cognitive Level

We allow the crew of the ship to think and use their brains, the logical part as well as the creative part, and we will reach the third rung on the energy scale transformation. Sailing the ship will be much more efficient, based on creative and productive thinking, the workers will become engineers and inventors who harness the wind, the sun and the engines on their journey. The resulting "intelligent" ship will move swiftly and efficiently, overcoming storms and obstacles. At this level, the ship and its crew will produce the highest energy coefficients of the cognitive level.

4.   The Spiritual Level

Let's imagine now that this advanced ship, with its team spirit, is sailing to the crew's destination. Its objective is their mission. It leads them to the realization of their aspirations, vision and purpose. In this instance, the energy coefficient is the highest, being that of the spiritual level of both mission and vision.

If you ask yourselves where you should invest your money, which ship will be the Ace – there is no doubt that the ship that reaches the highest level of energy coefficient is the Ace, the preferred transaction on the energy market.

The Organization Life Cycle and the law of C.H.E.

The term "organization life cycle" and the law of C.H.E was coined by Professor Adizes and discussed in his numerous books and articles, thus he introduced to professional consciousness the different characteristics of organizations according to their life cycles and the different needs and the specific handling required at each stage. The different stages of an organization's life cycle are characterized by their unequivocal need for different quotients as well as by different levels of energy as a result of different energy coefficients. The energy formula allows us to learn what type of energy the organization is connected to at different stages of its life. For instance, start-up organizations are characterized by their youthful enthusiasm. Despite their small size, they generate considerable energy, that is, the organization is deeply connected to the mission and vision. In other organizations, growth in mass is accompanied by decrease in the transformation scale, and they go from mission and vision to dealing with survival, that is, lower energy coefficients. In such situations, corporate energy depends on mass and not on transformation coefficients.

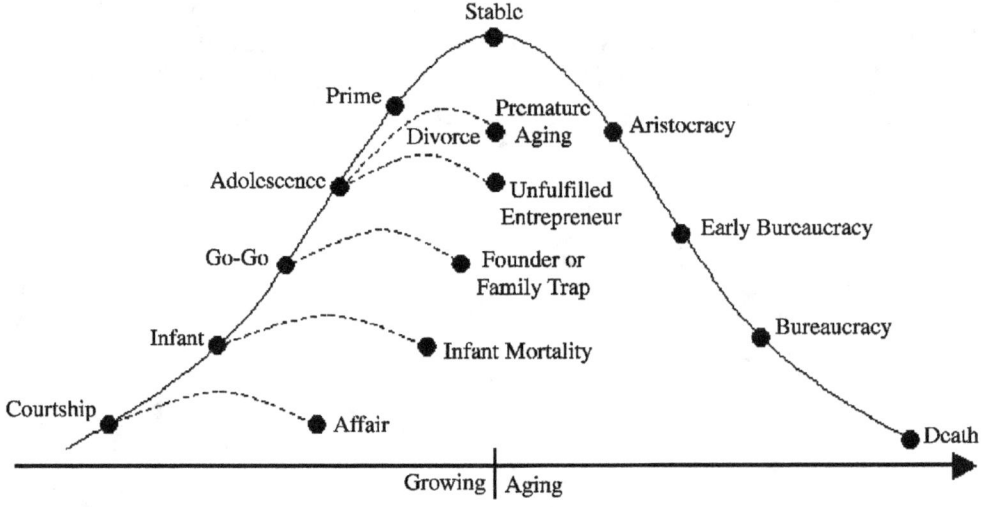

Source: Adizes's (1999)

In *Built to Last* (1995), Collins and Porras claim that organizations that maintain high levels of energy owing to high energy transformation coefficients will succeed over time. Conversely, shortage of energy in an organization might affect the organization and the individuals who work in it. A burnt-out organization which is not overhauled condemns itself to death. The means by which an organization can extricate itself from this situation are similar to the methods used to treat individuals lacking energy: External changes can be set in motion, such as a merger or an acquisition by a different corporate entity so that the new entity revitalizes the weaker one with fresh blood. Internal changes can also be implemented by hiring new workers whose energy level is high or by restructuring management in a way that will revive the organization.

The organizational endurance quotient is the second key factor in the energy quotient. This quotient refers to the way the organization deals with situations of hardship and failures which cannot be avoided. There are those who claim that the organizational endurance quotient is the most important factor for the success of the organization. As the pace of changes in the world becomes faster and more dynamic, the time allotted for achieving success gets shorter and, as a direct result, the percentage of mistakes and situations of hardship increase, so the capacity to overcome failure becomes essential. The better companies know how to deal with their mistakes and put them to constructive use, the better their chances of success.

The business world moves in waves of rise and decline affecting the business and its competitors. The way in which the organization copes with situations of adversity will determine its chances of success no less than the way in which plans its triumphs. When in dire straits, if the organization is wise enough keep it calm and doesn't allow the situation to drag it down nor try to learn negative formation or cover up failure, it will determine its starting point for the next wave. These actions affirm the organization's endurance quotient and its ability to deal with difficulty and failure.

According to this approach, successful companies are those that will be able to survive in "rough seas," which is why there is no point in searching for the formula for success and excellence, as many have in the past, but rather the formula to cope with stressful situations and failure. Organizations without any endurance quotient will fall apart in crises and will go about in no particular direction. According to this approach, instead of investing effort in the organization's growth, it is preferable to put effort into minimizing the downfall in times of recession and crisis. If we know how to soften the downfall, the increasing market forces will make the company grow from a higher starting point than that of its competitors. This approach maintains that the main effort in training a company must be directed at learning "how to fail" rather than "how to succeed."

It is possible to develop the endurance quotient through the courageous analysis of past failures and by drawing conclusions without trying to conceal any of those failures. Failure should not be perceived as a reason for giving up. It should be turned into an educational, fortifying experience, holding a lesson in reinforcing endurance and an opportunity for learning and growth.

Statements characterizing the EN.Q:
To what extent do the following statements characterize the organization?

- The organization's capacity to deal with difficulties and failures is effective.

- The organization knows how to extricate itself from difficult situations.

- The organization's endurance quotient is high.

- The work environment stimulates action.

- The organization is perceived as an invigorating and vital environment.

- The atmosphere in the organization is typically proactive and productive.

- The organization is seen as highly dynamic.

- The organization operates with much energy.

- The organization operates with enthusiasm and tempo.

- Work processes are promptly executed.

- Initiatives for action are encouraged.

- The organization is suffused with a sense of vitality and strength.

- Good organization and business infrastructures are in place.

- The organization is financially secure and has an efficient cash flow.

- The organization functions well under stress.

Organizational E.Q.

What does emotional maturity have to do with the business world? Is it not contradictory to follow such common beliefs as "the business world is a jungle devoid of sentiment" or "emotions and business don't mix"? These beliefs are gradually losing their relevance to the business world in the 21st century, not because of human and moral considerations but for practical reasons.

In a world of globalization, competition and rapid change requiring quick and efficient adjustment, emotional intelligence is turning into a business necessity. In a world where the customer is likened to a butterfly and one needs to find ways to "court" and attract him, sensitivity to the market and to the customer are required. There is no such thing as sensitivity to the market without sensitivity to others, and there is no sensitivity to others without emotional intelligence. Therefore, it is a quality we should look for in all workers, particularly those who deal directly with customers. Take, for example, a well-known hotel chain which implemented a new service strategy intended to provide personal care especially for businesspeople. One of the premises was that it was important to make the businessman feel at home so that he would come again to stay at the hotel later on a leisure trip. The chain looked for workers with good memories who would identify returning guests and remember their preferences, such as their favorite newspapers or foods. The chain was aware that the guest's entrance card makes it possible to access all the relevant information; in fact, the computer system remembers this information better than any human worker. However, the computer is unable to identify a guest's feelings – if he wants to be left alone or would prefer company, whether he is sad, happy or troubled. Computers don't have emotional intelligence; they feel no empathy; they are incapable of sympathetic communication with the guest.

There are three main orientations in modern management that require emotional and creative intelligence:

1. The need for sensitivity towards others, the market, the supplier, culture.
2. Corporate culture of responsibility, delegation of authority, a flat structure and creativity.
3. The organization as a "network" of teams and networking processes.

An organization with poor emotional intelligence has no emotional maturity. Such an organization will become "ill" by demonstrating insensitivity towards customers, its workers and the entire market. This is a common disease in large monopolies.

Teamwork

The story is told about a well-known company's chairman who fired the CEO in spite of his excellent business record. When asked why, he replied, "Because he just wasn't a team player." In modern organizations, the rigid, one-dimensional hierarchical structure has been replaced by a complex and flexible structure.

The "Peter principle" postulates that a person will be promoted up to a level beyond his competence, where he will stop advancing. Teamwork enables people to advance and express themselves beyond their natural abilities since, with teamwork, they get to perform jobs which seemed at the outset "too much for them." According to the SILVER ACE model, the more contradictory the characteristics of team members are, the larger the variety of requirements the team can handle but, at the same time, this also increases the likelihood of difficulty in creating harmonious cooperation among its members. In such situations, emotional intelligence plays a decisive part and it's critically important that all the participants be endowed with it. Emotional intelligence is the cement that keeps them together.

Successful cooperation between the entrepreneur (the right brain) and the manager (the left brain), requires a very high level of emotional maturity and emotional intelligence (E.Q.) to make the collaboration function efficiently. For these two forces to operate harmoniously without mutual emasculation, a close and tight relationship with a high degree of trust is needed, like the one existing sometimes between father and son. It does not have to be a father-son relationship in terms of a difference in ages, but in most cases the manager will be in the role of the experienced elder (chronologically or mentally), and the entrepreneur will be the creative partner.

One of the major aspects of an organization devoid of emotional intelligence is lack of teamwork. In today's organizations there is little to no chance of developing and surviving without teams to nurture a culture of cooperation and mutual understanding. The organizations that will succeed in the coming decades will be those sensitive to the needs of their workers and customers and even of their competitors. It took us a long time to understand that a sensitive man is no weaker than an insensitive man; the same goes for the corporate world. A sensitive organization is more resistant than the insensitive one due to the solid connection with its workers, its different components and between the organization and the environment, its customers and suppliers.

Developing emotional intelligence in the organization

Emotional intelligence within the team is a much more complex issue than self-consciousness and emotional control. Members of the team are required not only to get along with each other as people but to fit into a complete array while responding to the way each member of the team perceives himself in relation to the others and in relation to the organization.

A good business consultant should teach members of the organization to listen to others' viewpoints and positions and see them and the organization as one unit. Individuals must develop empathy towards the organization's members, customers, suppliers and community. American Express found a significant increase in sales and customer satisfaction following workshops designed to heighten emotional intelligence and awareness of others' feelings.

How do we develop the ability to be a team player? Primarily it will be through uplifting activities creating verbal and physical contact. Many workshops in this domain combine team missions taking place intentionally outside the formal framework of the organization. These are workshops of learning through adventures which team members take outside the organization, in nature, and their objective is usually twofold: the first is building and consolidating the team through action, leadership and authority; the second is learning and individual development of the ability to be a team player.

Modern management methods are not based on giving instructions, but on counseling and guidance for the workers who perform tasks, with considerable responsibility for the worker's personal and professional development. The manager must listen to his workers in order to turn them into responsible partners.

Statements characterizing the organization's E.Q.:
To what extent do the following statements characterize the organization?

- Teamwork in the organization is pleasant and efficient.

- The organization cares about its workers' morale.

- When a worker has a personal problem that interferes with his functioning, he gets support and backup.

- The work team is cohesive, based on support and partnership.

- The organization relates adequately to workers' personal problems.

- Communication between the different levels in the organization is friendly and informal.

- The organization shows consideration for workers' needs and acts with sensitivity and understanding.

- The organization is sensitive to the customers and wants to hear from them.

- The organization shows sensitivity to the environment and the community.

- The interpersonal atmosphere in the organization is positive.

- The organization relates to workers' feelings and cares for them.

- Team members usually have positive feelings for each other.

- Individuals like the people on their team and in the organization.

- Criticism is expressed in a positive and constructive spirit.

- The organization takes action to empower its workers.

Organizational V.Q.

The organization and the value system

The modern business world seemingly preserves Darwinian jungle characteristics. There is a genuine struggle for survival. No wonder that we use concepts such as "hunting," "pouncing" or "smelling blood." However, the nature of business is not just to select the strongest but also the most virtuous. Without an ethical code and regulations, no company can be sustained. Even criminal organizations like the Mafia or the Japanese Yakuza are characterized by a clear and tight system of sacred internal values. The credibility of organizations is an asset that can be converted to financial value, and it can affect the credit line the organization may obtain from a bank as much as any other business attribute. Businesses in the diamond industry are an interesting example of international operations dealing with considerable sums of money, based entirely on trust and a handshake. In *Trust: The Social Virtues and the Creation of Prosperity* (1996), Fukuyama talks about "the radius of trust," the ability to create connections of trust with business competitors and potential partners, with suppliers and customers, emphasizing its importance for ensuring the business long-term success. A survey of multinational corporations by The Economist showed that they form networks of extensive alliances glued tightly together through trust. In the survey, the representatives of those corporations were asked how they managed people working in other countries over whom they had no direct control. "By trusting them," was one of the answers.

The influence of a trust-based environment is far-reaching when it comes to the workers. It has been proven that these workers will have a more positive attitude towards their workplace and co-workers, and will be more open to sharing information, as well as considerate to others when operating. If a person is to realize his full potential, he needs people to trust him and give him the necessary space to express himself; he needs to know that he can trust the organization's value system as well as that of his colleagues. People trust their team not only because of the organization's E.Q. but also because they believe in the existence of a shared social and ethical code.

An advanced organization is flexible and relies on freedom of action and on the independence of its workers, more than on constraining laws, rules and control. This orientation requires trust between the organization and the workers through understanding that it is the right way to mobilize workers and increase their motivation. Instead of a hierarchical system of employee-employer, connections resembling family ties are created; the worker will define himself more by his commitment than his position, so that his value system becomes a central, critical issue.

Our value system is one of the key systems for maintaining and preserving energy – personal energy and that of the organization and the team. When there is no value system, considerable energy leaks out of the teams because team members are preoccupied with their own self-defense and survival.

All companies and cultures whose value systems were maintained by coercion lost their ability to adjust to current reality and eventually lost their humanity in time. In his book *Trust: The Social Virtues and the Creation of Prosperity,* which analyzes the financial success of certain cultures, Francis Fukuyama concludes that throughout history there has been clear preference for cultures with a value system fostering social trust. He perceives the moral component as a central motif for social-economic success. According to Fukuyama, cultures with a low level of trust can succeed only temporarily. Societies whose rules are imposed from above, by the church or by a political party, do not manage to maturely implement their value system in the population. The collapse of social trust in Russia and other East European countries was the main cause for the failure of communism.

Mutual Trust & Respect (MTR)
Mutual trust and respect is a concept presented by Professor Ichak Adizes, who developed one of the most advanced management theories in the world. In this context, respect means that I recognize your right to have different opinions than I hold to and to express them. Trust means that I can rely on you, that you don't want or don't intend to hurt me, and that we share common values so we can work together even when we have differences of opinion. In effect, MTR is the definition of a mature value system that makes it possible for teams to deal with internal conflicts, crises and change. These are essential conditions for synergetic teams: In the absence of trust and respect, considerable energy leaks out for self-defense and survival. It is impossible to establish mutual trust and respect without a certain level of value judgment.

Family businesses
A notable example of how a value system contributes to business success is the success of family businesses. Studies show that family-owned businesses tend to survive for long periods and succeed in adapting to changes since they are based on family values and allow partners to trust one another in situations requiring functional flexibility.

A classic example of family values combined with business success is the Rothschild family. Members of the family were able to set up a successful global business network because each one of them knew that all the other centers in the world were run by members of the family with the same value system and commitment. The same goes for criminal organizations such as the Japanese Yakuza or the Italian Mafia. The Mafia began as a family business that gradually integrated members from the outside but maintained family values and continued to nurture its members and demand their full commitment and devotion.

In the past, there was also room for organizations that operated like competitive predators in a wild environment without an outward-turning value system. Such organizations don't have a set of values that helps them to act in certain situations, outwards or inwards. Simply put, these organizations have no morals. The absence of a coherent value system can be reflected in several ways: Sometimes the system presents a certain set of values inwards and a different one outwards; at times, one's word is no one's bond; and at times, the approach is modified according to one's own interest. In any case, an organization with no value system has little chance to last for a long time, and it might be dangerous for its environment as well as its own components.

Organizations with little or no V.Q. will be improved by setting up a value system in the organization and absorbing it. More and more organizations implement processes which have to do with the shaping of the value system as part of their vision statement. They refer to codes of conduct and values, such as contribution to the community, not just to business objectives. These organizations emphasize the family values of the founding family thus generating family-oriented identification with the organization.

In the framework of the organization, we'll try to create a correlation between the individuals' value systems and that of the organization. Many companies adopt an ethical code of values as their emblem, which the organization tries to instill in its workers. I have found that an organizational value system is erected and reinforced through rituals, myths and "heroic" stories communicated through training, workshops and vision statements.

It's in the organization's interest to create congruence between an individual's values and those of the organization. In situations of incongruence, when an individual works in an environment whose value system is incompatible with his own, he is likely to burn out and lose energy and will eventually leave the organization. The aspiration to create harmony is a two-way process in which the individual adopts the organization's values but the organization also adopts the individual's values in order to create a harmonious environment.

Statements characterizing the organization's V.Q.:

To what extent do the following statements characterize the organization?

- The organization's personnel feel personally committed to the goals of the organization.

- The organization operates by a culture of corporate value.

- The workers know the norms of the organization and identify with them.

- The workers care about the organization and are dedicated to it and to their jobs.

- The organization informs its workers of its values and required procedures.

- The organization operates through a value system that its personnel are required to adhere to.

- The organization scrupulously hires workers who have values and personal integrity.

- The organization trusts its workers and delegates authority.

- The organization trusts the integrity of its workers.

- The organization cultivates personal responsibility.

- The organization is scrupulously fair towards customers, workers and the environment.

- The organization demonstrates responsibility towards the environment and the community.

- The organization has a clear set of rules and regulations.

- There is mutual trust and respect in the organization.

Organizational C.Q.

We live in a period of constant change, and no organization – no matter how big and strong – will be able to survive without coping with change. As the organization's natural environment changes at a faster pace, its change and chaos quotient will have to be more advanced. The high-tech world is characterized by an environment of extremely fast change, which is why high-tech organizations need to maintain a particularly high change quotient. Government agencies or monopolies are organizations that can succeed with a less developed change quotient than that of high-tech organizations. Nonetheless, an organization whose C.Q. is low will not be able to handle changes and uncertainty, and there are plenty of those. An organization incapable of changing is a rigid, bureaucratic organization which will have great difficulties responding to its environment.

A manager who walks into the room announcing, "We are going to make some changes here," will immediately identify the level of the change quotients of his workers by their reactions, which can range from fear and panic to enthusiasm and lots of energy. Many questionnaires refer to flexibility and adjustment capacity, but there is nothing better than a person's life story with regard to his ability to deal with changes in the past to show his attitude to situations of change and his ways of operating throughout those changes. The interviewer would do well to find out whether change is perceived as an important formative event, significantly a positive one, or does change give rise to fear and insecurity. That which applies to a person's life is no less true of an organization. We can look at the way a person or an organization relates the changes they underwent, which world of concepts they associate change with, and what personal or organizational myths have sprung from change.

Adding terms like "management" and "chaos" looks contradictory since the first and foremost characteristic of chaos is its untamed nature. However, innovative approaches to management posit that the organization exists in a chaotic environment; therefore chaotic management methods are established. Such methods stress the importance of undefined activities without any predetermined limits or organizational hierarchy and, true to their definition, consecrate no particular framework. This type of management has proved itself in certain situations in the competitive world, especially in rapidly changing and competitive environments. Chaotic management is intended to enable the organization to operate in a chaotic environment without being hampered by organizational structures. According to this approach, the consultant's role is not to put the organization in order but to "air" it and allow chaos in.

Separate sections of a business organization can change at different rates, which is the source of intra-organizational conflicts. The need for synergetic teams which include people of various skills necessarily creates tensions connected with conflict. An attempt to resolve conflict by creating harmony means losing the uniqueness and the contributions of the different members of the team. Modern organizational approaches claim that conflict will always exist, so one should act to change the prevalent attitude towards it, to recognize its positive side and accept its existence.

Quite a few consulting processes in organizations are engaged in teaching "enjoy it" techniques, which include softening up the organization, knocking it off balance and initiating a certain measure of disorder and conflict by generating change and dealing with the fear it entails. In many ways, the business consultant introduces C.Q. into the organization believing that it is necessary for instilling a new spirit within the organization and for reaching remarkable achievements. Curiosity and courage are two crucial characteristics of successful organizations: curiosity to study the environment and courage to carry out changes in light of the changing reality.

A dramatic example of C.Q. development is offered in Tom Peters' book *The Tom Peters Seminar: Crazy Times Call for Crazy Organizations* (1995), which deals with the importance of the change quotient. Peters describes Oticon, one of the world's leading hearing aid manufacturers, which experienced difficulties when the market shrank. The company president decided to carry out some major changes, ushering the organization towards a C.Q. atmosphere, including its chaotic aspect. He did it both physically and ideologically: He tore down all the walls and partitions between rooms, changed job descriptions, removed all outward signs of hierarchy, and sold the office furniture to the workers at an auction, in order to dramatically demonstrate drastic change and chaos. All the workers' stuff was stowed away in light trolleys which were easily moved around the wide open space of the office when trying to find a new place to sit and work every day. He created a reality of constant organizational change. As a result, the company succeeded in eliminating the formal organization and the fixation on its patterns, turning it into a flexible, constantly changing organization. This advantage was reflected shortly in financial success and record profits.

This is the secret, and sometimes the undoing, of start-up companies – maximal flexibility and the ability to adjust to that which happens through rapid changes without any "sacred" patterns or processes.

Statements characterizing the organization's C.Q.:
To what extent do the following statements characterize the organization?

- The organization is "open-minded" and encourages change.

- The organization has a positive attitude towards change in work processes.

- The organization is curious, attracted to novelty and innovation.

- The organization easily engages in new and unfamiliar operations.

- The organization adjusts to new situations quickly and efficiently.

- The organization efficiently handles conflicts without interference in ongoing work.

- The organization has a flexible ability to handle demands and changing situations.

- The organization functions well in times of chaos, uncertainty and ambiguity.

- The organization efficiently performs several processes simultaneously.

- The organization does not flinch from taking risks.

Organizational S.Q.

More than any other factor, the S.Q. represents traditional management. Being a manager means managing by re-establishing order in organizational chaos by setting objectives, goals, plans, budgets, constraints, etc.

The concept known as **SMART,** which can be found in every business consultant's toolbox, defines the characteristics of goals and objectives for an individual, an organization or a manager in terms of S.Q., representing the full set of S.Q. behaviors. The initials of the model stand for **S**pecific, **M**easurable, **A**ttainable, **R**elevant and **T**ime-based. When all these factors are implemented, one can make a work plan with objectives for the individual or the organization.

Lack of order and method in the organization is a "disease" typical of quite a few start-up companies at their outset. An organization which has no system of rules and procedures will have difficulties keeping on schedule and distinguishing the essential from the superfluous and will waste a lot of energy "reinventing the wheel" time and again. The S.Q. is the variable providing the organization with method, process, and regulations for dealing and coping with different situations, efficiency and energy conservation. Organizations with no balance between their system and structure and their change quotients will find themselves stuck in the turmoil between fixation and rigidity, movement and change.

A great many computer geniuses, exceptionally imaginative and creative, do not manage to realize their potential because of a lack in their efficiency and system and structure. Many start-up companies failed when they were unable to translate their ideas into S.Q. systems. Anybody involved in a start-up is perfectly aware of the ruthlessness of time; an "avatar" of S.Q. As soon as a group of young people becomes a business, the pressure of meeting deadlines, budgets and objectives begins. That is the toughest and most painful lesson for many young people who jump into the business world.

Venture capitalists and investors examine the value of start-ups based not only on the originality of their ideas but also according to their ability to operate in an organized and structured manner to achieve their goals. Analysts assessing a company's value need accessible data they can look at. Even when the company model is not based on profit but on activity, there is still a need to present something measurable which can point to a trend (users, satisfaction, speed of performance, etc.). A start-up with no system and structure will not succeed in creating a reliable business model, nor will it manage to obtain the funds it requires. One of the solutions for young start-up companies is employing a professional manager to be in charge of integrating the order and system and structure in their framework.

The domain of system and structure development reflects most of the modern managerial methods that have been emerging from engineering mind-sets, such as Management by Objectives (MBO), Just-in-Time (JIT), Total Quality Management, Kaizen and Six Sigma. Most management methods in place between the 1960s and the 1980s dealt with developing system and structure in one form or another. This dimension's proximity to the left intelligence quotient clarifies why these content-oriented areas are connected with engineering-style management. System and structure development can also rely on external mechanisms that include computerized tools, management systems, performance tracking systems or managing meetings.

Deficiencies in the system and structure of the organization can be dealt with through personnel changes: hiring managers whose system and structure is high; by introducing well-ordered management methods like Management by Objectives or Total Quality Management and standardization; or by implementing computerized systems and software. A large variety of management software currently available on the market can help organizations incorporate method, order and stability.

Statements characterizing the organization's S.Q.:

To what extent do the following statements characterize the organization?

- The organization keeps to a clearly formulated plan of operation that includes defined and measurable objectives.

- The organization has detailed and organized performance plans.

- The organization operates in a well-ordered, organized and methodical manner.

- The organization makes clear distinctions between the essential and the superfluous.

- The organization puts an emphasis on efficient performance.

- Processes are clearly elaborated.

- Communication is clear, focused and businesslike.

- Procedures and processes are well known.

- The organization's structure is formal, efficient and well understood by the workers.

- The organization's priorities are clearly defined and are characterized by its simplicity and thoroughness.

- The organization operates in keeping with clear standards.

- Processes in the organization are clear and defined.

- Tasks are performed by a method which is consistent or has another internal logic.

Organizational I.Q.-L

The organization's I.Q.-L determines the organization's level of intelligence, how well it learns from experience and makes logical decisions, if it has its very own SMART doctrine, professionalism and professional knowledge. An organization which has its own method and doctrine is likely to operate smartly. An organization with no I.Q.-L does not learn from experience, does not operate according to plan and does not base its activity on knowledge. In this day and age, such an organization will not manage to survive for long. There are organizations that suffer from "cognitive degeneration"; they gradually lost their ability to think, analyze and learn from experience, and they repeat past mistakes time and again.

These organizations can be assisted by investing in analyzing situations, drawing conclusions and through group learning. In recent years, many organizations have been investing in their knowledge management, a process that includes creating knowledge, accumulating knowledge, structuring knowledge and securing knowledge. Some organizations employ knowledge managers whose job is to create different activities for elevating the I.Q.-L level of the organization and its members. Certain management theories, especially Peter Senge's, as described in *The Fifth Discipline: The Art and Practice of the Learning Organization* (1995), discuss the "learning organization" as a place in which people "continuously reveal how they create their reality, and how changeable it is in their hands." Just as it applies to the individual, a learning organization is one that develops its cognitive muscle capacity.

This domain sees constant development of "organizational thinking agents," algorithms for information processing and for analysis of organizational databases enabling the organization to make intelligent decisions, and programs capable of learning from the past which remember accumulated experience and draw intelligent conclusions.

Statements characterizing the organization's I.Q.-L:
To what extent do the following statements characterize the organization?

- The organization operates intelligently.

- The organization learns from experience and draws conclusions.

- The organization is thoroughly professional and keeps up-to-date.

- The management team is highly professional.

- The organization invests in the development of the professional capabilities and skills of its workers.

- The organization expects high-level performance, both in quality and professionalism.

- The organization provides the required tools for the professional performance of tasks.

- The organization provides tools for learning and professional training.

- Decision-making processes are based on the logical analysis of options.

- The organization maintains processes for drawing conclusions and transferring information.

- The organization operates tools for safekeeping organizational information.

- The organization is considered an outstanding expert in its field.

- The organization implements methodical research for learning purposes.

- The organization has processes for analyzing information and processing data.

- The organization employs data processing and analysis in its decision making.

Organizational I.Q.-R

The organization's right intelligence quotient shows how innovative and creative it is, the extent to which it allows thinking out of the box and how open it is to discussion and diverse opinions. An organization with no I.Q.-R will lack imagination and creativity; it will be stuck in a routine that leaves no room for intuition. In our global, changing world organizations whose creativity has dried up are condemned to declining profit margins. Profitability solely based on streamlining processes tends to erode because of fierce competition. Significant profitability derives from invention and innovation, not from routine. In this respect, there is no doubt that a firm like Apple is an instructive example of the importance of the creativity quotient in organizational and business success.

Apple's legendary CEO, Steve Jobs, demonstrated the importance of the connection between organizational I.Q.-R and individuals endowed with creative thinking skills. Organizational I.Q.-R can also be created through individuals possessing such skills on the condition that the organization knows how to foster them and makes it possible for them to express themselves within the organization and realize their original creativity. When congruence appeared between Steve Jobs, an exceptionally creative leader, and Apple, a company that allowed the space needed for such creativity, the magic that turned Apple into a superstar appeared.

Methods and tools have recently been developed for the encouragement of creativity of the organization and its workers: professional teams, creativity development workshops, guided imagination, connecting with one's intuition, developing objectives and more. The organization or alternatively its organizational consultant should expose workers to the stimuli of innovative thinking, invention and "thinking outside the box."

Shoshana Zuboff of Harvard University argues in In the Age of the Smart Machine that companies that do not accept intuition will not survive. She also looked into ways and means to improve intuitive thinking capacity in organizations. A method that achieved great results was for workers and managers to rotate among different departments. Those among them who had participated in the rotation found that their intuitive thinking had improved.

Statements characterizing the organization's I.Q.-R:
To what extent do the following statements characterize the organization?

- The organization encourages innovation and creativity.

- The organization appreciates and allows intuitive thinking.

- The organization encourages new ideas and thinking outside the box.

- The working environment encourages initiative and putting forth new ideas.

- The organization dedicates time and resources for improvement and innovation.

- The organization puts an emphasis on research and development.

- The organization's atmosphere is one of innovation and boldness.

- The organization encourages sophisticated, crafty thinking.

- The organization is open to new ideas and implements them.

- The organization is considered innovative and creative.

- The organization has its unconventional way of solving problems.

- The organization is regarded as a trailblazer in its field.

- The organization efficiently identifies business opportunities.

- The organization seeks to find new ways of doing things.

Organizational A.Q.

The aspiration quotient and the organization's vision refer to the measure of the organization's "hunger" and "satiety." Does it aspire to be an empire or a shop, to become global or remain local? Does it have a sense of purpose and mission beyond its very existence? Is there a spiritual element too? Adherence to the organization's objectives has to be balanced by the change quotient, that is, the objectives must be changed in accordance with changing reality.

The aspiration quotient is one of the key characteristics of the organization's success: An organization devoid of vision and direction has no chance of becoming an "Ace." In *Built to Last,* an in-depth analysis of 18 successful organizations that survived for many years, Collins and Porras stress the importance of vision as a key factor in success.

An organization that lacks vision needs a complex process that requires its leaders to commit to a shared vision. The task of building a vision has to be led by the organization's managers and proprietors, but it must be adopted at all levels of the organization. Connection to vision should result from individuals' identification and enthusiasm.

Statements characterizing the organization's A.Q.:
To what extent do the following statements characterize the organization?

- The organization strives for excellence.

- The organization operates in accordance with high standards.

- The organization nurtures achievement and ambition among its workers.

- The organization and its managers set the highest, most ambitious objectives for themselves.

- The workers share the owners' ambition.

- The vision by which the organization operates is clearly defined.

- The organization's sense of purpose goes beyond day-to-day activity.

- The organization and its managers are resolved and determined to attain their mission.

- The workers are familiar with the company's vision and identify with it.

- The organization's strategy is clear to all its workers.

- The workers take pride in the organization being special.

- The organization leads its workers in accordance with vision and a clear picture of the future.

- The organization strives to be the best and most successful in its field.

- The workers feel that they are partners in the organization's mission.

- The organization seeks challenges and copes with them.

Organizational development through balancing

Without a clear assessment of the organization's SILVER ACE status, we may develop the wrong dimensions, or develop a certain dimension without its proper balance. Development of system and structure without flexibility could bring about a rigid system of laws and rules that would make the organization stagnate. The opposite process which organizational consultants are sometimes tempted to set in motion is developing interpersonal sensitivity in an organization devoid of procedures and control systems.

In an interview, William Green, at the time the chairman and CEO of the global consulting firm Accenture, described the managerial characteristics that led to the success of the company: "I needed to beef up my and the organization's analytic skills (I.Q.-L) because I'm an instinctive and intuitive kind of guy."

E.Q. and V.Q. – between sensitivity and values

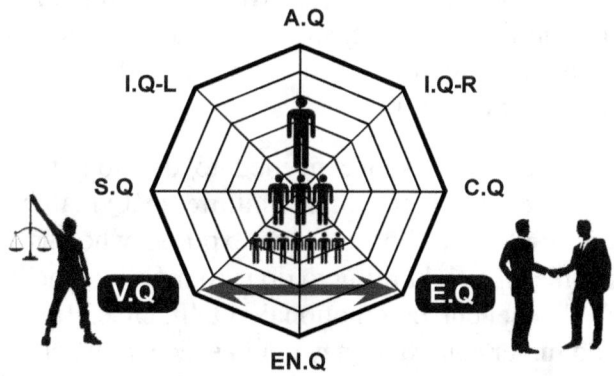

The proper functioning and collaboration between these two quotients necessarily require a subtle balance for an organization that strives to succeed. Disequilibrium in either direction could be problematic; exaggerating on the side of interpersonal sensitivity could give rise to over-sensitivity impacting the organization's welfare and efficiency. Conversely, principles without the balancing sensitivity would make the organization more rigid and less humane. Common tension between human resources and the budgeting department or between welfare and accounting is healthy. In order to sustain balance, energy must flow from right to left, from emotions to rules, otherwise all interpersonal sensitivity will be blocked and restrained. It is very easy for organizations to make processes and rules that inhibit the emotional domain, but such lack of equilibrium takes a heavy organizational toll; it will become an organization with no heart, without the energy produced by emotional connection.

A very large corporation decided to develop its directors' E.Q. in the training sessions its workers undergo. It invited leading, experienced psychologists to conduct workshops for personal, emotional and interpersonal openness, but the results were catastrophic. People voted with their feet; one group said something, and the other defended itself against what its members perceived consciously or unconsciously as threatening. The workshop was completely out of touch with the organization's culture. In SILVER ACE terms, it was an attempt to develop the E.Q. element without first checking if its balancing factors could sustain it. The development of a certain quotient without a complementary foundation between its balances is likely to lead to an unhealthy situation of disequilibrium.

Excessive openness without the right foundation is an erroneous and dangerous objective. Consultants who see interpersonal sensitivity as an end in itself without first probing the organization's situation can be likened to those who apply a medicine called "group dynamics" without having first diagnosed the patient's real need. Interpersonal openness is not an end in itself. It is true that most super Aces have high E.Q.'s, but it rests upon the solid foundation of a value system and logical thinking, upon clear "do and don't" rules. An organization cannot push its people to elevate their inner E.Q. if the organization itself doesn't possess the right cultural value system.

The organization referred to above needed to develop its E.Q. only if its corporate value system and corporate culture (V.Q.) allowed it. Clearly, a sensible person would not choose to be exposed where it could hurt him eventually. Sometimes the right thing to do is to mobilize the logical cognitive side (I.Q.-L) for the benefit of emotional intelligence. In other words, the participants would understand that they could succeed in achieving their goals through openness and cooperation. Only then can there be a will to learn; the importance of openness itself is not enough. Concurrently, the value system that ought to be developed should assure the participants that their openness will not be turned against them.

C.Q. and S.Q. – change and chaos versus order and efficiency

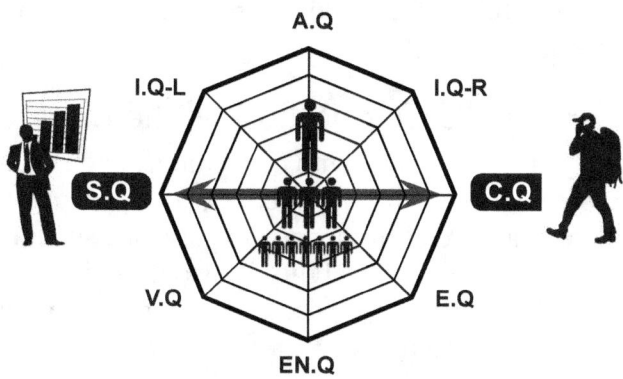

In an organization, this is the management axis. The manager's role, like that of a captain of a ship is to lead from change to stability and efficiency.

Every organization has units whose function is to express the C.Q. and others that have to express the S.Q. The tension between them is healthy and should exist. This is the classic relationship between development and marketing on the one hand and accounting and production on the other. Each of these cultures has its own language, values and approach. Each of these extremities threatens the other. This axis is the meeting place between harbingers of chaos and the initiators of order, between those who yearn for conflicts to be resolved and those who believe there will always be conflicts. The synergy that the organization should aspire to is not the minimizing of tension and gaps but an equilibrium between the extremities, when both system and structure and change quotients will be present most of the time.

The difficulty in the encounter of C.Q. and S.Q. is identical to that between people speaking different languages or worse, those who mistakenly believe they understand the other's language through their own world of concepts. One of the ways to create organizational synergy is to have everyone develop the knowledge, sensitivity and understanding of the different languages of the organization – to develop the balance of every worker.

Ned Herrmann, known for having developed a comprehensive brain dominance system (see "The SILVER ACE model"), specialized in the creation of complementary language-learning workshops. He taught S.Q. people (accounting, administration, purchasing) to play with clay or mud, draw with their hands and body, to express themselves through dance and so on.

He connected them to chaos, diversity and change. Conversely, he taught C.Q. people (marketing, entrepreneurs, developers) to produce work plans, time management charts, Excel spreadsheets and so on. Effective teams were thus created when people with high S.Q. and others with high C.Q. were able to join forces and complement each other.

Movement between C.Q. and S.Q. in the organization

A start-up is usually an organization with no hierarchy or clear task distribution, but it is also an organization with much enthusiasm. Despite the importance the change quotient is accorded in modern society, one should remember that between one change and the next, stability is also necessary. He who changes all the time doesn't change at all. The solution is not in restraining C.Q. but in developing and reinforcing S.Q.

When I investigated the characteristics of Aces, I met with one successful entrepreneur, among others. I learned from him the irrepressible need of entrepreneurs, especially those in high-tech, to be flexible and have a high C.Q. He told me about something that had happened to him one morning on his way to work. While he was listening to an economic news report on the BBC about a new development in Japan, he understood that the product his company had been working on for over six months was no longer relevant. He got to his office, assembled the development team and informed them, "We're off the project! We have to make a significant change of direction in light of the news report I have just heard." This is an example of the C.Q. full-blast. "So what did you do then?" I asked him, and he explained, "We immediately prepared new work plans, we changed our schedules, we defined new objectives and we set up organized and integral processes." That was S.Q. at its best.

At the organizational level, when the system and structure is too high, it will have a completely contradictory effect. There are many organizations whose high S.Q. level blinded them and prevented them from noticing the changes occurring around them. Numerous giant corporations went bankrupt after they had failed to read the map of their environment and didn't cultivate the flexibility required by the competitive conditions. When order and method exceed their instigators, the organization becomes a slave of the method it developed. This is the source of bureaucratic monsters which had defined rules of system and structure but have long forgotten why these rules had been set in the first place. When system and structure become the essence, the organization gradually becomes cumbersome and eventually too heavy – more clerks, more paperwork until it becomes an anachronistic fossilized dinosaur.

Chance management is another very good example of the relation and movement between the S.Q and the C.Q. It is an approach of transitioning individuals, teams, and organizations to a desired future state by better leveraging of the management axis and the chance axis towards a positive outcome.

Management and Chance are positioned on opposite sides of the chart (S.Q. and C.Q), and are seemingly in contradiction, though ideally in practice one has the capability to act on both.

One way of mastering chance management is through the management axis. Setting a top-of-mind purpose and framework that when confronted with a chance event, small or large, allows us to take a moment to "zoom out," spot the chance in time, and then zoom back in to reflect on the desired plan by getting the details right and improve the return on chance. In addition, our aim is to be able, despite having a set framework, not to narrow our choices only to that framework. We should leave room for new possibilities that are not necessarily in line with the mother plan and be open to a new chance that could improve the plan.

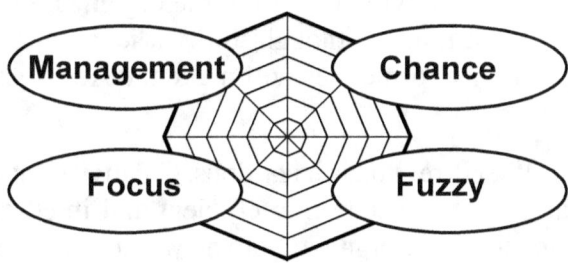

Even with the lack of a set framework, an unexpected and unplanned-for chance event can be transformed into good fortune if it is executed using the management axis skills. Chance happens to all, but turning chance into opportunity is the reward of the few – those who have a chance and take it.

Between I.Q.-R and I.Q.-L – balancing in the cognitive level of the organization

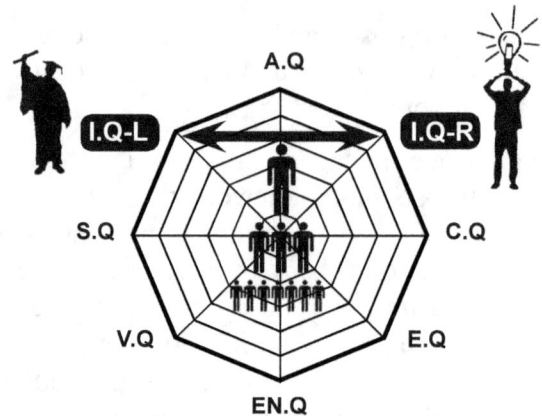

Movement between right-sided and left-sided thinking is the existential basis of modern organizations. Creativity, rendering the organization with uniqueness and the ability to turn a random thought into an idea which can be put into action according to a set of principles will make the Ace organization win the competition.

Lack of balance in either direction is hazardous. Creativity, intuition, originality and invention that do not translate into efficient and intelligent performance endanger the existence of the organization, as would the opposite situation of lots of highly systematic, scientific and linear thinking without any creative originality.

Balance is also connected to the power relationships within the organization – between representatives of the right side and those of the left side, between engineers and programmers against marketing people and developers. The more we develop each quotient on the axis, the wider the disparity and the stronger the tension: We should not revoke it under any circumstances by closing the gap but by managing and balancing the tension.

Counterbalances in the organization

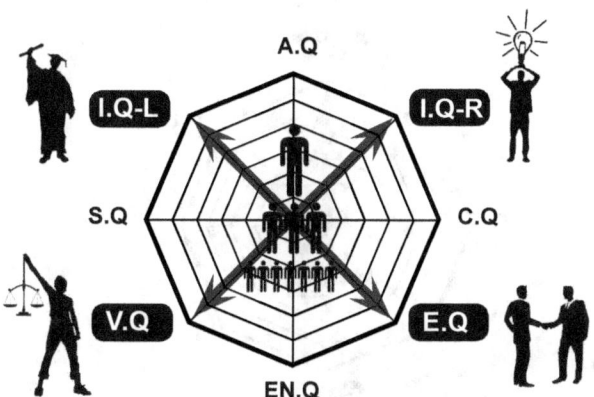

1. E.Q – I.Q.-L

The organization's emotional intelligence (sensitivity to others, empathy, love) and its logical, scientific, intellectual and calculating aspect must be balanced.

Lack of balance in one direction will cause the organization to become cold and alienated towards others, its workers and customers, whereas lack of balance in the other direction will render the organization sensitive and empathetic yet without any clear measurable results.

2. V.Q – I.Q.-R

Balance is absolutely indispensable between the organization's value system and its creativity and iconoclastic quotient.

Lack of balance in one direction will make the organization creative yet without any rules, iconoclastic. Without a value system, such an organization would be dangerous. Lack of balance in the other direction, that is, a value system of rules and laws but no intuitive creativity the organization will become rigid up to freezing point.

Balance in the vertical axis: A.Q. – EN.Q.

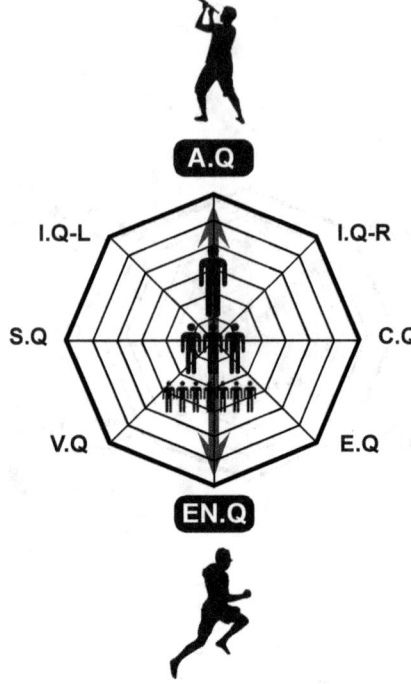

The balance of an organization's spiritual energy (A.Q.) with its survival energy, strength and power (EN.Q.).

An organization with a high EN.Q. which has a solid and stable business structure, profitability and high cash flow, strength and power but no vision, no sense of purpose or spiritual energy resembles a powerful dinosaur on the brink of extinction.

However, even an organization with a strong sense of purpose, vision and spiritual energy that lacks a strong body to carry it will not manage ultimately to survive and stand on its own and will need the support of another body.

This connection between business and social mission, between profitability and ideals has been gaining ground in the last few years as has the recognition that giving only financial support to an organization in crisis without any vision or mission would eventually turn out to be completely useless.

Organizational energy centers and the crystal principle

An optimal organization will have "four aspects":

Strong – the physical level. The organization's business and financial structure is stable and strong.

Warm – the emotional/social level. Sensitivity, empathy, trust and responsibility.

Intelligence – the cognitive level. A creative, knowledgeable organization functioning as per its own axiom.

Vision – the spiritual level. Vision, purpose, inspiration, ambition.

Organizations capable of creating four clear foci for the above mentioned needs will be more stable and resistant. Organizations investing in the development of only one will not survive for long.

An organization is just like an individual oriented to create optimal energy and thus must implement the "crystal principle." According to this principle, the four main energy foci on the energy transformation scale, the physical, emotional/social, mental and spiritual levels must sustain direct and reciprocal relations. In the structure of a crystal, each focus must be in direct relation with the others, and each center must take the other three into account.

Figuratively speaking, any idea evolving from one focus must be checked and seen by all the other foci; any organizational development or invention must be in congruence with the rest. Any business idea should undergo a reality check on the one hand and a test of vision on the other. My advice to any organization and any person: Do not adopt any idea or orientation before putting it to the test of the other three aspects. Organizations that have taken a certain path or adopted a certain process even though they were incompatible with one of the foci realized very soon they were in a state of severe energy drain.

The organizational human energy reactor

from **Ladder** ⟶ to **crystal**

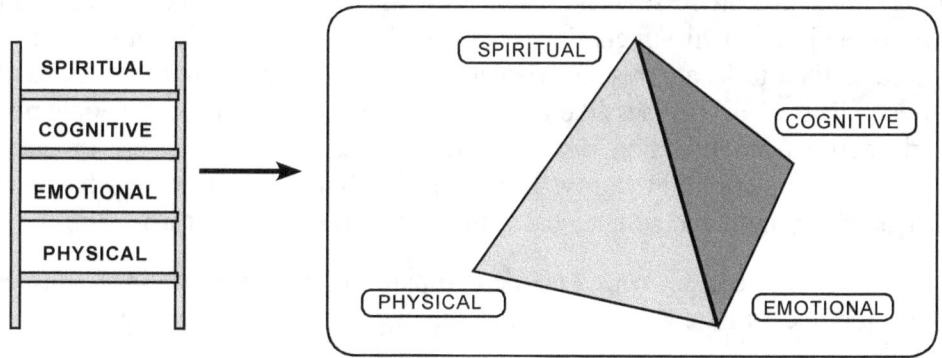

Recruitment, assessment & compensation
the SILVER ACE way

The secret of successfully recruiting and preserving workers lies in having congruence of the SILV.R ACE characteristics of the person with the process and working environment. The person's characteristics should not be in contrast with the processes and environment in which he operates. Having defined the SILVER ACE characteristics and those of the job and the person most suited for it, we have also defined the work environment suitable for him as well as the way he would be recruited and preserved. In this context, no contradictions can be created.

The parallel between the worker's characteristics and those of the organization and its recruitment applies to all aspects. Do not try to recruit accountants through a colorful and creative process that will attract the wrong people. However, one cannot recruit highly energetic people without investing energy in the process itself. People who inspire enthusiasm in others need situations and actions to excite them. We are attracted to energetic people and energy processes. Therefore if, for example, we look for enthusiastic salespeople, we need to excite all the suppliers involved in the recruitment process, such as manpower firms and assessment experts, so that their enthusiasm will infect the candidates.

Energy recharging should continue even after the worker is hired. A worker required to sustain a high level of energy in his work will not be capable of doing so in an environment which is low on energy and depressing, let alone in an energy-guzzling environment. In order to preserve workers, the organization must invest in creating and building up enthusiasm, optimism and a positive approach. It is important to provide the workers, as early as the recruiting stage and the conversation about their terms of employment, with what we look for in the process.

It is impossible to recruit people endowed with high emotional intelligence (E.Q.) through alienating processes lacking empathy, and there is no chance of preserving such people in an environment devoid of E.Q. If we need people with high S.Q., focused on their tasks and results oriented, the right corporate environment has to be methodical, clear, businesslike and results oriented as well. Such people need clearly defined remuneration systems and work processes. They are in search of fairness, simplicity and clarity. Therefore their recruitment process has to be efficient, transparent and simple, just as the employment contract with them.

I was called in to consult with a textile company on improving their recruitment system for selecting and preserving machine operators, many of whom left the company shortly after having been hired. When I analyzed the job, I found that the job requirements were very simple and didn't require sophisticated thinking of any kind and that the job was suitable to people looking for job security and uncomplicated work. As we analyzed the resignation processes, we discovered that there were those who left after the first week, whereas others left after three months. Further analysis showed that this was a classic case of an integration process incongruent with the skills required for the job. All the candidates came from Arab villages in the West Bank, and they had a variety of skills and abilities. The integration process required on-the-job training by the supervisor in charge of the production line with the machines the new worker was to operate. In order to get acquainted with the situation, the rural worker had to have high adaptability to the noisy and strange industrial environment and show his ability to learn and quickly understand the training given by an impatient supervisor tired of having to repeat and explain things to workers who then quit. At this early stage, those who found it difficult quit or were fired, and those who stayed were young men of high I.Q.-L and C.Q., who proved to be quick, intelligent, talented, resourceful and highly capable of changing and adapting. However, those workers would leave after three months because the job itself didn't interest them and because they had other opportunities elsewhere. In fact, the suitable candidates for the job were those who saw it as challenging and those who did not easily adapt to the outside world, those exact workers who were compelled to flee from an integration process that was incongruent with the SILVER ACE of the qualified candidate.

Clearly, changes had to be made by establishing a new integration process that corresponded with the skills of the desired person: learning slowly, step by step, becoming familiar with the environment. Offering appropriate training and integration would help them stay because the job matched their abilities. For these workers, the job allows for the full use of their abilities rather than wasting them. With a different integration process, through the implementation of an external training unit allowing time to learn step by step, change decreased drastically, which ensured the suitability of such processes to the desired worker's SILVER ACE. Ignoring this is like a manager who hires salespeople who are good at manipulating customers but who states that he finds direct, honest and reliable reports to be of utmost importance.

The image of the organizational SILVER ACE

The image of the organization's SILVER ACE represents how the organization is perceived by its people, and it is not an objective assessment. An outstanding organization is constantly working on developing its eight organizational muscles/quotients and is constantly examining the bodies responsible for the quotients and their status in relation to the rest.

In order to have an organizational map, one should fill in on the SILVER ACE map the score obtained for each quotient on the SILVER ACE based on the characteristics listed in each section. In addition, one can consult the SILVER ACE organizational questionnaire and its analysis, available on the book site.

It is also possible to draw a joint map of the team, the department or management in order to see how people in the organization assess it in terms of the model's characteristics.

In sessions with managers, it is recommended to occasionally fill out the organization's SILVER ACE directly on the map.

We used to put up a large poster of the SILVER ACE; the managers and those workers who were already familiar with the concepts were asked to place stickers on the map to indicate their own perception of the organization. The image obtained provides significant information on the organization and its employees:

How is the organization perceived by its people in terms of different indexes?

Which are the strong or weak points of a given organization?

On what issues do members' evaluations of the organization differ?

Which groups exist in the organization?

Where are there significant gaps between balances and in which direction?

Who is responsible for the different quotients?

In comparison with a previous evaluation (if there is one), is there any improvement?

Energy-oriented management = "Holistic management"

Energy is dynamic and just like a car battery it has to be charged constantly. I have learned that the key to success lies in recharging energy in each of the different levels of the SILVER ACE. A person or an organization wishing to succeed should look for ways to recharge their energy in physical, mental, emotional and spiritual terms. This understanding lies at the basis of most organizational workshops. When you see a team coming back from a workshop, the most conspicuous thing is the increase in the participants' energy levels. The workshop can focus on topics connected with strategy, vision, cooperation or time management, it doesn't matter what exactly. In any case, the participants come back filled with new energies for action and change.

Using this approach, we made a variety of tools and methods for developing the organizational SILVER ACE, such as "Ace Workshop," aimed at elevating a person's energy level in all dimensions. We set the replenishment of energy and the health of the organizational body as our central goal, more important than achieving other objectives. The participants confirmed that after the workshop they found they could solve problems they hadn't even discussed during the workshop, which was clear proof that opening up "obstructions" to energy flow generates adequate energy balance between the different elements of the organization and its management.

The organization itself, apart from its executives, is an entity that requires energy balance. An organization needs physical energy which is expressed through infrastructure and financial capacity. It also requires cognitive energy, work methods and procedures. Interpersonal energy is expressed through relationships between management and the team, between the employees themselves, and finally between the organization, its suppliers and customers. The organization also has its spirit and soul expressed through vision and mission. The "Ace Workshop" deals with all these different aspects.

The SILVER ACE perceives energy transformation as the basis of all activity. Success is thus a function of the difference between levels of energy generated for the benefit of success and worn-out energy. The main message here is that it is worthwhile to go from resource management to organizational energy management. A meeting planned in accordance with a precise schedule will not be useful if it lacks constructive energy, or worse, if the meeting actually consumes energy.

The management of people must be energy oriented. The organization has to strive for every single worker to make full use of his abilities, as this will make full use of the entire organization's SILVER ACE. The manager's role is to push employees to make full use of their abilities and attain maximal levels of energy. In this type of management the individual and the organization suit each other, just as the individual is suited to the job, which gave rise to the concept of "people management." This is a holistic approach that perceives the organization and the individual as a single system with common interests.

Holistic management characteristics:

- In-depth knowledge of the SILVER ACE potential of every worker.

- Understanding personal vision and mission.

- Transition from exploiting to bringing out the worker's potential and making full use of it.

- Making the structures and job descriptions of the organization more flexible in order to make full use of potential.

- The manager as partner and supporter of individual development.

- An organization that integrates peer management will provide its workers with support systems and reasons to develop all of the organization's energy centers, such as:

    * **Physical** – a gym, which is a way to get out of our comfort zones.

    * **Emotional/Social** – a room designed for interpersonal encounters, workshops, building trust and mutual respect.

    * **Cognitive** – rooms for thinking, libraries and information centers, a room for brainstorming and creativity.

    * **Spiritual** – a room for meditation, relaxing music, a place for reflection.

Be the ACE you are!!!

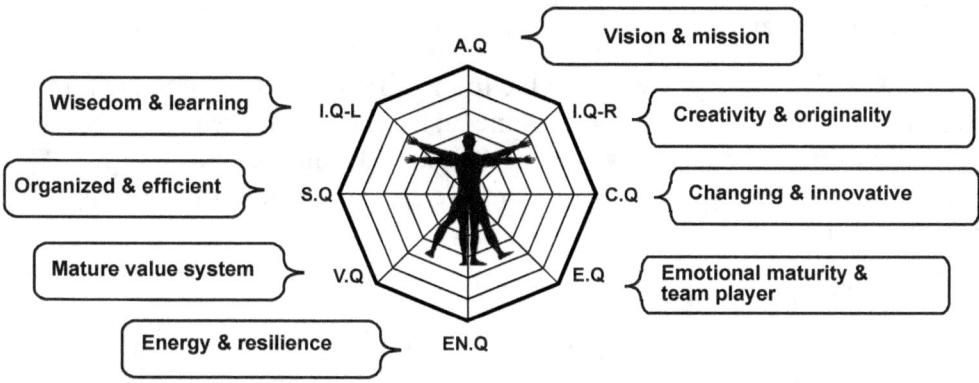

Developing one's SILVER ACE potential to the maximum is every person's mission in life.

Individual exercises

"I don't try to dance better than anyone else. I only try to dance better than myself."

Mikhail Baryshnikov

The 21st century, with the ever-growing competition between humans and computers, requires humans to aspire to being who they really are, to express the variety of their capacities, and to develop their potential to the fullest.

Humans strive by nature to locate and exhaust their various capacities and potential. People may be Aces of different sizes and brilliance, but it is the duty of each one to realize one's very own Ace. Those who are true to themselves and their origins will succeed and realize their potential.

Successful people manage their resources and realize their projects. They invest every effort and resource necessary in order to attain their objective; they muster their maximum energies with their passion for doing; moreover, and this may be all the more true nowadays, they are flexible and adaptable, and welcome change as they understand the opportunity it holds. They also have values and interpersonal sensitivity. Therefore, in order to be the real you, you should be able to bring together these different worlds – spirit, emotion, intellect and matter, creativity and wisdom, flexibility and order, sensitivity and values.

The Individual SILVER ACE map

In Appendix 1, you will find a diagram on which you can sketch an individual SILVER ACE map.

Assisted by this map, you will be able to identify your strong points and your weak ones; which dimensions are balanced; in which ones are there gaps; what your natural tendencies are; what your position would be in a SILVER ACE team; which training and development are recommended for realizing your potential to its fullest.

Personal assessment

The SILVER ACE is a conceptual model not a diagnostic one, which is why there are many valid and reliable tests for some of the different quotients (such as the I.Q.-L) but not for others (such as the energy quotient or the change quotient). There is not yet a standard set of SILVER ACE tests; for the moment there is only a small collection of tests for the different quotients. Nonetheless, we can draw an individual map based on one's personal self-evaluation, which even though subjective and lacking objective standard scores, is valuable as a picture of how the person perceives himself.

When I first started as an occupational psychologist, I believed in the power of tests – I almost worshipped them. I found it extraordinary that by asking a person all sorts of strange questions, and finally adding up, subtracting and calculating the data, one can reach some conclusions about that person's personality and abilities. One day, I was introduced to a new test in occupational psychology (out of respect, I will not mention its name). The test was about 500 questions long and it took a long time to complete. Once you coded the answers, you could sort them to different domains and obtain a diagram with multiple indicators about the person's occupational profile.

Mirona Greenberg, the founder of the Adam Institute and one of the originators of occupational psychology in Israel, a wise and experienced professional, suggested something that at the time seemed revolutionary to me. "Let's give it a try," she said, "instead of giving the person the test itself, let's give him the final result page of the occupational parameters, we'll add a few words of explanation and ask him to fill out the final result himself, without this whole tedious and complex process." To my amazement, I discovered that in most cases we obtained the same results. In most cases, people knew about themselves exactly what we were trying to learn about them through devious ways. So we simply asked and they simply answered.

The Power of Gaps

The drawback of subjective evaluation lies in the inaccuracy of comparisons; to compare those who "elevate" and those who "demean," those who think that a grade of 7 out of 10 is one befitting gods, and those who see a 6 as a crushing failure. Its strength lies in the gaps within the very same world of concepts. The authentic significant information is in the gaps appearing in the way the person refers to himself. When a person whose average is 5.8 grades himself as 6.8 or 4.8 in a certain domain, he indicates a significant gap in his world of concepts. For example, a below average C.Q. indicates that the person perceives his ability to change as a weak point. For this reason, we suggest drawing the person's subjective average line on the SILVER map and then examine the different scores obtained.

The truth is in the gaps:

1. **A gap in a person's personal general average** indicates the subject's weak and strong points according to his own perception of himself.

2. **Gaps in the balances**: The model emphasizes the different balance systems through six pairs of balances. Unbalanced pairs indicate problematic areas that require development, nurturing or partnership.

Sketching the individual map

There are two ways to self-evaluate in order to draw the individual SILVER ACE:

1. **Directly:** Perform a direct evaluation of the score for each quotient. Refer to each quotient while examining the guiding statements listed at the end of each quotient and honestly determine the score that genuinely represents you.

2. **By means of the questionnaire** available on the website: WWW.THESILVERACE.COM/Q

Analyzing the individual SILVER ACE map (see Appendix 1)

1. **How does it seem? What does it look like? What is the meaning of its shape?**

2. **Gaps compared with the average**:

   What are the strong points? – The gap above the general average.

   What are the weak points? – The gap below the general average.

3. **Gaps between balances:**

   Examine the six pairs of balances. Which ones are balanced and where do you find gaps? How big are the gaps and in which direction?

Developing Balances

People tend to stay in the comfort zone of their skills. Those who have a dominant advantage tend to maintain it and keep developing it. "When all you have is a hammer, everything looks like a nail," as Maslow said. Humans tend to further develop what is already developed because this is where they get the most reinforcement and encouragement. You should remember that if you develop only your stronger leg, you will continue to limp!

The SILVER ACE model puts the emphasis on the importance of developing the complementing counterbalances. This is the only way to truly become an Ace. Developing the counterbalances not only enables a person to be whole and holistic, but almost paradoxically enables the dominant side to develop more. Nature is not interested in creatures with disproportionate abilities, and the more a certain ability grows disproportionately, the more difficult it becomes to continue developing. Nature will not allow the right hand to grow regardless of the size of the left hand. This is why one should not be surprised that the development of balancing quotients does away with blockages even on the dominant side.

THE SILVER ACE GYM

Developing the quotients – rooms for developing aptitude

The potential of every muscle or organ in our body is a genetic given, but realizing it depends on the individual.

The eight dimensions of the SILVER ACE are like the eight muscles required for succeeding in the occupational world of the 21st century. It is not possible for every person to nurture all eight dimensions of the model, and sometimes it may be preferable to make up for any lack through synergetic teamwork, a process which reinforces the SILVER A.E.

In order to develop physical fitness, one has to identify the weak muscles and see that they are developed. For that purpose, gyms offer various equipment that makes it possible to set an individual training program catering to individual needs. You can train according to those individual strong and weak points and concentrate on the weaker muscles, those insufficiently developed because of our tendency to stay in the comfort zone of our strong muscles. It is also necessary to dedicate internal and external space on which we should focus in order to develop other aptitudes, not physical ones, with different accessories, pleasant atmosphere, music and different training techniques.

This is what we call **"The SILVER ACE gym."**

We can picture the facilities as eight different training rooms on **five floors**:

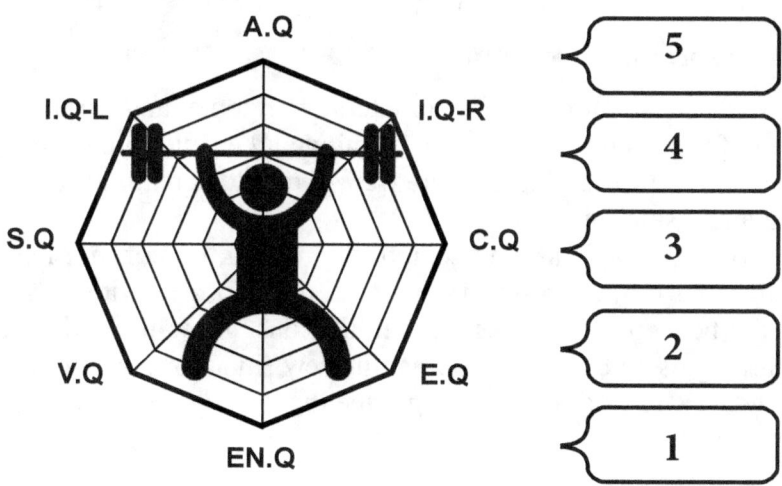

A.Q.

Gym for developing the A.Q.
Build your own vision and mission, strive for the summit!

This room is where we try to connect to what is above and beyond us – sitting and meditating, listening to celestial music, watching the sunset, clearing our heads of noises and listening to the silence, reflecting on spiritual matters, pondering over personal vision and comprehending what our aspirations mean, what is our commitment to achieve them.

- What are we most passionate and enthusiastic about?

- What is our life's mission?

- What mark would we care to leave behind?

- What are our dreams? What would we wish to realize, given the opportunity?

- What kind of new future would we like to create? What is the meaning of our existence?

I.Q.-R ☞

Gym for developing the I.Q.-R
Be creative, original and intuitive!

This is where we should exercise our lateral, horizontal and parallel thinking – the sort of thinking that opens up the mind and enables movement without searching for solutions. This is where we will develop creativity, associations, intuition and visual thinking.

In this room, we shall take up sculpting, drawing, humor, music, dancing, being silly and brainstorming in order to develop creativity and thinking outside the box, free ourselves from inhibitions, allow uncritical affection, break paradigms and patterns, to imagine new situations, train our intuition, learn how to listen and rely on our gut feelings.

I.Q.-L ☞

Gym for developing the I.Q.-L

Be wise, logical, knowledgeable learners!

Here we'll develop vertical, logical and linear thinking. We shall practice mental exercises, problem solving and analysis. We shall expand our knowledge and learning, we shall try solving all sorts of logical problems, we will read encyclopedias and surf the internet. We shall do crossword puzzles, Sudoku, trivia or mathematical exercises, we shall adopt tools and methods in order to draw conclusions and make decisions.

C.Q. ☞

Gym for developing the C.Q.

Have courage for change and curiosity for diversity!

Fear of change and uncertainty can be paralyzing. We shall try to be conscious of this fear and cope with it. One can get help through classic psychological therapy, self-awareness workshops, rock climbing, or getting out of one's comfort zone. Trying to befriend uncertainty on several domains concurrently can also help. We shall learn to enjoy the "roller coaster" adventure of change, and we shall find that any change carries with it a challenging and exciting opportunity.

S.Q. ☞

Gym for developing the S.Q.

Be organized, plan in advance, be methodical!

We'll exercise ways to manage time, plan tasks and create priorities. We shall look at how we should attain our objectives; adopt new habits through strict practice; initiate organizational processes which will promote efficiency and saving; study theories of organization and method and consult with experts; use software and other tools for effective time management.

E.Q. ☞

Gym for developing E.Q.

Be a humane, sensitive, empathetic and considerate team player!

Nurturing emotional intelligence through investing in contact with friends; participating in workshops designed to improve teamwork, self-awareness and being attentive to others. In this room, we'll learn, experience and get acquainted with our emotional world as well as that of others. Group dynamics can assist in getting to know our emotions and those of others and expressing those emotions. Sensitivity should be nurtured with maturity.

V.Q. ☜

Gym for developing the V.Q.

Hold to your values, be reliable, respect and trust others!

This is where one develops one's values, ethics, integrity and responsibility. Team members will converse trustingly with each other, involving their value systems and close environment. Individual values and those of the organization will be examined: What are the "do's" and the "don't do's"? learn theories of ethics and books on how to deal with moral dilemmas.

EN.Q. ☞

Gym for developing the EN.Q.

Be energetic, vital, strong and powerful!

This time, it is a real gym in which we shall do sports and allow our bodies to be at their optimum energy. We'll go back to nature, take care of our health and focus on positive thinking; cope with difficult tasks and prove to ourselves that in the face of difficulties, we don't break down; we'll learn to manage our energy capital, how and with what we should refill our energy; get to know energy multiplication in action and find where we lose energy; learn about personal energy loss mechanisms and how to prevent energy leaks; develop the endurance quotient to sustain us against distress and failure and reduce their duration and influence.

Personal profile vis-à-vis that of the occupation/position/ organization

As a holistic model, the SILVER ACE relates to a person, an occupation, a job, or an organization. The quotients that characterize each one of them make it possible to obtain their maps.

"Be that which you are to the fullest" is realized when a person fits in with the potential of his skills, his personal SILVER ACE and his occupation, his job, and the characteristics of the organization than we get Holistic system.

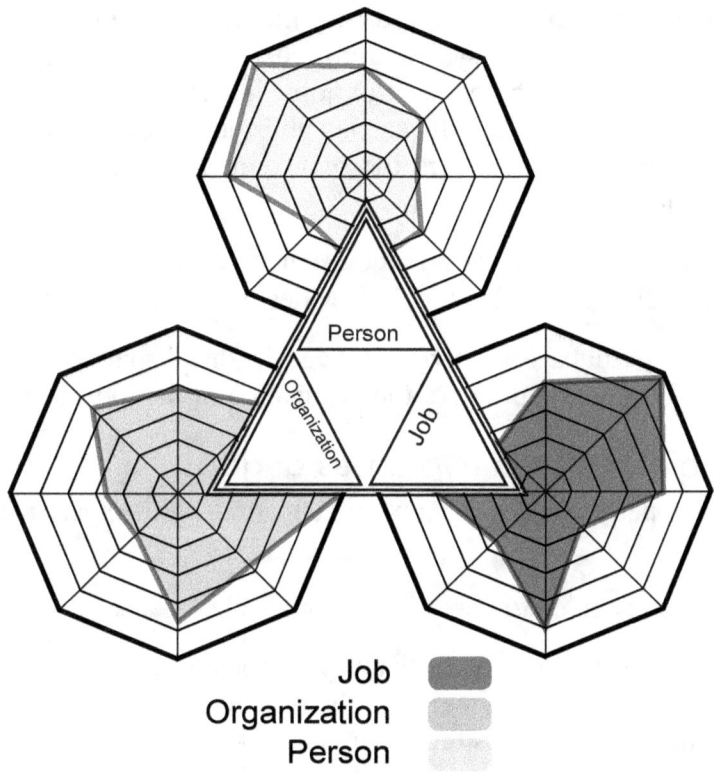

Job
Organization
Person

A person's mission in life to become a complete SILVER ACE is affected by the occupational and organizational environment. Gaps may be challenging or depressing. Fulfilling that mission is the ability to express the creative potential in a bureaucratic organization which represses any breaking of patterns or thinking out of the box, in an organization insisting on strict regulation of roles and procedures.

When a person's quotients and those of his environment or occupation are not balanced, energy loss will inevitably ensue.

Comparing the personal SILVER ACE profile with that of the job/occupation:

Every job/occupation has its own SILVER ACE characteristics indicating the skills required and their levels. Comparing one's personal profile with that of the occupation makes it possible to examine compatibility/incompatibility with the job.

The occupation/job can be characterized by the same terms a person would characterize himself: What is the creative thinking quotient of the job? What is its wisdom and professional knowledge quotient? What is its change quotient? What is its system and structure? You should take note of the overlapping between the occupation/job characteristics and the personal individual map as well as the disparities and their types: Is your potential higher than the job requires? Are the requirements of the job higher than your own quotient level?

Although this is a subjective estimation, when compared with the personal assessment, which is subjective too, it provides significant information.

One of the major hubs for energy leakage is the disparity between one's personal SILVER ACE and that of the occupation or the job.

Energy drain occurs in two cases of gaps:

1. Difficulty in performing one's job or occupation while experiencing lack of success

2. No expression is given to personal potential causing a sense of uselessness

In the first case, one has to see in what way personal capacity can be expanded in places where the job requires it. In the second case, the job itself can be enlarged to enable full expression of personal potential.

When one's full personal potential is not realized in a certain job, it may be expressed as dissatisfaction with one's salary or pay. We found in many cases a paradox: The organization pays high wages for an unchallenging job in which one's personal abilities and skills are scarcely realized.

Comparison with the organization's SILVER ACE:

The organization is an entity that has a SILV.R ACE of its own (see the chapter on the organizational SILVER AC.E).

Sketch the characteristics of your organization: How intelligent, creative, flexible, etc., is the organization? In this case, it is also possible to directly characterize the organization (see Appendix 2). Compare your organization as you perceive it to your own personal SI.VER ACE and the potential you want to express. Where are the gaps? Are they a challenging or repressive factor?

- **Gaps and lack of balance between one's personal SILVER ACE and the organization, the environment and the job cause burnout and energy loss!**

- **Bear in mind that you are the one paying a heavy personal price when you are in an environment or a job at which you do not realize your potential!**

- **The organization is wasting resources worth money – you are wasting your life!!!**

Be the ACE you are!!!

It's your life's mission and the key to your success!

Appendix 1 - The SILVER ACE personal map

Go through the different quotients and characteristics and give yourself an overall grade according to the scale below. Try to assess yourself in relation to your cohort. Relate to your life experience, to your school friends, your friends from the military and from work, to the people you meet in clubs, at the garage, on the street and in social gatherings. Place yourself on the scale with regard to each quotient.

The next step is to indicate on the map that you'll find in these pages, the marks you have gotten, according to the instructions.

Drawing your personal SILVER ACE map

1. **Drawing your personal profile:** Take the empty SILVER diagram below and report the grades you obtained for each of the dimensions; connect the dots and color the inner surface so that your SILVER ACE shape is visible.

2. **Drawing your average:** Use a different color to symbolize your overall average line so that you will be able to tangibly see the quotients and areas either below or above your average.

Appendix 2 – The organizational SILVER ACE map

Go over all the different quotients in the organizational chapter, the characteristics and key questions for each, and give the organization an overall grade according to the scale below.

Record the grades on the map. Connect the dots in order to obtain the organization's map shape. You can also draw the results obtained by other members of the organization in order to make comparisons.

Very low	Low	Below average	Above average	High	Very high	Excellent
1	2	3	4	5	6	7

Result summary:

Quotient	Name	Score
A.Q.	Aspiration and Ambition quotient	
I.Q.-R	Right Intelligence quotient	
I.Q.-L	Left Intelligence quotient	
C.Q.	Change and Chaos quotient	
S.Q.	System and Structure quotient	
E.Q.	Emotional intelligence quotient	
V.Q.	Value quotient	
EN.Q.	Energy and Endurance quotient	
Total	Total average	

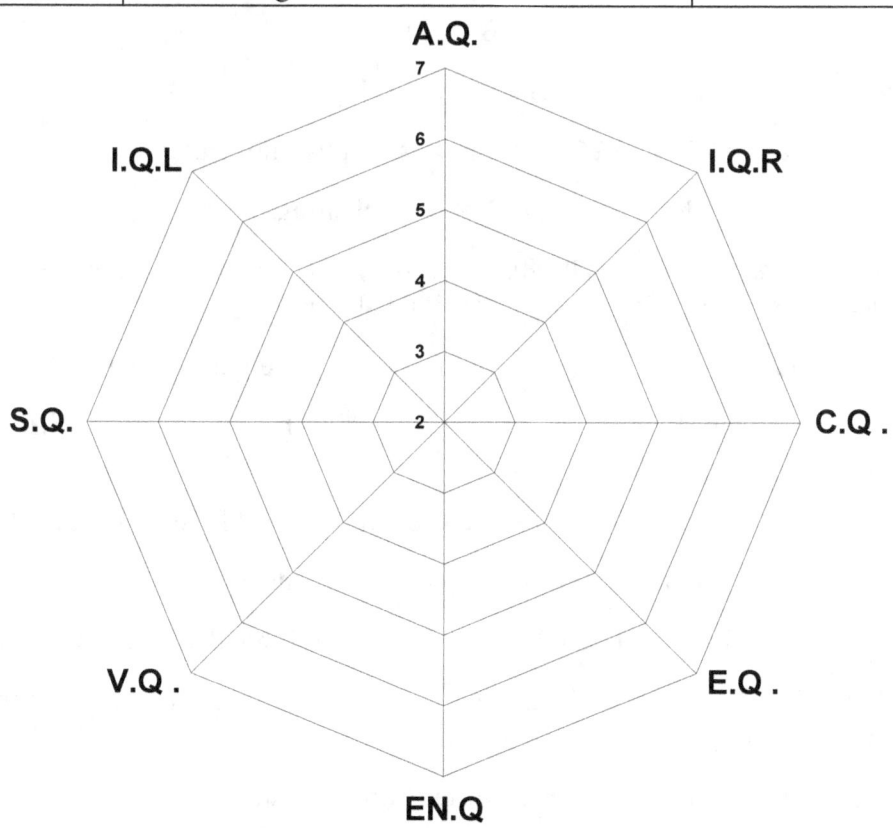

Bibliography

Adizes, I. (1980). How to Solve the Mismanagement Crisis. Tcherikover Publishers.

Adizes, I. (1992). Mastering Change: The Power of Mutual Trust and Respect. Adizes Institute Publications.

Adizes, I. (2004). Managing Corporate Lifecycles. Adizes Institute Publications.

Arica, Y. (1999). What's In The Future? Modan Publishing.

Ariely, D. (2009). Predictably Irrational. Matar Publishing.

Ariely, D. (2010). The Upside of Irrationality. Amazon.

Barabási, A.-L. (2004). Linked: The New Science of Networks. Mishkal Publishing.

Baron-Cohen, S. (2006). The Essential Difference: Men, Women and the Extreme Male Brain. Am Oved Publishing.

Beck, D. E., & Cowan, C. C. (1996). Spiral Dynamics. Blackwell Publications.

Bodanis, D. (2002). $E=mc^2$. Keter Books.

Buber, M. (1964). I and Thou. Bialik Publishing.

Collins, J. & Porras, J. (1995). Built to Last. Opus Publishing.

Collins, J. (2001). Good to Great. Pecker Publishing.

Cooper, R. & Sawaf, A. (1998). Executive EQ: Emotional Intelligence in Leadership and Organizations. Pecker Publishing.

Covey, S. (1996). The 7 Habits of Highly Effective People. Or Am Publishing.

Covey, S., Merrill, A. R., & Merrill, R. R. (1994). First Things First: To Live, to Love, to Learn, to Leave a Legacy. Simon and Schuster.

Davis, S., & Meyer, C. (2000). Future Wealth. Harvard Business Press.

Day, L. (1997). Practical Intuition. Pecker Publishing.

de Bono, E. (1967). The Use of Lateral Thinking. Johnathan Cape.

de Bono, E. (1995). Serious Creativity: Using the Power of Lateral Thinking to Create New Ideas. Branco Weiss Institute.

du Sautoy, M. (2006). The Music of the Primes. Mishkal.

Frankl, V. (1970). Man's Search for Meaning. Dvir Publishing.

Fukuyama, F. (1996). Trust: The Social Virtues and the Creation of Prosperity. Free Press.

Gegax, T. (2000). Winning in the Game of Life. Three Rivers Press.

Gilley, K. (2000). The Alchemy of Fear. Pecker Publishing.

Gleick, J. (1991). Chaos: Making a New Science. Maariv Library.

Goleman, D. (1997). Emotional Intelligence. Matar Publishing.

Hampden-Turner, C. (1981). Maps of the Mind. Collier Books, Macmillan Publishing.

Handy, C. (1990). The Age of Unreason. Harvard Business School Press.

Herrigel, E. (1990). Zen in the Art of Archery. Dvir Publishing.

Herrmann, N. (1988). The Creative Brain. Brain Books.

Hutchison, M. (1986). Megabrain. Ballantine Books.

James, J. (1997). Thinking in the Future Tense. Free Press.

Johnson, S. (1998). Who Moved My Cheese? Pecker Publishing.

Kahneman, D. (2005). A Perspective on Judgment and Choice: Mapping Bounded Rationality. Keter Books.

Kurzweil, R. (2000). The Age of Spiritual Machines. Penguin Books.

Kurzweil, R. (2005). The Singularity Is Near: When Humans Transcend Biology. Penguin Books.

Kurzweil, R. (2012). The Singularity Is Near: When Humans Transcend Biology. Kineret.

Leakey, R. (1998). The Origin of Humankind. Hed Arzi.

Levin, S. (1979). Moral Character Shaping and Teacher Training in Character Education. Otzar HaMore.

Lynn, A. (2002). In Search of Honor: Lessons from Workers on How to Build Trust. Pecker Publishing.

Maddox, R. (1995). Inc. Your Dreams. Penguin group.

Maslow, A. (1954). Motivation and Personality. Harper.

Matthews, G., Zeidner, M., & Roberts, R. D. (2007). The Science of Emotional Intelligence. Oxford University Press.

Misztal, B. (1996). Trust in Modern Societies: The Search for the Bases of Social Order. Polity.

Papp, P. (1983). The Process of Change. The Guilford Press.

Peters, T. (1995). The Tom Peters Seminar: Crazy Times Call for Crazy Organizations. Matar Publishing.

Pink, D. H. (2009). A Whole New Mind: Why Right-Brainers Will Rule the Future. Matar Publishing.

Pinker, S. (2004). How The Mind Works. Matar Publishing.

Ratey, J. (2005). A User's Guide to the Brain: Perception, Attention, and the Four Theaters of the Brain. Zmora-Bitan Publishing.

Reik, T. (1983). Listening with the Third Ear. Farrar, Straus and Giroux.

Ridley, M. (2000). The Origins of Virtue. Zmora-Bitan Publishing.

Ring, I. (1999) Morals for What? Sifriat HaPoalim – HaKibbutz Haarzi.

Senge, P. (1995). The Fifth Discipline: The Art and Practice of the Learning Organization. Matar Publishing.

Shlain, L. (1991). Art & Physics. Quill, William Morrow.

Shlain, L. (1999). The Alphabet Versus the Goddess: The Conflict Between Word and Image. Penguin.

Stoltz, P. (1997). Adversity Quotient. Wiley and sons.

Toffler, A. (1971). Future Shock. Am Oved Publishing.

Toffler, A. (1992). Powershift: Knowledge, Wealth and Violence at the Edge of the 21st Century. Maariv Library.

Wilber, K. (2006). A Brief History of Everything. Kineret Zmora-Bitan Dvir.

Yanai, O. (1998). Everyone Has a Path. Modan Publishing.(Heb)

Yanai. O. (2000) Career your passion.

Zohar, D. & Marshall, I. (2001). Spiritual Intelligence. Keter Books.

Zuboff, S. (1988). In the Age of The Smart Machine. Basic Books, Harper Collins.

Thanks,

Many professionals have joined together in the developing of the model and the book, some directly and some indirectly by serving as teachers and students. I wish to thank them wholeheartedly:

The thinking group at the Adam Institute that went along with me in the initial development stage of the model;

The various professionals who used it for different developments in the domain of human resources;

The people who went hand in hand with me while writing the book:

Orly Pecker, who pushed me into writing what was on my mind; Dorit Landes, who was my writing mentor in writing the first draft; Daphne Mor-Haim, who zealously edited the last version of the book; Dr. M. Shachak for translating the book with all her heart; and to Netta Ness, my partner in the creation of the SILVER ACE ACADEMY.

Thanks to my family for their support and their learning to speak SILVER ACE.

To my first born, Gonni, who established and manages the House for Career: "Career your passion" for encouraging me and pushing me into practicing what I preach; to my daughter, Nattali, who meticulously worked on the design, the presentations and the visual material for this book as well as preparation for workshops and building my website; and to my youngest son, Elad, for taking care of the technology of the site as well as organizational and individual computerized diagnosis tools, including the "M.S.A. assessment " based on SILVER ACE.

Special thanks to my life companion and professional thinking partner – Dr. Orenia – my life with whom is a wondrous journey of multidimensional thinking, emotional depth and intellectual curiosity. This model was devised and the book was written through the fertile dialogue between us. Our ability to meet and reach an agreement through all the layers of the SILVER ACE and its quotients is magic that fills me with infinite happiness.

Dr. Dov Yanai - Professional Experience

Dr. Dov Yanai is a world renowned Management Consultant and expert in the human side of management and Human Potential development. Consulting, corporate management, boards of directors and business owners in aligning the human capital and corporate strategy.

Had a diverse fields of academic studies: Math, Physics, Psychology, and Business-Management. Human Resource and Organizational Development and Future studies.

Dr Yanai served as chairperson of the Occupational Diagnostic Institutes and was an advisor to government bodies in the area of human employment solutions.

He also chaired the Israeli Future Society and was among the founding members of the Israeli Science & Consciousness Association.

Dr. Yanai has researched the different human profiles of managers and entrepreneurs, and has recently been the head of Human-Energy research Lab in the Tel-Aviv University.

As an entrepreneur, he established numerous well known and successful companies in his professional line of expertise, among them the Adam–Institute. A group of Professional Psychological Services in the area of Human Resources and guided it to its position as Israel's leading institute in the field of human assessment, diagnostics and development, Career consulting, Management development.

He is acting president of Genesis - Management Consulting Group and that of AMI - the Family Business Consulting Center.

Among his public activities: He was the elected president of the Israeli Student Union, Played active role in the National Worker Union and was elected member of his town council.

He developed The Silver Ace model. Mapping of Human intelligences for the 21st Century, as a unified theoretical model and language for the characterization of people and organizations.

Recently established the Silver Ace Academy, determined to spread the Silver Ace teachings for the realization of human potential to firms and individuals of all ages, from school-age to retirement.

He is a sought-after specialist in his field and takes part in many professional conferences.

His book The Giant and the Dwarf was published in 2013. It is a tale for adults about freedom, self-inquiry and empowerment.

Dr. Dov Yanai   dovyanai@genesis-gr.com